SOLVING THE WORK/FAMILY PUZZLE

SOLVING THE WORK/FAMILY PUZZLE

Bonnie Michaels

President
Managing Work & Family, Inc.

Elizabeth McCarty

Vice President and General Counsel
Managing Work & Family, Inc.

BUSINESS ONE IRWIN
Homewood, Illinois 60430

© 1992 MANAGING WORK & FAMILY, INC.

This publication is designed to provide accurate and
authoritative information in regard to the subject matter
covered. It is sold with the understanding that neither the
author nor the publisher is engaged in rendering legal, accounting,
or other professional service. If legal advice or other expert
assistance is required, the services of a competent
professional person should be sought.

*From a Declaration of Principles jointly adopted by a Committee
of the American Bar Association and a Committee of Publishers.*

Sponsoring editor: Jeffrey A. Krames
Project editor: Jane Lightell
Production manager: Bette K. Ittersagen
Jacket designer: Kay Fulton
Designer: Jeanne M. Rivera
Art manager: Kim Meriwether
Compositor: BookMasters, Inc.
Typeface: 11/13 Palatino
Printer: Arcata Graphics/Kingsport

Library of Congress Cataloging-in-Publication Data

Michaels, Bonnie.
   Solving the work/family puzzle / Bonnie Michaels and Elizabeth
McCarty.
      p.   cm.
   Includes bibliographical references and index.
   ISBN 1-55623-627-1
   1. Work and family.   I. McCarty, Elizabeth.   II. Title
HD4904.25.M53   1992
646.7—dc20   91–46296

Printed in the United States of America
1 2 3 4 5 6 7 8 9 0 K 9 8 7 6 5 4 3 2

Preface

You do not have to live your life off balance. It is your responsibility to discover what is best for you and bring peace and harmony into your life.

Finding a balance between work and family life is hard work. But it can be done.

I grew up in the 1950s in a middle-class family. The reality for my mom and dad was that money was always tight. We moved out of the city in the early 50s and settled in a subdivision development of unfinished homes. My father became ill, and it was my mother who finished building the home. It was my mother who found ways to make extra money by baby-sitting and working part time in retail. When my sister was 10, my mother became a full-time employee out of necessity. My sister was a latchkey child. My mother had the same worries that every parent has today. My husband, from an immigrant family, arrived in the early 50s and spent most of his childhood alone, with a neighbor, or in front of the TV set. His parents also had to work.

As an adult, I've experienced marriage, divorce, single parenting, blended families, grand parenting, and caregiving for elders. Finding the balance is a challenge every day. My personal experiences motivated me to gather and share ideas that are working for me and others. Through my work, I have also seen that a satisfying balance between work and family life is achievable, not the impossible dream we are often told it is.

I see the difficulty and struggle my own daughter, a single parent of a three-year-old, faces everyday. She is surrounded by a loving and supportive extended family. She has alternative sources of child care when needed. She has financial backing, good loyal friends, and information to guide her. Yet she alone has to deal with the ear infections, the fevers, the nightmares, the ups and downs of child development, the demands of work, and the juggling to pay the bills, get more education, and have some social life.

As I reflect on my own life, it's easy to see that if I had had more information, resources, and support, it wouldn't have been so difficult.

So what got me through single parenting? What does my daughter use to get through her difficult days alone? First, all of us have one thing in common: a strong will to survive. I learned it from my mother. She learned it from hers. And my daughter learned it from me.

Second, there's hope, hope that things will get better, easier. And finally, there is the desire and perseverance to make it better.

I truly believe things can get better and easier for all of us who work and have families. It happened for me. I raised my daughter to believe it. It will happen for her some day. I talk every day to men and women who have seen it come to pass.

In 1983, I interviewed 35 women, aged 23 to 85 years, to find out how they got through difficult times. They had experienced a variety of work/family conflicts such as divorce, single parenting, role conflicts, death of a spouse, and caregiving for elders. They were of different ethnic groups; one had survived World War II and the Nazi occupation of Germany. I asked them to comment on how they got through the difficult times. The common theme was support—formal or informal.

Here are a few select quotes that encompass many of their thoughts about how they survived difficult times:

> "Having people believe in you . . . being there no matter what."

> "I've got good friends . . . there's a real sharing of personal feelings."

> "I look to my mother . . . her courage."

> "I can call men and women friends in the neighborhood . . . even in the middle of the night. I feel comforted with the support system around me."

> "I told my problems to lots of people. They, in turn, took care of me. I didn't want advice. I just wanted them to be there."

> "I ask for TLC. It comes in whatever form a person is willing to give."

"I've always been an optimist. I've taken anything that was negative and have been able to see the options for changing and turning it around."

"I don't want advice, just someone to be there. A hug or a touch."

I have been hearing similar stories in the course of my work ever since. Their courage, stamina, optimism, and willingness to ask for and receive support are a great inspiration.

I hope this book inspires you the way those men and women have inspired me.

Good luck in managing your work and family life.

If you'd like to share your stories of success with me, please write to me:

Bonnie Michaels
Managing Work & Family, Inc.
912 Crain St.
Evanston, IL 60202

Acknowledgments

To my husband, Michael, who is a constant reminder of what is really important. To my daughter, Anna, for helping me find the way and whose courage is an inspiration. To my grandson, Tristan, who makes me smile and motivates me to make this world a better place for children. To my mother, Dorothea, who has always shown me the value of strength and perseverance. To my father, Joe, who instilled a sense of humor.

Thanks go as well to my sister, Kaylyn LoCoco, and other family members, Len LoCoco, Mark and Leah Seef, for providing love and inspiration. Thanks also to the many friends who have provided emotional support during difficult times: Joan Ruez, Susan Moss, Louise Love, Judy Chiss, Gerry Shavitz, Bob Peller, Ernie Miller, Leonie Norton, Jenny Blackton, Jo Anne Davis, Ronna and Alan Kaplan, Howard and Carol Kirsch; and to the professionals who have supported the idea of "managing work and family": Mary E. Longe, Marina Eovaldi, Joanne Koch, Hedy Ratner, Val Mrak, Richard Roby, Candice Hadley, Phil Lanier, and Sharon Spence. And finally, to Elizabeth McCarty, whose partnership, contributions, and friendship made this book possible.

B. Michaels

To my family—my parents, Daniel and Constance McCarty, for their unfailing love and support and my mother's experiences as an elder caregiver; my sister, Claire, who helped express the principles of communication and listened to me complain when the going was hard; my sister, Margie, who contributed stories and ideas from her work with the elderly, my brothers, Dan and Brian, brothers-in-law, Joe and Bob, and sister-in-law-to-be, April, for their encouragement, support, and humor—and my extended family of friends, especially Zora, Steve and Siobhan

Shinn, Janet Kerrigan, Betty Sassanno and Ross Goldstein. Deep-felt thanks also go to Bonnie whose friendship, generous spirit, and devotion to families has inspired me and helped me find my niche.

E. McCarty

Our joint thanks to the many individuals and families, too numerous to name, who have contributed so generously to this book, sharing their stories and experiences and telling us which strategies have worked for them.

We also wish to thank the following people who were very helpful in the development and preparation of the book: Lesli Siegel, who worked as hard as we did in preparing the manuscript and took charge of the bibliography; Amy Kraable, Amy Chamberlain, and Ann Burlebach who helped with research; Claire McCarty Kilian for help and advice on the communication chapter; and Janet Kerrigan, Candice Hadley, Joanne Koch, and Beverly Kaye for their friendship and help with review of the manuscript. Our thanks also to Mary Longe of Longe Life Libraries, Deerfield, Illinois, who contributed substantially to our resources lists, to Elizabeth Bodie of ElderLink, Inc., Chicago, Illinois, who provided resources and guidance in the complex subject of elder care, and to Anna Michaels' generous contributions to the single parenting section.

B. Michaels and E. McCarty

Table of Contents

Preface   *v*

Acknowledgments   *ix*

Chapter One
INTRODUCTION   1

The Big Puzzle—Historical Context, 1
Where This Book Comes In, 3
What Topics Are Covered Where, 3
Your Puzzle, 4
Notes, 6

Chapter Two
CREATING A WHOLE LIFE PLAN   7

Creating a Whole Life Plan, 7
   Goals—The First Step in an Action Plan, 9
   Creating a Fantasy Plan, 13
   Identify Your Goals, 13
   The Big Picture, 17
Alternate Career Paths, 20
   Barrier 1: Fear, 21
   Barrier 2: Expectations, 23
   Career Path Decisions, 28
   Alternative Career Path Options, 29
   Alternative Full-Time Work Options, 30
   Less Than Full-Time Alternatives, 31
   Flexibility: Unplanned Events, 33
Resources, 33
Notes, 35

Chapter Three
MANAGING GUILT   36

Healthy and Unhealthy Guilt, 37
   The Sources of Unhealthy Guilt, 38
   The Results, 39
   The Cure, 39
Specific Anti-guilt Strategies, 40
   Are My Children OK?, 41
   Are My Elders OK?, 43
   Is My Spouse/Partner OK?, 44
   Are My Friends OK?, 45
Get Rid of Guilt, 45
Resources, 46
Notes, 47

Chapter Four
COMMUNICATING TO GET WHAT
YOU NEED   49

Communication Skill Assessment, 50
What Is Communication?, 50
   The Elements of Effective Communication, 50
   Active Listening, 59
   Effective Confrontation, 63
Communicating with Children, 67
   Play, 72
Communicating with Adolescents, 73
Communicating with Elders, 76
Communicating with Spouse/Significant Other, 81
Communicating with Your Supervisor, 85
   Handling Telephone Calls, 88
Resources, 90
Notes, 91

Chapter Five

ORGANIZING FOR LIFE MANAGEMENT   95

Identifying Your Priorities, 96
    The Status Quo—Where Does Your Time Go Now?, 98
Making Time, 100
    Option 1: Choose Not to Do It, 104
    Option 2: Postpone Responsibilities, 105
    Option 3: Delegate, 106
    Option 4: Do It Better (and Reduce Time Spent), 113
    Option 5: Barter, 115
    Option 6: Hire Help, 116
    Revised Weekly Planner, 117
Putting Priorities and Organization into Action, 117
    Celia and Jim's Story, 117
    Weekly Routines, 118
    New and Reaffirmed Priorities, 120
    Making It Happen, 122
Summary, 123
Resources, 123
Notes, 125

Chapter Six

BEGINNING A FAMILY . . . WHILE HAVING A CAREER   130

Deciding to Have a Family, 130
Assessing Your Career and Family Values, 131
Planning Your Leave of Absence, 135
    Working Out Your Leave with Your Partner and Family, 135
    Getting Support from Your Supervisor, 137
    Planning For Your Replacement At Work, 139
Maternity Leave, 140
Paternity Leave, 142
Child-Care Arrangements, 146
Planning Your Return to Work, 146

Reentry Shock, 147
Summary, 147
Resources, 147
Notes, 148

Chapter Seven
FINDING AND MANAGING QUALITY
CHILD CARE   149
Child-Care Options, 150
   Child Care in Your Home, 150
   Care for the Child at Work, 153
   Family Day-Care Homes, 153
   Day-Care Centers and Preschools, 154
Be Flexible . . . Be Patient!, 154
What Is a Good Child-Care Program?, 156
   Characteristics of Child-Care Programs, 156
Determining Your Child-Care Needs, 161
Selecting a Child-Care Provider, 163
   Step One: Get Started Early, 163
   Step Two: Narrow the Field of Choices, 164
   Step Three: Screen Providers by Telephone, 165
   Step Four: Check References, 166
   Step Five: Interview and Observe, 167
   Step Six: Revisit with Your Child, 168
   Step Seven: Establish a Professional Relationship, 168
   Step Eight: Time Together, 171
Child-Care Checklists, 171
Preparing for Child Care, 175
   Preparing Yourself, 176
   Preparing Your Child for Child Care, 176
   Preparing Your Caregiver, 177
What About Child Abuse?, 179
Meeting Special Child-Care Needs, 180
   Care of Sick Children, 180

Emergencies, 181
Holidays, 181
Overnight, 181
Backup Care, 181
Children with Special Needs, 182
Care for School-aged Children, 183
When Can Children Take Care of Themselves?, 183
The Benefits of Self-Care, 184
The Risks of Self-Care, 184
Deciding About Self-Care, 184
Communication with Self-Care Children, 185
Resources, 187

Chapter Eight
CARING FOR ELDERS   194
Our Population Is Aging, 194
Becoming an Elder Caregiver, 195
When Does It Start?, 195
Where to Begin, 199
Get Help, 200
Education and Information, 200
Professional Help, 201
Elder-Care Options, 203
Moral Support, 203
Elder-Care Services, 204
Assistance in the Elder's Home, 207
Adult Day-Care Center, 210
Special-Care Community or Facility, 210
Adult Care in Your Home, 215
Long-Distance Caregiving, 217
The Caregiver: Taking Care of Yourself, 217
Conclusion, 220
Appendix A: Home Equity Conversion:
Mortgage Insurance Demonstration Program, 221

Appendix B: Medicare Coverage, 222

Appendix C: Medicare Supplement
Insurance Policies, 225

Appendix D: Long-Term Care Insurance Policies, 226

Resources, 228

Notes, 234

Chapter Nine

MANAGING SPECIAL FAMILY SITUATIONS   235

Single Parenting, 235

   Becoming a Single Parent, 236

   Life as a Single Parent, 237

   Final Thoughts, 245

Blended Families, 246

   Deciding to Remarry and Become Part of
   a Blended Family, 246

   Strategies for Blended Families, 249

Business Travel while Caring for Others, 250

   Before You Leave, 251

   Taking Care of Yourself While Traveling, 254

   Reentry, 255

   A Learning Experience for All, 255

   Take the Children with You, 256

Resources, 257

Notes, 258

Chapter Ten

GETTING THE ORGANIZATION TO
WORK WITH YOU   259

Corporate Culture, 259

What Can Be Done?, 261

   Education and Information, 261

   Policies and Benefits, 262

How Can You Help Start a Work/Family
Initiative at Your Company? 263
Resources, 264
Notes, 265

Chapter Eleven   TAKING CARE OF YOURSELF   266

Bibliography   271
Index   283

Chapter One

Introduction

THE BIG PUZZLE—HISTORICAL CONTEXT

The struggle to find a balance between work and family is not a new issue, nor is it a "women's issue." While it is true that the number of women working outside the home has risen steadily since 1970, the vast majority of women have always worked so that they and their families could survive, juggling work and family time.

For generations, men and women worked side by side while they raised their families together. The Industrial Revolution brought about a significant change. Men and women left the farm or family business for factories and other places of work.

> American women have often diverged from the model of the home-bound, domestic mother. The child-centered housewife is actually a relatively recent historical development and is a social position that has generally been reserved for the more privileged members of the female population. . . . [T]hroughout the early stages of industrialization, women contributed directly to the economic support of their families in a variety of ways.[1]

Men became the breadwinners as a middle class emerged. Middle- and upper-class women remained at home. Gradually, the myth grew that women were not capable of doing "men's jobs," that their place was in the home. Nevertheless, many women worked, albeit in "women's jobs"—clerks, typists, factory workers, teachers. These women were made to feel that their work was temporary, a short-term effort until their husbands were able to support them. The reality was that most of these women were in the work force to stay, but with little chance for advancement.[2]

Then came World War II and Rosie the Riveter. Women entered the workplace in large numbers, doing jobs previously done by men. After the war ended, some of them stayed, even if demoted.[3] Women have been entering the work force in increasing numbers ever since.

> In 1940, only 9 percent of the women with school-age children were working. By 1948, that figure had more than doubled to 20 percent, and by 1972, the figure was 50 percent. In 1982, 65 percent of women with children under age 18 were working. The most dramatic rise was among working women with pre-school children: In 1948, 10 percent of these women were working. By 1960, the figure had risen to 19 percent; by 1971 to 30 percent; and by 1982 to 50 percent.[4]

In 1990, 53 percent of women with preschool-age children worked; 66 percent of all mothers worked. Many of these women are single parents. Twenty-five percent of American children live in single-parent households, most headed by women. Most women are employed full time; 25 percent of working women are in part-time positions. Most women work because of economic need and contribute either all or a significant percentage of their family income.[5] The presence of women in the work force seems here to stay.

The high number of working women is impacting the workplace in many ways. The changing work force has required that the corporation deal with employees' needs for family-responsive programs. Businesses are increasingly offering benefits and services that assist their employees to manage work/family conflicts. Our work with companies has shown that they are looking for creative solutions so that they can be more "family friendly."

Changes in work itself have also put pressure on the family. Work has expanded. The average American works significantly more hours a week than she or he did in 1960. Americans are also chronically fatigued, having lost sleep to the increased demands on our time.

Technology has increased the pace of our lives. Overnight deliveries, faxes, satellites, and new forms of media bombard us for attention. Our society has become more dangerous as crime and drugs pervade every stratum of society.

All of these factors have combined to put tremendous pressure on individuals and families trying to live balanced, happy lives. It is going to take a united effort of individuals, employers, government, and community organizations to support the changing work force and their families. We are a nation in crisis with regard to supportive services for children and elders. The future success of our country depends on the quality of the care and education we are providing today for our children. We must all work together to support working families.

WHERE THIS BOOK COMES IN

In the meantime, workers who have families are struggling to find their way. That is why this book has been written. Through our work, we try to promote and help individuals and their families reach balance, with and without the support of their employers. This book is a compilation of what we have learned through our organizational assessments, focus groups, training programs, research, seminars, and speeches and the wonderful ideas and stories people have shared with us in the course of our work, some of which we have shared with you. (Their names have been changed to give them anonymity.)

Solving the Work/Family Puzzle may not answer all of your questions relating to managing work and family, but we know from our workshop and consulting experience that if you try, you can always find creative answers to difficult questions.

This book addresses each of the various phases in an individual's adult life. Whether you are single or married, have children now or may in the future, or are an elder caregiver today or expect to be tomorrow, you will be able to think through the challenges presented by working while maintaining a satisfying personal and family life. You will have the opportunity to make discoveries about yourself and your family, to clarify your values and priorities, and to find ways to redesign your life to achieve your goals.

WHAT TOPICS ARE COVERED WHERE

In Chapter Two, "Creating a Whole Life Plan," we work on identifying our values and goals to design a whole life action plan that can be the basis for finding and achieving a satisfying balance.

We also look at the value of planning to achieve goals over time and examine some alternatives to traditional paths. In Chapters Three, Four, and Five, we discuss the basic skills we all need to achieve balance between all of the pieces of our lives—dealing with guilt, communicating effectively, and organizing for life management. In the remaining chapters, we look at applying those skills to various aspects of work/family life. Chapter Six, "Beginning a Family . . . While Having a Career," deals with questions about adding children to career and how to have a successful leave of absence following the birth of a child. In Chapter Seven, we look at ways to find, evaluate, and manage quality child care. The many aspects of elder care are the subject of Chapter Eight. The special needs of families with single parents, blended families, and parents who travel are examined in Chapter Nine. In Chapter Ten, we look at the ways our employers can help, and how you can work with your employer to get assistance and cooperation to achieve balance between work and family. Finally, in Chapter Eleven we stress the importance of taking care of yourself.

YOUR PUZZLE

Finding the balance between work and family can be like solving a puzzle. Some puzzles are complicated; some are simple. The work/family puzzle is usually a complicated one with many pieces to fit together. You maneuver the pieces until they fit, try different ideas and options, put aside what doesn't work, and experiment until it feels right. We hope you will use this book to begin to put the pieces of your puzzle together in a new way.

Your work/family puzzle is similar to the puzzles of others all over the world. You may find yourself identifying with some of the stories shared here. But your puzzle is also unique because you and your family members are unique. To make your unique pieces fit, you need to look at the big picture. Begin to look at your life as a whole.

Like most intricate and complicated puzzles, it takes time and hard work to solve the challenge of combining work and family so that you are happy in both areas. It takes patience, perseverance, and an understanding of the challenges you face daily. Don't look for "the" answer. There are no black-and-white solutions. It may take trial and error. It takes re-solving the puzzle when the pieces get out of line. Finally and most importantly, it takes the belief that you can, in fact, solve the puzzle.

To really meet the challenge of the work/family puzzle, you must be willing to open your mind to options. You must be willing to change your current way of operating at work and at home. It is difficult to change how we operate. We develop habits that are hard to break. Most of us have also developed patterns of doing things that reflect the way our parents did them. Because many of our lives bear little resemblance to those of our parents (or bosses), those patterns may not serve us well. As we discuss different options, begin to examine whether you are currently operating in the way best suited to get what you need so you feel in control of your work life and your family life.

Ask yourself, "How creative am I in problem solving?" Your ability to be creative is very important. Unfortunately, many working parents don't have the time to creatively solve their problems. Many people barely make it through the day. It's important, however, to make the time to find more creative ways of solving the work/family puzzle. Dedicate one weekend or a vacation day to you and your family and work together to find a better, more satisfying way to live.

Some of the alternatives we explore in this book may be new to you; some you may have heard before. You may not get all the solutions you need from this book, but we hope you will have many new ideas and options to try. It's important to acknowledge that it's *how* you approach these options that makes a difference. A lot is being written about work and family today. Most people read about other possibilities, but then do not put them into action.

This book is active, not passive. To be most effective, it requires participation from you and other family members. There are questionnaires to fill out and exercises to practice. All are designed to help you work through the issues and find a balance that works for you. Use them. Write in your answers. Make notes in the margin. Mark up a calendar. Do whatever it takes to make the information helpful to you. We invite you to read the whole book or only those chapters that deal with topics affecting you today. Read them in any order you choose (though we suggest you start with Chapter Two, which will help you develop a whole life plan as a base for all other planning, and at least skim the basic skills chapters). To solve the work/family puzzle and make all the pieces fit, you will need to invest some time and thought. Then you need to *do*—put your plan into action.

We will not discuss the stages of children's development, parenting skills, or the aging process and its effect in depth. This book is also not about making career changes or the psychological aspects of working and caring for others. We have included resources at the end of each chapter so that you can read more about subjects that interest you or affect your life.

We hope you will find this book a helpful guide to new ways of putting your puzzle together and a source of useful information. At the least, we hope to give you confidence to pursue your unique path to balance and a satisfying work and family life.

NOTES

1. Kathleen Gerson, *How Women Decide About Work, Career and Motherhood* (Berkeley and Los Angeles, Calif.: University of California Press, 1985), p. 3.
2. John P. Fernandez, *Child Care and Corporate Productivity Resolving Family/Work Conflicts* (Lexington, Mass., and Toronto: Lexington Books: D. C. Heath and Company, 1986), p. 7.
3. Ibid., p. 8.
4. Ibid.
5. U.S. Department of Labor, Women's Bureau, *20 Facts on Women Workers*, No. 90-2, September 1990.

Chapter Two

Creating a Whole Life Plan

"If I had known what it was like to have it all, I would have settled for less."

Lily Tomlin

P ersonal relationships, money, status, children, power, pleasure, security, time and family/self/partner, and contentment are some of many goals most of us aspire to achieve. It may be possible to achieve many of these goals, but *which* goals you choose and *how* and *when* you achieve them are important factors to consider. It is the rare individual who can have it all at the same time—and enjoy it!

CREATING A WHOLE LIFE PLAN

Whole life planning means setting goals for the *whole person*—social, intellectual, spiritual, and physical goals. It means striving to achieve balance and harmony in all areas, setting realistic goals, and reaching them.

> The challenge to develop, balance, and harmonize working and loving is with us every day, regardless of the presence or absence of a job or a loved one. When we establish long-range life goals, when we think about our aspirations in terms of career and family, we are thinking about integrating work and love. We make choices, consciously or unconsciously, about the kinds of people we want to be, by arranging the mix between work and love in our own personalities.[1]

The Roles We Play

Most of us play many roles in our lives—worker, boss, son/daughter, mother/father, sister/brother, friend, neighbor, and so on. Each role plays a part in our puzzle. In the circle below, draw in the roles that you play, trying to proportion one to another.

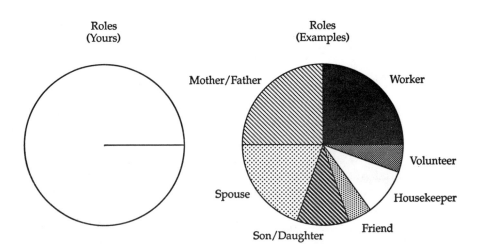

The activities we engage in depend on our roles. These activities can generally be classified into three groups: work, family, and self. Using the following checklists, indicate which specific pieces are part of your puzzle.

Work	*Family*	*Self*
_____ Job	_____ Spouse	_____ Exercise
_____ Commute	_____ Infant	_____ Religion
_____ Business travel	_____ Toddler	_____ Recreation
_____ Business	_____ Preschooler	_____ Time alone
entertainment	_____ School-age child	_____ Sleep
_____ Work at home	_____ School-age child	_____ Volunteering
_____ Training courses	_____ Teen	_____ Community
_____ Education/classes	_____ Teen	_____ Service
_____ Readings	_____ Children's activities	_____ Hobby
_____ Committees	_____ Elder/mother	(Describe) _____
_____ Professional	_____ Elder/father	_____ Hobby
organization	_____ Elder/mother-in-law	(Describe) _____

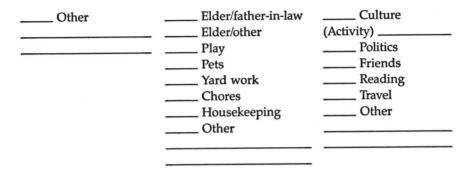

_____ Other	_____ Elder/father-in-law	_____ Culture
_____	_____ Elder/other	(Activity) _____
_____	_____ Play	_____ Politics
	_____ Pets	_____ Friends
	_____ Yard work	_____ Reading
	_____ Chores	_____ Travel
	_____ Housekeeping	_____ Other
	_____ Other	_____
	_____	_____
	_____	

Are you happy with the balance in and between these three areas? Do you wish you were able to check any items that are not now present in your life? Do you wish you could erase some of the checks? If you feel out of balance, either because there is too much on your plate, too little, or an unsatisfying mix, you may want to identify where the dissatisfaction comes from. Try using the accompanying Life Satisfaction Index.

Goals—The First Step in an Action Plan

To establish a successful whole life plan, we need to start by identifying our goals, those things that will make us happy. One way to zero in on your goals is to identify your values. Then you can choose goals compatible with those values.

The following questions will help you clarify the values that you bring to career and family life. Family and cultural values are the belief system with which we were raised. They often relate to how people *should* behave, how they *should* interact, and what they *should* do. For example, would you agree or disagree with the following statements:

A family should have dinner together.

A wife should make breakfast for her husband.

Children need a home-cooked meal every day.

Couples should spend all of their free time together.

Time spent on me is not as important as time spent on others.

Cleanliness is next to godliness. (Translation: My housecleaning takes priority over play.)

Fill in the accompanying Values Clarification Exercise to identify your values.

My Life Satisfaction Index

Circle your response to the following statements. "Enough time" means the amount of time necessary for you to feel satisfied.

		Never	Rarely	Sometimes	Frequently	Always
1. a.	I spend enough time with my spouse/partner; or	1	2	3	4	5
b.	I want a spouse/partner and am actively looking for one.	1	2	3	4	5
2.	I spend enough time with my children.	1	2	3	4	5
3.	I spend enough time with my elders.	1	2	3	4	5
4.	I spend enough time with my friends.	1	2	3	4	5
5.	My career does not interfere with my personal life.	1	2	3	4	5
6.	I make time for spiritual growth.	1	2	3	4	5
7.	I am satisfied with my physical condition.	1	2	3	4	5
8.	I spend enough time on my own intellectual stimulation.	1	2	3	4	5
9.	I spend enough time alone or doing things just for me.	1	2	3	4	5
10.	I am generally happy.	1	2	3	4	5
11.	I enjoy my work.	1	2	3	4	5
12.	My personal life does not interfere with my work.	1	2	3	4	5
13.	I experience joy in my accomplishments, my relationships, my children.	1	2	3	4	5

Now add up your points and look at where you stand overall.

46–60 You are pretty happy with the way things are. Read on if you would like to make life even better.

31–45 You are satisfied more than not. As you read the chapter, pay close attention to those areas where your satisfaction level is low.

21–30 Tired of feeling so-so? Take charge and replan!

13–20 Time for a major overhaul. This book is a good first step.

Values Clarification Exercise

Answer the following questions to start to examine the "shoulds" that may be driving you. Remember, there are no right or wrong answers. If none of the options works for you, write in your own answer. The questions are designed to get you to think about what matters to you.

1. Where does a person's primary responsibility lie?
   a. To work   b. To family   c. To oneself   d. _____

2. A woman who works and has children:
   a. Can't be a good   b. Can't be a good   c. Can be a good   d. _____
      mother   worker   mother and a
                                                  good worker.

3. A man who takes time off from work to take care of his children is:
   a. A wimp   b. A good father   c. Jeopardizing his   d. _____
                                           career

4. There needs to be harmony and balance between work and home.
   a. True   b. False   c. It depends   d. _____

5. I work because (choose the option which is *most* true):
   a. I want to   b. I have to   c. My spouse/family d. _____
                                           wants me to

6. My work is:
   a. More important   b. As important as   c. Not as important   d. _____
      than my personal   my personal life   as my personal
      life   life

7. I believe that a person must:
   a. Keep work and   b. Devote equal   c. Find their own   d. _____
      family separate   time to work and   balance between
                          family   work and family

8. How do you define success?
   a. More money   b. Status/power   c. Personal
                                           harmony

   d. Spiritual growth   e. A strong family   f. Other (describe) _____

9. If you had more successes, would it help you maintain a happy balance in your life?
   Yes   No   Don't know

10. I believe my relationship with my wife/husband is primary (i.e., more important than my children/elders).
    Yes   Sometimes   No

11. What regrets do you have about the way you are living your life, things you wish you could change?
    1.
    2.
    3.

12. What accomplishments are you most proud of?
    1.
    2.
    3.
13. What were your goals when you finished school?
    1.
    2.
    3.
14. What are your most important family values (the "shoulds" or beliefs you grew up with, whether or not they were acted on)?
    1.
    2.
    3.
    4.
    5.
15. What are your most important family norms (those behaviors that are typical of your family, i.e., anger is not to be expressed; self-sufficiency is our goal)?
    1.
    2.
    3.
    4.
    5.

Once you identify what "shoulds" are driving you, you can look at whether what you *should* do is what you *want* to do.

Examine the values and norms you identified in questions 14 and 15.

- Where did these beliefs come from (you, your spouse, your parents)?
- How happy are you with the values and norms you have incorporated into your own life?
- Do you feel guilty if you are not meeting them?
- Does anyone notice if a rule is broken?
- How important is each value or norm to the successful functioning of your family?

- How many of the values or norms conflict? Example: "Family members should help each other" (value) versus "Don't ask for help" (norm).

Decide which of your answers reflect your goals, hopes, and dreams and which reflect a "should" you choose not to do anymore.

Creating a Fantasy Plan

Another way to identify goals that will make your life full is to identify fantasies. By knowing your fantasies, you can construct a whole life plan that includes them. Many people fail to even try. They put barriers in the way, such as:

- "I can't."
- "I shouldn't."
- "I can't afford it."
- "My mother/father wouldn't approve."
- "This isn't the way it's done."
- "How could I?"

Well you *can*. This is the only life you have. If you don't live it fully the way *you* want to, you're cheating yourself and your family. Keep in mind that you are a role model for your children. If they see you denying yourself the right to the things you want, will they feel free to go after their own goals?

It often helps to visualize what you want life to look like. You can do this quite literally with powerful results. Cut pictures out of magazines and make a collage on a big sheet of cardboard of the things you want in your life—the type of house, job, relationships, pets, activities. You might be surprised at the pictures you respond to and what your finished picture shows you. Keep it visible to help keep you on track.

Identify Your Goals

List the five things you would most like to accomplish in each area. Don't stop yourself. Don't eliminate those things you think you couldn't or shouldn't do. Dare to dream.

Work	Family	Self
1. _____	1. _____	1. _____
2. _____	2. _____	2. _____
3. _____	3. _____	3. _____
4. _____	4. _____	4. _____
5. _____	5. _____	5. _____

For each of the goals you have identified, ask yourself the following questions.

Is my goal specific, measurable, and clearly defined?

Is my goal flexible (do alternatives exist)?

Is my goal something *I* want (not what others want for me)?

Is my goal possible (within my physical, mental, and emotional abilities)?

Is my goal powerful, representing something I feel passionate about?

Is my goal big enough?

If you answered no for any goal, rephrase or replace it with a goal that meets these criteria.

A family plan.   None of us lives in a vacuum. If you are married or living with someone, the values, goals, and priorities of your partner play a major role in your ability to accomplish your goals. Other family members also affect us. Ask your partner, or anyone else who plays a major part in your personal life, to do the Values Clarification Exercise and identify his or her own goals. Then discuss each of your goals and priorities, how conflicts can be resolved, and how you can help each other achieve your goals.

Also share your goals with other family and friends. By verbalizing the goal and making it public, you acknowledge it to yourself as well as to others and get support. Others will help you and provide resources in ways you could never predict.

Next, you need to identify the actions you need to take to achieve each of your goals. What do you need to do to accomplish your goals? Do you need to take classes or have more time for yourself? What would it take? Use another sheet if you need more room. Leave the time frames blank for now.

My Action Plan

I will get there by taking the following steps.

Action	*Time Frame*

Work Goal 1:
1. _____ by _____
2. _____ by _____
3. _____ by _____
4. _____ by _____
5. _____ by _____

Work Goal 2:
1. _____ by _____
2. _____ by _____
3. _____ by _____
4. _____ by _____
5. _____ by _____

Work Goal 3:
1. _____ by _____
2. _____ by _____
3. _____ by _____
4. _____ by _____
5. _____ by _____

Work Goal 4:
1. _____ by _____
2. _____ by _____
3. _____ by _____
4. _____ by _____
5. _____ by _____

Work Goal 5:
1. _____ by _____
2. _____ by _____
3. _____ by _____
4. _____ by _____
5. _____ by _____

Family Goal 1:
1. _____ by _____
2. _____ by _____
3. _____ by _____
4. _____ by _____
5. _____ by _____

Family Goal 2:

1. _____ by _____
2. _____ by _____
3. _____ by _____
4. _____ by _____
5. _____ by _____

Family Goal 3:

1. _____ by _____
2. _____ by _____
3. _____ by _____
4. _____ by _____
5. _____ by _____

Family Goal 4:

1. _____ by _____
2. _____ by _____
3. _____ by _____
4. _____ by _____
5. _____ by _____

Family Goal 5:

1. _____ by _____
2. _____ by _____
3. _____ by _____
4. _____ by _____
5. _____ by _____

Self Goal 1:

1. _____ by _____
2. _____ by _____
3. _____ by _____
4. _____ by _____
5. _____ by _____

Self Goal 2:

1. _____ by _____
2. _____ by _____
3. _____ by _____
4. _____ by _____
5. _____ by _____

Self Goal 3:

1. _____ by _____
2. _____ by _____
3. _____ by _____
4. _____ by _____
5. _____ by _____

Self Goal 4:
1. _____ by _____
2. _____ by _____
3. _____ by _____
4. _____ by _____
5. _____ by _____
Self Goal 5:
1. _____ by _____
2. _____ by _____
3. _____ by _____
4. _____ by _____
5. _____ by _____

The Big Picture

It is important to look at the big picture when you create a whole life plan to help you to realize that life is (we hope) long. There may be many opportunities for you to reach your goals. In setting time frames for your action plan and goals, also consider how the three sets of goals interrelate. Which goals can you do at once, and which may be more appropriately pursued later in your life? Delaying some goals while you work on others is often referred to as sequencing.

Sequencing. Sequencing is defined by Arlene Rossen Cardozo as:

> . . . the solution more and more women choose of having it all—career and family—by not trying to do it all at once, at all times in their lives. Women who elect to sequence, first complete their educations and gain career experience, then leave full-time work during the years they bear and mother their young children, and then—as their children grow—innovate new ways to incorporate professional activities back into their lives, so that mothering and profession don't conflict. These women—who have clearly separated the work of the house from the raising of their families—are neither "housewives" nor "jobwives" but are persons to themselves.[2]

This principle can be applied by both men and women. It doesn't mean giving up goals or balance. Rather, it means focusing on the balance at each stage of your life and setting goals throughout your life. The way you achieve balance now may be different five years from now.

Bonnie's Story

During my single-parent days, it was difficult to achieve all the spiritual and intellectual goals that were part of my whole life planning. More time was devoted to raising my child and working. Nevertheless, I exercised regularly, saw friends, and learned to find little ways of keeping intellectual and spiritual growth alive. I also set some long-term career goals. Now that my child-raising days are over, I spend more time growing spiritually and intellectually, building my consulting business, and relaxing with my spouse. My responsibilities as a grandmother, daughter, and daughter-in-law are minimal, but caring for elders will probably take more time in the near future. I have tried to anticipate what the responsibilities may be, but it is too soon to know for sure.

Lifeline.   What will your lifeline look like?

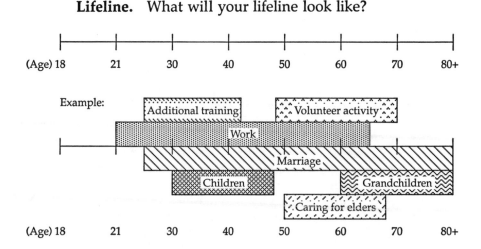

Setting goals over time.   Now let's prioritize the goals over time. Go back to your action plan and fill in the time elements

(1 month, 6 months, 1 year, 3 years, 10 years). You can now translate your actions and goals into a whole life plan. Simply list the actions you need to take in the time frame you have chosen. Use the accompanying chart, or devise one of your own.

My Whole Life Plan

Time Frame	Goal*	Action
1 month		
6 months		
1 year		
2 years		
3 years		
4 years		
5 years		
6 years		
7 years		
8 years		

*Goal: Work Goal 1 = WG1
     Family Goal 3 = FG3
     Self Goal 2 = SG2

9 years		
10 years		
15 years		
20 years		
25 years		
30 years		
50 years		

Every once in a while, pull out your plan. Have you achieved your short-term goals? If yes, give yourself credit and revel in the accomplishments. If not, figure out what went wrong. Did it turn out to be something you didn't really want? Did another goal pre-empt it? Do you want to build it into a later stage? If you are serious about living a conscious life, take the time every year to do another set of short-term goals for the coming year. What new goals can you add? Which old goals can you reaffirm? Take control and do what you want to do with your whole life. It is yours—and it is the only one you have.

ALTERNATE CAREER PATHS

For men and women with aspirations to achieve goals in all three areas of life—work, family, and self—choosing alternate career paths may be one way to fit it all in. In the traditional linear path, an individual moves up the pyramid, increasing his or her power, status, and work load with each rise. For individuals with family responsibilities, this linear career path may not always work. Individuals who wish to spend more time with family may need to reevaluate their career plan.

When deciding what you want to do about your career, you have four basic options.

1. You can keep on your present track.
2. You can stop working, permanently or for a set period.
3. You can change jobs, companies, or careers.
4. You can modify your career path by choosing an alternative track.

If you've chosen options 1 or 2, you can skip the rest of this chapter. If you've chosen options 3 or 4 (or wish you could), read on!

Choosing an alternative career or alternative work option is not a new concept but one that still has not been widely accepted. Many factors weigh heavily on families that decide to try a different road. Many of you may be worried about the consequences of alternative career paths. Questions may come to your mind such as:

Will I ever meet my goal of a high status and power position?

If I choose an alternative working option, will I be taken seriously at the job or will I be seen as lacking commitment?

If I take a family leave, will I have a job when I return?

Can my family get by with less money?

There is no *one* right way. There are only options to choose from. Many individuals look for role models to help them make the decision. But in the end, only *you* can make the decision about what is right for you and your family.

A number of barriers get in our way of choosing an alternative path. Let's look at the most common obstacles, and what we can do to overcome them.

Barrier 1: Fear

Fear is probably the most common barrier to making good decisions for ourselves and our families. Fear is reflected in our everyday language. In Susan Jeffers' book, *Feel the Fear and Do It*

Anyway, she describes her "pain to power" theory of language—how the language we choose colors our vision of what is possible.[3] She gives examples of phrases that prevent us from making good decisions about our lives ("pain") rather than phrases that give us control ("power"). For example, instead of saying "I can't," you might choose "I won't." "I can't" implies external forces are preventing you from doing something or you are just not competent to do it. "I won't" says you have chosen not to do it. "I could" (a decision based on choice) is more powerful than "I should" (where the choice is removed). Similarly, "What will I do about this?" is more empowering than "What can I do?"

When thinking about your alternatives with career and family, "I will handle this by doing _____ " is the most important phrase you can utter. If you really believe you can handle whatever comes your way, you will probably be successful with the choices you make regarding work and family.

Lisa's Story

Lisa is a human resource professional. She did not want to work full time while her baby was under one year old, but she also didn't want to give up her job, so she negotiated a job-sharing arrangement. The arrangement went well for three months. It then became apparent that her partner in the job-sharing position did not communicate effectively with her supervisor, the human resources director. The director finally said Lisa would have to return full time. Lisa wasn't ready to return full time and was determined to make job-sharing work. She worked with the human resource director and her job-sharing partner to improve the communication.

After two months, Lisa's boss still was not satisfied and asked her again to return to a full-time position. Lisa outlined another alternative work plan for her boss. This plan included three days in the office and two days at home. She asked her in-home caregiver to work five days a week to allow her to concentrate on her work on the days she was at home. Her two days at home allowed her to see her child frequently, continue to breast-feed, and eliminate time commuting. Her boss was willing to give it a try. The arrangement satisfied everyone for six months, when Lisa decided to return to work full time.

Lisa's story is one of problem solving and using the "pain to power" theory. She chose "I know I can handle it." When one situation didn't work out, she came up with another solution. She overcame the fear and made it work.

Removing the fear exercise. Have you thought about choosing an alternative career path or work option? What is stopping you?

1. What fears does the situation invoke in you? Describe them.
2. How can you take charge of those fears? Describe your actions.
3. What investigation or homework have you done to identify your options?
4. If you were let go from your job, what would you do?
5. If another fear happened, what would you do?

Barrier 2: Expectations

High expectations of yourself and your partner can be another barrier to making an effective decision for work/family balance. In the last chapter, you identified the values with which you grew up. Those values affect the expectations you have for your life. If you have set a tight timetable for achieving some important career goals such as power, money, or status, you may have little room for family time while you are achieving them. The urgency to have all our career goals met early in life is common. Many individuals believe that if they do not have money, a house, and long-term security early in their lives, they will never achieve it. If you have chosen to delay pursuit of marriage and/or children, great. You are not alone. But if this isn't OK with you, you may need to allow yourself some career flexibility. Give yourself permission to achieve your work goals within a longer timetable that includes time for family, and you may be closer to finding a balance that feels right to you.

Gary and Sue's Story

Gary and Sue have a three-month-old child. As a couple, they had decided Sue would stay at home for a year and then return to her job. In the meantime, Sue was offered a new position in the company that required frequent travel. It was a terrific opportunity for her to reach some of her career and financial goals sooner than she had planned. As a couple, they agreed they still believed one parent should be home with their child for at least a year. Gary decided to ask for a nine-month leave from his job as a newspaper reporter. Gary's boss was shocked and very unsupportive even though the company had a family leave program (without job guarantee). Gary's boss told him he would ruin his career and image in the company and refused to guarantee him a position when he returned. Gary and Sue decided their commitment to family was very important. They felt secure that Gary would find another job if the company wouldn't take him back.

Sue took the new job and Gary took his leave. He checked in with his boss regularly. Six months later, Gary's boss told him the department was trimming positions and his old job would not be available. At that point, Gary began to investigate freelance writing positions. After three months, he began to get some freelance work he really enjoyed. Today he loves his work; has a steady, adequate income; and has the flexibility to work at home and be near his daughter, even though they now have hired a caregiver. Sue enjoys her new responsibilities as well. Their daughter is thriving.

Gary and Sue were honest about their values and priorities and had the courage to put them into action. Their worst fears (Gary's job loss) were realized, and they were able to find solutions. Gary and Sue were not concerned about how their role reversals would be perceived by others. They were both comfortable with their solution to balancing their work and family.

Take a close look at your work life and compare it to the goals you identified earlier in this chapter. Are they compatible? We all need hopes and dreams. We need to be sure our dreams are really our own and not the reflection of the expectations of our parents, our spouse, or society. We need the courage to go after our unique goals.

Linda and Laura

Linda and Laura are both associate attorneys at a large law firm. They started at the same time. Both were married. They chose the same legal specialty. After three years, Linda and her husband decided to start a family. Linda knew that having a family might derail her progress toward partnership, but she wanted to start her family and delaying her career didn't bother her. After her baby was born, she returned to work part time. She remains a valued attorney but will not make partner with her class.

Laura has decided to hold off starting a family until after she makes partner. She and her husband have decided her career aspirations will be better served and that having children later is fine with both of them.

Neither approach is better or worse, just different.

Removing high expectations exercise.

- Clarify your values, goals, and expectations of yourself.
- Discuss them with your partner, as well as your partner's expectations of you.
- Develop a long-term financial plan.
- Be creative about your career.
- Look for role models who have achieved what they want in a creative way.
- Confront your fears. Ask yourself what is the worst that can happen and how you will deal with it.
- Listen to your inner self. If you are happy, trust that you are on the right track.
- Have courage.

Justin's Story

Justin was trained as a teacher. His specialty was music education. After college, he was fortunate to get a job teaching band in grade school for several years. During those years, he also developed a talent for writing scripts for school plays. He did it mostly for fun.

After Justin was married and his wife was expecting, he felt a conflict between his career and new family life. His parents had instilled strong values about being a good provider. His teacher's salary alone would not enable his wife to stay home after the baby was born. Justin investigated new possibilities of using his creative writing talents. Soon he was hired as a writer for corporate sales meetings and industrial shows. The increased income allowed his wife to stay home with their new child.

After two years, Justin realized he did not like the corporate environment and missed working with children. He and his wife discussed his dissatisfaction at length. He realized he was trying to meet expectations set up by his parents. He valued different things. He and his wife worked out a financial plan that included her return to work. Justin began looking for another teaching job. Six months later, Justin landed a job and his wife returned to work. Justin is happy with his work and his schedule allows him to be home by 3:30 p.m. to spend time with their child.

Justin's example is a good study of being creative and open to change, of problem solving, and of listening to the inner self. It took courage to try a new career and then admit it was not one that satisfied his needs. But by admitting his true priorities to himself and his wife, he is back living a life he loves.

Career and other choices can be affected by many outside forces. Things happen serendipitously. How we deal with these unplanned circumstances can be a barrier, or we can look for ways to turn those barriers into possibilities. It takes a willingness to change and take risks.

Alternative career exercise.

- Be open to change.
- Have a vision of what is possible.
- Get the training, skills, or experience you need.
- Believe you can be successful in your new career.
- Develop a contingency plan for if things don't work out.
- Do it.

Over the years, we've known many men and women who have tried alternative careers and lifestyles. All of those individuals had a vision and belief that they could find a better way of working and having a satisfying personal life. Their courage and support have been inspirational in the development of our business and our personal lives.

Bonnie's Story

The circumstances of my family life have often dictated changes in my career—financial responsibilities, my first husband's illness, and being a single parent. As I look back, I am amazed that I have found satisfaction and fulfillment in many careers. As a young person, I was trained in the theater. I truly believed nothing else could bring me the satisfaction I got from dance. Financial circumstances, however, forced me to look at alternative career paths.

When I made the decision to train and work with children in early childhood education, I began to see all the creative ways in which I could use my theater skills in my work with children. Once I opened my mind to that, I found a special niche in my work that encompassed all I had learned in my previous career. My new career also allowed me the flexibility I needed to care for my family. Eight years later, economic need dictated another change. As a single parent, I needed to earn more to care for my daughter. My previous experience gave me the courage to see how my skills could translate to the business community in writing, training, and communication.

Finally, I have brought all three areas of experience and expertise together as a small-business owner and consultant. I am glad for the opportunities I have had to learn and grow. In retrospect, the forced career changes were really a blessing. It pushed me to try different careers and explore skills I never knew I had.

If you wish to consider an alternative career path or work option, here are some questions to answer to help you determine what is best for you.

Beth's Story

My career has been a well-planned accident. I graduated from college with a liberal arts degree, a love for writing and travel and no clue about what I wanted to "be." I thought being an international banker sounded good. I worked as a credit analyst in a bank for three years. Frustrated with the length of the track to lender, I moved to an old-line finance company and the promise of a new job in industry. I *hated* it. I felt smothered by my supervisor, a control-oriented manager, and the rigid organizational structure.

The only job in which I could envision myself being happy was corporate counsel. They got to travel and no one yelled at them if they were five minutes late. So I went to law school. I interned at a law firm my second summer and became intrigued by litigation. For eight years, I worked as a litigator in large law firms. I liked parts of the job very much but still didn't fit well into the corporate environment. I wasn't happy with the hour commitment that left me very little time for a personal life. So I took a hard look at my skills and what I enjoyed and jumped at the chance to co-run a small business.

I think I've finally found my niche. I have a great partner with whom I communicate very well. My finance and legal background as well as the persuasive writing and negotiating skills developed during my years as a litigator all translate well and support me in my new roles as business owner, writer, consultant, and trainer. I still work hard but with much more control over my time. I make less money, but the trade-off of time and flexibility makes it well worth it for me. I'm looking forward to finding a partner, creating a family to balance out my new life, and planning my life as a whole, not just from job to job.

Career Path Decisions

Answer or fill in the following questions.

1. What is my greatest fear?

2. If I chose an alternative career path or work option, I will need to deal with the issues of: (e.g., my partner complaining that my lower salary is not fulfilling my end of the bargain.)

3. If I revise my career plan and I'm unsuccessful reaching my new career goals in my present organization, I can _____ .

4. If I choose a linear career path and I notice my children are having difficulty adjusting to other caregivers and my work schedule, I will _____ .
5. If I choose an alternative work option to help with my ailing mother and my organization doesn't support the decision, I will _____ .

These are only a few of the questions that may help you determine a decision for yourself that helps you create a better balance in your life. When you have completed answering the questions, share them with your partner or friends. Get some feedback. Keep talking and looking for answers that fit you. Consider some of the following options.

Alternative Career Path Options

• *Plateau:* Maybe where you are is where you want to be, at least for now. Where is it written that you must seek (or take) a promotion *now*. Maybe your role as a manager fits into your life. But if you became a vice president, the extra work demands just would not fit. It may be appropriate to coast for a while.

• *Different company:* If your company has not adopted policies that support your ability to balance work and family, consider changing employers. There may be a company that could offer the same or a comparable job whose overall philosophy meshes with your own.

• *Different shift:* For some people, it is possible to achieve a family balance by working other than a daytime shift. Many parents choose this option so that one parent is always caring for the children, either because of financial considerations or because they feel strongly that they want to be the primary caregivers. In one family, for example, Patti, the mother of an infant and a six-year-old, works three days a week. Her husband Rick, a pressman, switched to the third shift after the baby was born so that he could care for the baby while his wife worked and be home when their first-grader gets home. (When the baby is awake more, they plan to have a sitter come in for the mornings while he sleeps.) They have found they actually see each other more often and are happy about the care for their children. A different shift would also be a good solution for someone who wanted to go back to school but could not afford to quit working and didn't want to or couldn't attend night school.

• *Smaller company:* Often, but not always, a smaller company will be more flexible and may not require the ("face") time a larger organization demands. It depends on your job and the employer and you should investigate thoroughly. Of course, less time also generally means less money.

• *Different location:* Your salary may go farther in a different part of the country or in a smaller town. Staying close to other family members can keep your support network strong. Both career and lifestyle decisions are big factors here, but it's something to consider. Many families are choosing relocation "back home" to help them balance.

• *Self-employment:* Do you have the kind of job you could do on your own, on a freelance or consulting basis, maybe making less money if you choose to work less but with greater ability to control your time? Or maybe you have the experience or backing to run a small business. Again, do your homework and plan carefully. Many types of businesses will require substantially more than 40 hours a week, especially in the early years. The great majority of small businesses fail in the first year and even more within three years. Careful research and planning is crucial.

Alternative Full-Time Work Options

Many companies offer alternatives to the traditional 9-to-5, 40-hour workweek. If you want to continue working, but would like to change your hours, see if your employer (or another employer) offers any of the following options for your type of work:

Flextime: Full-time work with flexible starting, quitting, and lunch times, generally within limits set by management and/or approved by your supervisor. Currently, flextime is available to 13 percent of the U.S. work force. Examples: Sarah, a secretary, works from 7:30 A.M. to 3:00 P.M. (rather than 9:00 A.M. to 5:00 P.M.) so that she can be home with her children after school. Marty, a systems analyst, works 8:00 A.M. to noon and 2:00 P.M. to 5:00 P.M. He spends the two-hour lunch period taking care of errands and chores and catching up on his business reading to free his evening and weekend hours for his family.

Compressed workweek: A 40-hour workweek compressed into less than five days. Examples: Mary, a quality inspector, works 10 hours a day Monday through Thursday and has Friday off, so she can attend a weekend college program without collapsing. Ken, an emergency room technician, works three, 12-hour days and is on call for an additional shift every other week. The flexible schedule lets him spend significant time with his two children (and allows his wife to do temporary work on his days off).

Telecommuting/work at home: All or part of the work is done off-site, usually at your home. Examples: Sonia, a court reporter, works at home two days a week to save on her lengthy commute and spend time with her baby. She covers hearings and depositions or is in the office three days a week. Frank, a computer programmer, works at home four days a week, connected to the office by computer. He works in the office one day a week. His schedule allows him to live in the country because he has to do the long commute to his city employer only one day a week.

Less Than Full-Time Alternatives

Less than full-time work for one partner is a balancing solution chosen by many couples, particularly those who are the parents of young children, if they can afford it.[4] Discuss the reasons for altering your career path with your partner. Several mothers have told us that when they went to part-time work, their husbands assumed they would take on full responsibility for chores, become supermom. As one wife told her husband, "I am taking the time and delaying my career to be a better mother to our child, not to be a better wife or homemaker." Stick to your goal. Use the extra time as you intended.

Part-time: Working fewer than five days a week. In most companies, salaries and benefits will be prorated. Example: When Sylvia had her baby, she wanted to decrease the number of hours she worked. As a lawyer at a large law firm, Sylvia had regularly worked 55 to 65 hours a week. She knew her employer would not permit her to cut back her hours and remain on partnership track. Instead, she negotiated a part-time schedule. She carried a reduced caseload. She still works five days a week but now averages 35 hours a week (8:00 A.M. to 3:00 P.M.).

Job-sharing: Regular part-time work in which two people share the responsibilities of one full-time position, with salaries and benefits prorated. Example: When Patti had her first child, she went back to work as a legal secretary full time. After six months, she was exhausted and unhappy with the amount of time her child was in family care. Another secretary was in the same boat. Together, they approached two lawyers and asked if they could job share. The lawyers agreed to give it a try. Six years (and three job-share partners) later, Patti still works three days a week and has had a second child.

Temporary work: Certain jobs allow you to work full or part time when you can, such as nurses, paralegals, secretaries, writers, and journalists. Example: Jennifer is a paralegal. She has substantial care responsibilities for her parents. She works through a placement agency or takes short-term jobs with law firms. When her elder-care duties get to be too much, she refuses assignments.

Voluntary reduced work time: Where one person reduces his or her work hours for a specified period, generally with a corresponding reduction in pay. Example: Monica's father had a stroke and her mother needed help with his care. After a couple of weeks, Monica realized her work and family were both suffering from the new responsibility. She negotiated an arrangement with her supervisor that allowed her to cut back her hours from 40 to 30 a week for two months until she could get her parents' situation stabilized.

Phase-in: An employee returning from a leave of absence phases back into full-time work by working increasing numbers of hours over a specified period. Example: Sarah is an account executive for an advertising agency. When she had her baby, she took her 6-week paid leave and asked for 10 additional weeks unpaid. Her manager believed he couldn't do without someone in her job for four months. Sarah proposed that she come back for two days a week for weeks 7 to 9, three days for weeks 10 to 14 and four days for weeks 15 and 16. She agreed to be available for meetings and to do work at home as necessary. Her manager agreed.

Flexibility: Unplanned Events

Even under the best circumstances, you will have to adjust your life plan. Change is our only constant. It keeps life interesting. You change; family circumstances change. No plan would be perfect without room to change or adjust your goals. Your ability to be flexible and accept what cannot be changed and yet achieve some degree of balance in your whole life is important. Don't lose sight of that vision!

RESOURCES

Abraham, Danielson, Eberle, Green, Rosenberg, and Stone. *Reinventing Home: Six Working Women Look at Their Home Lives.* New York: Plume, 1991.

Ashery, Rebecca Sager, and Michelle Margolin Basen. *Guide for Parents with Careers: Ideas on How to Cope.* Washington, D.C.: Acropolis Books, Ltd., 1991.

Bartholomew. *I Come as a Brother.* Taos, N.M.: High Mesa Press, 1986.

Blotnick, Srully, Ph.D. *Otherwise Engaged.* New York: Penguin Books, 1985.

Bolles, Richard Nelson. *What Color Is My Parachute?* Berkeley, Calif.: Ten Speed Press, 1991.

Brooks, Andree Aelion. *Children of Fast Track Parents: Raising Self-Sufficient and Confident Children in an Achievement Oriented World.* New York: Viking Press, 1989.

Cardozo, Arlene Rossen. *Sequencing: Having It All But Not All At Once.* New York: Atheneum Publishers, 1986.

Conrad, Pam. *Balancing Home and Career: Skills for Successful Life Management.* Los Altos, Calif.: Crisp Publications, 1986.

Covey, Stephen R. *Seven Habits of Highly Effective People.* New York: Simon & Schuster, 1989.

Donkin, Scott W. *Sitting on the Job: How to Survive the Stresses of Sitting Down to Work: A Practical Handbook.* Boston: Houghton Mifflin, 1989.

Edwards, Paul and Sarah. *Working from Home: Everything You Need to Know About Living and Working under the Same Roof.* Los Angeles: Jeremy P. Tarcher, Inc., 1990.

Eyre, Linda and Richard. *Lifebalance: Priority Balance, Attitude Balance, Goal Balance in All Areas of Your Life.* New York: Ballantine Books, 1987.

Feinstein, Karen Wolk, ed. *Working Women and Families*, vol. 4. Beverly Hills, Calif.: Sage Publications, 1979.

Fulghum, Robert. *All I Really Needed to Know I Learned in Kindergarten.* New York: Ivy Books, 1986.

Gabany, Steve G., Ph.D. *The Working Person's Survival Guide.* Terre Haute, Ind.: Hunt & Peck Publishing, 1990.

Gerson, Kathleen. *Hard Choices: How Women Decide About Work, Career and Motherhood.* Berkeley and Los Angeles: University of California Press, 1985.

Grollman, Earl A., and Gerri L. Sweder. *The Working Parent Dilemma: How to Balance the Responsibilities of Children and Careers.* Boston: Beacon Press, 1986.

Hallett, Jeffrey J. *Worklife Visions.* Alexandria, Va.: American Society for Personnel Administration, 1987.

Hewlett, Sylvia Anne. *When the Bough Breaks.* New York: Basic Books, 1991.

Hochschild, Arlie Russell, with Anne Machung. *The Second Shift: Working Parents and the Revolution at Home.* New York: Viking Press, 1989.

Jeffers, Susan, Ph.D. *Feel the Fear and Do It Anyway.* New York: Ballantine Books, 1987.

Judson, Sylvia Shaw. *The Quiet Eye.* Chicago: Regnery/Gateway, 1982.

Kahn-Hut, Rachel, Arlene Kaplan Daniels, and Richard Colvard, ed. *Women and Work: Problems and Perspectives.* New York: Oxford University Press, 1982.

Kanter, Rosabeth Moss. *Men and Women of the Corporation.* New York: Basic Books, 1977.

Kaye, Beverly. *Up is Not the Only Way: A Guide for Career Development Practitioners.* San Diego, Calif.: University Associates, 1985.

Kimball, Gayle, Ph.D. *50/50 Parenting: Sharing Family Rewards and Responsibilities.* Lexington, Mass.: Lexington Books, 1988.

Kimball, Gayle, Ph.D. *The 50/50 Marriage.* Boston: Beacon Press, 1983.

Klinman, Debra G., and Rhiana Kohl. *Fatherhood U.S.A.* New York: Garland Publications, 1984.

Labich, Kenneth. "Can Your Career Hurt Your Kids?" *Fortune,* May 20, 1991.

Lewan, Lloyd S. *Women in the Workplace: A Man's Perspective.* Denver, Colo.: Remington Press, 1988.

Lewis, Hunter. *A Question of Values: Six Ways We Make the Personal Choices that Shape Our Lives.* San Francisco: Harper Collins Publishers, 1990.

Lindbergh, Anne Morrow. *Gifts from the Sea*. New York: Pantheon Books, 1955.

Magid, Renee. *The Work and Family Challenge*. New York: American Management Association Publications, 1990.

Magid, Renee Y., with Nancy E. Fleming. *When Mothers and Fathers Work: Creative Strategies for Balancing Career and Family*. New York: AMACOM, 1987.

Olmstead, Barney, and Suzanne Smith. *Creating a Flexible Workplace*. New York: AMACOM, 1989.

Parke, Ross. *Fathers*. Cambridge, Mass.: Harvard University Press, 1981.

Paulson, Pat A., Sharon C. Brown, and Jo Ann Wolf. *Living on Purpose*. New York: Simon & Schuster, 1988.

Rohrlich, Jay B. *Work and Love: The Crucial Balance*. New York: Harmony Books, 1980.

Satir, Virginia. *Helping Families to Change*. New York: J. Aronson, 1975.

Satir, Virginia. *Meditations and Inspirations*. Berkeley, Calif.: Celestial Arts, 1985.

Satir, Virginia. *The New Peoplemaking*. Mountain View, Calif.: Science and Behavior Books, Inc., 1972.

Smedes, Lewis B. *Choices: Making Right Decisions in a Complex World*. San Francisco: Harper & Row, 1986.

Tilly, Louise, and Joan W. Scott. *Women, Work, and Family*. New York: Holt, Rinehart & Winston, 1978.

NOTES

1. Jay B. Rohrlich, M.D., *Work and Love: The Crucial Balance* (New York: Harmony Books, 1980), p. 232.
2. Arlene Rossen Cardozo, *Sequencing* (New York: Atheneum Publishers, 1986), p. 17.
3. Susan Jeffers, Ph.D., *Feel the Fear and Do It Anyway* (New York: Ballantine Books, 1987), pp. 33–46.
4. Kenneth Labich, "Can Your Career Hurt Your Kids?" *Fortune*, May 20, 1991, p. 52.

Chapter Three

Managing Guilt

As we grow older, our duties, responsibilities, and roles too often assume control of us. No longer free to express our moods, needs, and fantasies, many of us find our security in the act of pleasing others. Our natural moods and impulses feel shameful, and we gradually learn to block them out, resigned to live in a state of unhealthy guilt where the futile effort to please everyone, do good, be "perfect," and keep ourselves safe and secure in the process keeps us prisoners of the urge to do what we think we "should" do. In saying yes to guilt, we begin saying no to life.[1]

Joan Borysenko, *Guilt Is the Teacher, Love Is the Lesson*

Guilt is like a black fly looking for a place to bite. There seems to be no way to avoid it.[2]

Rabbi Harlan J. Weschler, *What's So Bad About Guilt*

*W*orking Mother magazine says 16 percent of 3,000 working mothers surveyed suffer intense guilt because they work.[3] Most women work because they want to or need to, as do men. So why feel guilty? Only one in five women reported they are guilt-free about balancing work and family. The majority of women surveyed admit they feel at least occasional twinges of guilt. They also acknowledged that their guilt was self-inflicted.

In our workshops and focus groups, many parents tell us that "feeling guilty" is a frequent occurrence. Men and women feel guilty about the same things—children, spouses, elders, and work. In short, no aspect of our lives escapes. Guilt is sometimes felt more intensely by single parents who feel guilty about the absence of the other parent in their children's lives, guilty about not being a better parent, or guilty about doing things for themselves. Many of us feel guilty about everything at one time or another. Guilt can interfere with any healthy whole life plan. It can also take away the energy you need to balance your life.

HEALTHY AND UNHEALTHY GUILT

In *Guilt Is the Teacher, Love Is the Lesson,* Joan Borysenko describes two types of guilt—healthy (productive) and unhealthy (debilitating). Healthy guilt "teaches us conscience by providing emotional feedback about the consequences of hurtful behavior."[4] Unhealthy guilt is the culprit that creates stress, unhappiness, and lower productivity. "Unhealthy guilt causes life to become organized around the need to avoid fear rather than the desire to share love."[5] Healthy and unhealthy guilt translate into other emotions and tendencies.[6]

Healthy Guilt	*Unhealthy Guilt*
Responsibility	Fear
Self-inquiry	Unworthiness
Forgiveness	Perfectionism
Self-esteem	Overachievement
Self-awareness	Self-blame
Personal growth	Anxiety

The Sources of Unhealthy Guilt

Guilt can often be triggered by fear.

- Fear our children won't turn out OK.
- Fear our elders won't love us anymore.
- Fear that if we displease a friend, that person will abandon us.
- Fear that if we anger a loved one, she or he will cease to love us.

Guilt can also be triggered by the demands of others on us. Consciously or not, others may try to manipulate us by pushing our guilt button.

Child:
> "You're never home. You're always working or traveling."
>
> "You love work more than you love me."

Elder:
> "You never come to see me. You're always too busy."

Spouse/partner:
> "Since you went back to work, this house is never clean."
>
> "Since you took that promotion, you never have the energy to go out."

Co-worker:
> "You're no fun since the baby."

Supervisor:
> "You can't work on this project. It'll put too much stress on your family."

Old tapes from our parents or other role models play over and over in our heads and add to our guilt. Phrases like, "Mothers/ fathers must be at their best at all times," or "Children need their mothers at home."

Finally, guilt can be triggered by demands we make of ourselves, particularly when our roles conflict. For women, the role conflict between working and being a "Donna Reed" type of a mother can create stress and feelings of guilt. Dr. Renee Hermann, psychiatrist, describes women as still having the burden of "making everything right." She says women in particular are trained to believe they are responsible for other people's happiness.[7] This is a heavy burden to carry.

For men, the dual responsibility creates a different set of stresses. Role models in the past promoted "being the breadwinner." Men who choose to take time off to be with their families risk being labeled a "wimp." Most corporate cultures still reward those who work long hours and sacrifice family time for the job. In such an environment, a man who wants to leave on time or not travel during family time is regarded as not dedicated to his work or the corporation. Promotions and performance evaluations may be hurt by choices to spend more time with family.

Single parents, who have the greatest burden in working and parenting, often feel guilty that their children don't have male or female role models. Many single parents have told us how they are constantly trying to prove to society that they and their children are OK.

The tugs and pulls for both working men and women are heightened by new studies and media reports saying our children are in crisis. Parents, who average only 17 hours a week with their children, are charged with neglect.[8] Television and news stories portray horrifyingly inadequate child care. Natural concern and worry plague parents as well. Similarly, we worry about elders who need us, and we may feel guilty that we are not doing enough.

The Results

Unchecked guilt can have many unpleasant side effects:

- Stress.
- Fatigue.
- Depression.
- Anxiety.
- Burnout.
- Mood swings.

The Cure

Unhealthy guilt often comes from not making conscious choices.[9] If you feel in control of your life, it is easier to dismiss the negative feelings. If your priorities reflect your values and the time spent in each of your roles reflects your priorities, you are less likely to suffer role conflicts and the guilt that results. Remember why you have made your choices and reaffirm those decisions when conflicts occur.

Why do you work? Answer the question for yourself. Why do you work? Some answers might be:

- I want to.
- Money.
- Intellectual stimulation.

- I like my work.
- Balance.
- Challenge.
- Status.
- Security.
- To be a good role model for my children.
- Excitement.
- Community service.
- To get out of the house.
- Friendship.
- Self-worth.

Think also about what benefits your family gets from your working. How does your partner benefit (lifestyle, conversation)? Your children (role model, confidence, and independence)? Your boss (good work, perspective)? Don't focus only on the paycheck. Think about other benefits.

Compartmentalization also helps. When you are at work, work. When you are home, be with your family. When you're doing chores, do chores. When you have set aside time for yourself, take it.

Finally, get support. Ask your family and friends to give you positive feedback and try not to push your guilt button to get what they want. Join a support group where you can give and get validation for your choices. If your feelings of guilt overwhelm you, get professional advice. Learn to limit your guilt to the healthy guilt level.

SPECIFIC ANTI-GUILT STRATEGIES

The best way to deal with guilt is to recognize when we are feeling it, analyze whether the cause is real or imagined, and then either fix it or dismiss it. Stay grounded in reality, not the "what if" world. Answer the fear-provoking questions. Take stock. Are your children OK? Is your spouse or partner OK? Is your relationship OK? Are your elders OK? Are you OK? If everything is OK, forget the guilt and move on. If something is not OK, figure out what you need to do to fix it. Then *do* that, and move on.

Are My Children OK?

Don't dwell on questions that have no answer. For example, "Is my child going to turn out OK?" Who knows? All you can do is your best. You can answer the question, "Is my child OK right now?" Don't engage in the "who is the better mother" debate. Just evaluate whether your child is thriving.

Your child's development depends on several factors:

1. *The physical, emotional, intellectual characteristics your child was born with* (genes, heredity, and so on). Many child experts believe the genetic makeup of an individual plays an equal part with the environment the child grows up in. Children are born with a particular temperament or way of behaving which influences the lifestyle they develop over time. According to the authors of *Parenting Young Children*, heredity, family atmosphere and values, role models, parenting methods, and the child's position in the family are all factors that influence lifestyle.

2. *Parenting skills.* Even though you as working parents may spend less time with your children than the hired caregiver, your role in nurturing the values and total growth and development of your children is of vital importance. One mother told us she used to feel guilty when she missed a "first." Now she takes the attitude that the first time is the first time her daughter does something new for her. Dr. Sanger agrees. She says, "Achievements don't become truly real in a child's mind or imagination until they have been validated by mother's presence."[10]

Working parents often complain about exhaustion and lack of energy to be an active parent. Be clear about your priorities. Make time for your children. Negotiate time off with your employer if necessary.

Increasingly, isolation from parents is a problem even when the family is physically together. Beginning in infancy, children are highly attuned to their parents' moods. When parents have little left to give to their offspring at the end of a stressful day, the kids' disappointment can be crushing. Eleanor Szanton, executive director of the National Center for Clinical Infant Programs, a nonprofit resource center in Virginia, says, "What happens between parents and children during the first hour they are reunited is as important as anything that happens all day. If the mother is too exhausted to be a mother, you've got a problem."[11]

"Security, trust, a sense of mastery and competence, humor, curiosity—all qualities that matter to a child's future—originate not in *what* a woman does with her child but in *how* she does it; in other words, in the sensitivity of her interactional and relationship skills."[12] The same factors play a role in successful fathering.

3. *The quality of child care.* Numerous studies have cited the importance of a skilled caregiver who can promote the proper development of a child. There is no question that the quality of his or her child-care program will play an important role in how your child develops. Child care should be stable, warm and loving, and skilled.

Says Barbara Reisman, executive director of the Child Care Action Campaign, a nonprofit educational and advocacy organization in New York: "Despite all the questions that have been raised, the bottom line is that if the quality is there, and the parents are comfortable with the situation, the kids are going to be fine."[13]

If your child is achieving all he or she should at his or her age (see the development charts at the end of Chapter Four) and is happy and healthy, you and your child are doing great.

Give yourself the following reality test to help you identify how much of the guilt you experience in connection with your children is unhealthy guilt.

Reality Check

1. Under my circumstances, I have chosen the best caregiver for my child(ren).	Yes / No
2. I feel confident in my parenting skills or am getting the education I need to be the best parent I can be.	Yes / No
3. I ask for and get the support I need.	Yes / No
4. I know my child(ren)'s special traits and characteristics.	Yes / No
5. I am comfortable with the amount of time I spend with my child(ren) each week.	Yes / No
6. My child(ren) is(are) healthy, happy, and thriving.	Yes / No

If you circled "Yes" in response to each statement, ignore those guilt feelings until they go away. If you circled "No" to a question, take action to address the problem—and eliminate the guilt. Are there other aspects of your parenting role that trigger guilt feelings? If so, figure out what you need to do to fix the problem, and then do it. If you are doing the best that you can and your child(ren) are OK, give yourself credit and don't lessen your accomplishment by allowing yourself to feel unwarranted guilt.

Are My Elders OK?

With our elders living longer, we are presented with caregiving roles for which we are not prepared. As with parenting, you want to feel like you are doing a good job. Ask yourself the question, "Does work interfere with my ability to be a loving and caring daughter or son?" One of the ways to validate your role as a daughter or son is to distinguish between what you *can* do to ensure the safety and care of an elder versus what you *cannot* do to alter their physical, emotional, and intellectual situation. Every caregiving situation is different, depending on the elder's physical, emotional, intellectual, and financial state. If your guilt stems from things you cannot change, it is unhealthy and unproductive. When the feeling surfaces, say to yourself, "I am doing all I can—I can't feel guilt about things I cannot control."

Give yourself the following reality test to help you identify how much of the guilt you feel in connection with your elder is unhealthy guilt.

Reality Check

1. Under my circumstances, I have chosen the best caregiver for my elder.	Yes / No
2. I feel confident that I have educated myself about the aging process and my elder's options so that we can make sound decisions about care.	Yes / No
3. I ask for and get the support I need.	Yes / No
4. I know my elder's physical, emotional, and financial needs.	Yes / No
5. I am comfortable with the amount of time I spend with my elder each week.	Yes / No
6. My elder is getting the best possible care and is as well as can be expected under his or her circumstances.	Yes / No

If you circled "Yes" in response to each statement, ignore those guilt feelings until they go away. If you circled "No" to a question, take action to address the problem—and eliminate the guilt. If there are other things that trigger guilt feelings, assess whether or not you can do anything to fix the problem. If you can, do it. If you cannot, make a resolution not to punish yourself with guilt about things you cannot change.

Is My Spouse/Partner OK?

Common remarks such as, "Since you went to work, we never have a decent meal," or "You spend more time with your secretary than you do with me" can hurt. You may find yourself questioning your choices. Am I a bad partner because I work, or travel, or go to school? Believing that you are a good partner is essential to maintaining a stable relationship.

Role conflicts for men and women can easily cause guilt as each partner tries to find the balance between being fulfilled, contributing financially, and being a supportive partner. Keeping in touch with each other by listening, clarifying, and probing should be a daily occurrence. Your partner's needs change as she or he goes through life's different cycles. Talk openly about your conflicts, needs, and feelings.

Give yourself the following reality test to help you identify how much of the guilt you experience in your relationship with your spouse or partner is unhealthy. (The same questions can be applied to your relationships with friends or other adult family members.)

Reality Check

1. I spend time alone with my spouse/partner each week.	Yes / No
2. My spouse/partner and I communicate often and effectively.	Yes / No
3. I ask for and get the support I need; we work together to organize and manage our responsibilities.	Yes / No
4. I know my spouse/partner's needs and try to meet them.	Yes / No
5. My expectations of myself and my spouse/partner are realistic.	Yes / No
6. I am the best spouse/partner I can be.	Yes / No

If you circled "Yes" in response to each statement, ignore those guilt feelings until they go away. If you circled "No" to a question, take action to address the problem—and eliminate the guilt. Finally, ask your spouse/partner if she or he is happy. Talk about ways you could make life better together. If things are fine, enjoy it and don't let guilt feelings get in the way.

Bonnie's Story

On one of my husband's assignments, he commuted to Mexico City, leaving on Monday and returning on Friday. We both complained about the lack of time together, so I joined him for a week. I worked on this book in his hotel room during the day. We could at least have breakfast and dinner together. My husband felt less guilty for being away, and I felt more satisfied.

Are My Friends OK?

Occasionally a friend or other family member will hit us with a remark like, "You never have time for lunch!" or "So where have you been?" Most of us immediately fall into the trap of defending ourselves and our lives.

The next time a friend, family member, or spouse throws one of those guilt phrases your way, be prepared to use good communication skills. Most likely, there is an underlying message in their statement. Work to uncover the hidden message. Are they frustrated, overworked, confused, or just missing you? Probe to find out what you can realistically do to satisfy you both. Push feelings of guilt out of the way. They will only interfere with positive problem solving and take away from the energy you need to fulfill your many roles.

GET RID OF GUILT

Here is a final list to help manage your guilt feelings daily.

1. Analyze the feeling, find the cause.
2. Look at what you are doing that's good (providing love, support, financial security).

3. Learn to say no to things you can't provide for others.
4. Trust your instincts.
5. Share your ideas with others.
6. When in doubt, get some professional help.

The "I'm Guilt-Free" Exercise

Take a minute to go through the following meditation exercise. Find a comfortable, quiet place. Relax your body and close your eyes after reading the following meditation. Quietly give yourself a mental pat on the back.

"I'm doing the best I can everyday. I provide love and support for my family, friends, co-workers, spouse, elders in many ways. I do this with love and honesty. I am glad to be me. Now it's time to take care of me by taking this moment and enjoying the beauty and peacefulness it brings to me."

Let's kick the guilt habit forever!

RESOURCES

Borysenko, Joan. *Guilt Is the Teacher, Love Is the Lesson.* New York: Warner Books, 1990.

Bradshaw, John. *Healing the Shame that Binds You.* Deerfield Beach, Fl.: Health Communications, 1988.

Briles, Judith. *Confidence Factor: How Self-Esteem Can Change Your Life.* New York: Mastermedia, 1990.

Burke, Jane B., and Lenora M. Yuen. *Procrastination: Why You Do It, What to Do.* Reading, Mass.: Addison-Wesley Publishing, 1983.

Caine, Lynn. *What Did I Do Wrong? Mothers, Children, Guilt.* New York: Arbor House, 1985.

Dinkmeyer, Don, Gary D. McCay, and James S. Dinkmeyer. *Parenting Young Children.* New York: Avon, 1969.

Feinstein, Karen Wolk, ed. *Working Women and Families*, vol. 4. Beverly Hills, Calif.: Sage Publications, 1979.

Gerson, Kathleen, *Hard Choices: How Women Decide about Work, Career and Motherhood.* Berkeley, Calif.: University of California Press, 1985.

Harris, Amy Bjork, and Thomas A. Harris, M.D. *Staying OK.* New York: Avon Books, 1985.

Harris, Thomas A., M.D. *I'm OK, You're OK*. New York: Avon Books, 1969.

Jeffers, Susan, Ph.D. *Feel the Fear And Do It Anyway*. New York: Ballantine Books, 1987.

Kaufmans, Gershen. *Shame: The Power of Caring*. Cambridge, Mass.: Schenkman Publishing Company, 1985.

Kottler, Jeffrey A. *Private Moments, Secret Selves: Enriching Our Time Alone*. Los Angeles: Jeremy P. Tarcher, Inc., 1990.

Labich, Kenneth. "Can Your Career Hurt Your Kids?" *Fortune*, May 20, 1991.

Sanger, Sirgay, M.D. and John Kelly. *The Woman Who Works, The Parent Who Cares*. New York: Harper & Row, 1987.

Satir, Virginia. *Making Contact*. Berkeley, Calif.: Celestial Arts, 1976.

Schaef, Anne Wilson. *Meditations for Women Who Do Too Much*. San Francisco: Harper & Row, 1990.

Shaevitz, Margorie. *The Superwoman Syndrome*. New York: Warner Books, 1984.

Shwebel, Andrew. *Guide to a Happier Family: Overcoming the Anger, Frustration and Boredom that Destroy Family Life*. Los Angeles: Jeremy P. Tarcher, Inc., 1989.

Swigart, Jane. *The Myth of the Bad Mother: The Emotional Realities of Mothering*. Garden City, N.Y.: Doubleday Publishing, 1991.

Weschler, Rabbi Harlin J., Ph.D. *What's So Bad About Guilt?* New York: Simon & Schuster, 1990.

NOTES

1. Joan Borysenko, Ph.D., *Guilt Is the Teacher, Love Is the Lesson* (New York: Warner Books, 1990), p. 1.
2. Rabbi Harlin J. Weschler, Ph.D., *What's So Bad About Guilt* (New York: Simon & Schuster, 1990), p. 16.
3. Karin Rubenstein, "Guilty or Not Guilty?," *Working Mother* Magazine, May, 1991, p. 53.
4. Joan Borysenko, *Guilt Is the Teacher*, p. 9.
5. Ibid., p. 20.
6. Ibid., pp. 35–43.
7. Lynn Caine, *What Did I Do Wrong? Mothers, Children, Guilt* (New York: Arbor House, 1985), pp. 184–85.

8. Kenneth Labich, "Can You Hurt Your Kids?" *Fortune*, May 20, 1991, p. 38.
9. Karen Wolk Feinstein, ed., *Working Women and Families* (Berkeley, Calif.: Sage Publications, 1979), p. 289.
10. Kenneth Labich, "Can You Hurt Your Kids?" p. 52.
11. Sirgay Sanger, M.D. and John Kelly, *The Woman Who Works, The Parent Who Cares* (New York: Harper & Row, 1987), pp. 177–78.
12. Kenneth Labich, "Can You Hurt Your Kids?" p. 44.
13. Sirgay Sanger and John Kelly, *The Woman Who Works*, p. 189.
14. Rick Fields and editors of *New Age Journal, Chopwood Carry Water* (Los Angeles: Jeremy P. Tarcher, Inc., 1984), p. 286.

Chapter 4

Communicating to Get What You Need

No pleasure has any savor for me without communication. Not even a merry thought comes to my mind without my being vexed at having produced it alone without anyone to offer it to.[1]

Montaigne, *Essays, III.9*

I believe in both Show and Tell. My attitude is that I am always talking to one person, and if I am going to address you in any form, I ought to give you every advantage I can to understand what I have to say. This emphatically does not mean that I underestimate your intelligence. It means that I am aware how complicated communication is. It means that I would rather err on the side of telling you too much than run the risk of leaving you confused.[2]

Robert Fulghum, *Uh-Oh*

Good communication is an art. Researchers have studied human communication closely with fascinating results. Hundreds of books have been written on the subject (some of which are listed at the end of this chapter). While we can't discuss all aspects of communication here, we can remind ourselves of the basic principles and practice them to enhance communication with our family, friends, and co-workers.

How often have you walked away from a situation wondering what was just decided? Or been unsuccessful again in your attempt to get your toddler to pick up his or her toys? Or hung up the phone with your elderly parent frustrated because you never reached an understanding? Or failed to get your point across when explaining to your supervisor that you need some flexibility? The application of good communication skills can make these kinds of exchanges productive.

COMMUNICATION SKILL ASSESSMENT

To help you assess your communication skills, answer the accompanying questionnaire. Be honest. If you are brave enough, ask other family members if they agree with your self-assessment.

While this is not a scientific assessment of your communication skills, it should give you a good idea about areas of your communication that could use practice, and it lets you hone in on those sections as we cover the various elements of communication.

WHAT IS COMMUNICATION?

Experts say communication is the giving and receiving of information through words, gestures, and writing. The goal is *effective* communication. When a message sent by one person (the speaker) is the same as that received by the other person (the listener), you have achieved effective communication. The messages sent and received are positively and negatively affected by many variables.

The speaker is half of the equation. Body language, attitude, tone, voice quality, timing, and setting all contribute to the message sent as do the words themselves. The listener is the second half of the effective communication equation. Successful exchanges are promoted by active listening. Active listening requires the listener to restate or paraphrase the speaker's message, verbal and nonverbal, and ask questions until the listener is clear about what the speaker is saying. The speaker is primarily responsible for giving an accurate message, but both parties must work together for mutual understanding. The accompanying diagram illustrates the main elements of effective communication.

The Elements of Effective Communication

Words: accurate messages.   The trouble often begins in giving the message. If the message given by the speaker is

How Do I Communicate?

	Never	Rarely	Sometimes	Frequently	Always
1. I am aware of my body language.	1	2	3	4	5
2. I ask questions and/or admit when I don't understand.	1	2	3	4	5
3. I focus on the matter at hand.	1	2	3	4	5
4. I listen well.	1	2	3	4	5
5. I don't interrupt.	1	2	3	4	5
6. I am aware of the emotional aspects (feelings) of a conversation.	1	2	3	4	5
7. I am good at confronting problems and reaching solutions and compromises.	1	2	3	4	5
8. I feel comfortable talking about personal issues.	1	2	3	4	5
9. I am approachable and open.	1	2	3	4	5
10. I accept what I hear without being judgmental or critical.	1	2	3	4	5
11. I am consistent in each aspect of my communication (words, feelings, body language are the same).	1	2	3	4	5
12. I think (about what I want to say and when I want to say it) before I speak.	1	2	3	4	5
13. I express my feelings readily.	1	2	3	4	5
14. I don't take everything personally or make it about me when it is not.	1	2	3	4	5
15. I consider all of the relevant factors in solving a problem.	1	2	3	4	5

Now look at where you stand overall.

61–75 Excellent communicator.

46–60 You are generally understood and understand others.

31–45 You probably have frequent misunderstandings but may not see communication as the problem.

15–30 Practice the skills we have discussed to achieve more effective communication.

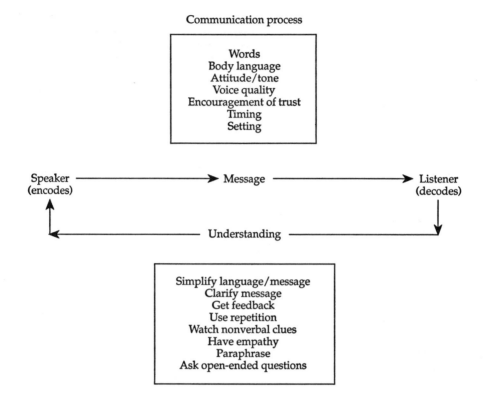

Communication process

Words
Body language
Attitude/tone
Voice quality
Encouragement of trust
Timing
Setting

Speaker ————————————→ Message ————————————→ Listener
(encodes)   (decodes)

←———————————— Understanding ————————————

Simplify language/message
Clarify message
Get feedback
Use repetition
Watch nonverbal clues
Have empathy
Paraphrase
Ask open-ended questions

inaccurate or unclear, then the response of the listener can be inappropriate.

For example, let's take a busy, tired couple discussing the upcoming weekend schedule. One spouse says, "I'm really tired and don't feel like doing anything this weekend." What she or he means is, "I'm tired now and don't want to add anything to our weekend plans so I can get some rest." The listener thinks it means his or her spouse doesn't want to attend a dinner party they had agreed to attend on Saturday night. The listener doesn't ask any questions, and they both go to bed without discussing it further. The next day she or he calls the host and cancels. When Saturday afternoon arrives, the spouse who complained of being tired begins getting ready to go out and is shocked to learn the party was canceled. An argument results. If the speaker had said what she or he actually meant, there would have been clear communication from the start. And if the listener had asked questions or clarified to make sure she or he understood the meaning the speaker intended, the misunderstanding could have been avoided.

Field of experience. What words mean to another person may be different from what the same words mean to you. Each of us has experienced a different set of circumstances (our "field of experience"). Our perceptions, needs, and values may be different, interfering with our ability to communicate clearly. Our cultural background and gender also influence our communication style. The same message can mean different things to different people.

Message	Meaning to Person A	Meaning to Person B
Don't spend too much.	Less than $50.	Less than they'd intended ($100).
Give it to me when you can.	As soon as possible.	In a reasonable amount of time.
Do you want to go to Mom and Dad's for Christmas?	Do you want to go?	I want to go, will you go with me?

Too often we assume listeners, who think and act like they understand, do understand our message, when they don't. Misunderstanding rather than effective communication results.

The only way you can be sure the message the listener received was the one you intended is to ask for feedback and check the other person's understanding. You can use a few techniques to help make sure the message you intend is the message received by the other half of your conversation equation.

Use appropriate language. Think about what it is you really want to say. It sounds simple but how often do we actually *think* before we speak? Be clear on what it is you are trying to say. Then use words you think are appropriate for your listener. Try not to use abstract or complex language. Rather, use straight simple sentences. This doesn't mean use simple words or a limited vocabulary. It means saying what you want to say as clearly as possible and not hiding the message in a lot of unnecessary verbiage.

Don't overload.   We've all experienced machine-gun communicators who talk faster than we can listen. Or we try to cover a lot of new material all at once. Regulate the information flow to a reasonable level.

Use repetition.   If you get a confused look as a response, try repeating the message in different words or at a different time. Repetition can help make your message clear. It forces both the speaker and the listener to check the meaning of the message.

Get feedback.   Assume you've been misunderstood. Follow up your message and ask for feedback. Ask the listener to repeat the message back to you as a check. If you are not sure the message is the one you intended, question the listener to see if she or he really understood you.

Body language.   We've discussed the importance of clarifying our words. However, the silent language expressed by our bodies, expressions, and gestures is just as important as the words. Some experts say over 50 percent of our messages are said with body language. We must be aware of our body language and integrate it into our conversations so that it is consistent with the words.

Because of the importance of body language, our observation skills need to be developed as thoroughly as our listening skills. What does body language tell you and how can you use what you see to help you with effective communication? As the speaker, you can watch the listener for nonverbal clues that can help you determine whether or not the listener understands your message. If a speaker is having difficulty expressing himself or herself in words, pay attention to the gestures or the body posture. What can you as the listener observe in the body language that you aren't getting through the words?

For instance, consider young children whose vocabulary isn't developed. If you've been observant, you know their body language signals hunger, distress, confusion, or joy well before they can express those feelings in words. Sometimes adults also have difficulty expressing themselves, but clear messages are radiating from their facial expressions and gestures. Or our words may not accurately reflect our feelings. Our spouse may say she or he agrees, for example, but the tension in his or her body and the failure to make eye contact says the opposite.

Body language exercise. Here's an exercise that can help make you more aware of the power of communication through facial expressions, gestures, and other body language. Get a pencil and notepad. Turn on the television but turn off the sound. A talk show is best. Sit down and observe the guest's behavior closely. Take notes on what you see.

Did the person express emotions? What kind?

Did the person seem relaxed or tense?

Did the person listen to the host?

Could you guess the subject matter of the conversation?

What else did you discover about this person just by watching them?

Try watching a dramatic show with the sound off. You may be amazed at how well you can follow the plot just by watching the action and the characters' body language.

Now that you've had an opportunity to practice with a stranger, begin to use your heightened observation skills on members of your family and friends. Take a few minutes every day to observe a family member's body language. Answer the following questions.

1. What have you noticed that you didn't notice before?
2. How will that information be useful to you in the future?
3. What will you do differently the next time you have a conversation and you notice the same body movements or expressions?

To make family communication as effective as possible, share this information with every member of the family. Have each member go through the body-watching exercise. Discuss as a family what you have learned.

Let's look at an example of how body language can assist people in getting the information they need.

Jim and Carol's Story

Carol and Jim have been married for three years. They successfully work through issues requiring compromise and negotiation
most of the time. One of the reasons they succeed is that they are
very observant of one another's body language. Jim has a habit of
lifting his shoulders up and down when he is feeling stressed.
When he does this, Carol usually begins a conversation with, "It
looks like you've had a rough day! What happened?" This approach immediately acknowledges how Jim is feeling and allows
him to get things off his chest before they discuss any issues that
might require compromise.

Jim has also done his homework with Carol's movement idio-
syncrasies. Carol often has a difficult time expressing her feelings,
so Jim isn't always clear where she stands on certain issues. Jim
knows that she gets an eye twitch when she is really upset. She
doesn't say anything and the rest of her body is completely calm,
but her eye twitches. That is a clue to Jim that the conversation has
touched a nerve. It gives him the opportunity to comment on what
he sees. "Does this subject upset you? Can you tell me why?"
They can then move on from there.

Attitude/tone. When you are having a conversation with
others, the conversation is often affected by the attitudes the
speaker and the listener bring with them and the tone of their expressions. For example, say to yourself, "I'm glad you're finally
home!" Depending on the words you emphasize and the tone
you use, the same sentence can mean very different things.

You can't change the other person's attitude. You can be aware
of it and acknowledge that what they feel is real. Use active listening and turn your observation into a question or comment.
"You seem upset," or "Are you angry?" Often by acknowledging
the other person's feelings, you can help that person get past the
emotion and express his or her message more clearly.

You *can* control your own attitude and your tone of voice. Because your attitude and tone will provoke a reaction from your
listener, try to make it one of cooperation. You know that if you
are angry, that's the tone you will use. Some of us yell. Others get
icy. Either way, the listener is likely to be bristling or defensive

before you finish the first sentence. Decide whether you need some time to cool off or otherwise adjust your attitude to make the conversation more effective. Be conscious of your attitude and the tone of your communication and adjust the tone to evoke a productive reaction from the other person.

Voice quality. Sometimes we are unaware that the level and pitch of our voice can affect the success of a conversation. For example, a whiny, high-pitched voice puts many people off. A calm, even-pitched voice can promote listening and a calm atmosphere.

If you haven't already heard your normal, everyday voice on audiotape, record your voice so you can hear what you sound like. Ask yourself: How might the quality and pitch of my voice affect others? Does it promote understanding and conversation? If necessary, get a speech therapist or vocal coach to help you adjust your voice quality. Actors and speakers get coaching to promote good voice quality and reduce accents or other speech habits that hamper their ability to communicate. So should you if your present voice quality is hurting your communication with loved ones and/or co-workers.

Be empathetic/encourage trust. Empathy is "the action of understanding, being aware of, being sensitive to, and vicariously experiencing the feelings, thoughts, and experience of another"[3] An empathetic speaker puts himself or herself in the listener's place. Can you anticipate how your listener will react to your statement? Can you say it differently to bypass a defensive response? If you know that the subject is a sensitive one, try phrasing it as an "I" message, where the focus is on you rather than the other person.

"I think we need to take a hard look at our budget."	versus	"You spend too much money."
"I feel that you don't listen to me."	versus	"You never listen."

You may want to consider outlawing the words *you always* and *you never* from your house. They are rarely accurate and very inflammatory to your listener. Practice being an empathetic speaker and you will find others will respond in kind. If you can speak into an atmosphere of trust, developed over time, you are more likely to develop a pattern of successful communication and understanding.

Timing. The timing of a conversation can also affect the outcome. The speaker needs to consider the best time to engage in certain communications. If you try to have a serious, or even significant, conversation while everyone is rushing around getting ready for work or school, it isn't likely to be successful. Choose your timing. The moment you think of the topic may not be the moment to talk about it.

Mike's Story

Mike wanted to talk to his wife, Trisha, about a job offer he had received. It would mean relocation to another state. As Trisha walked into the house from work, two hungry children in tow, he announced, "I've been offered a job in Philadelphia! What do you think?" Both children started to cry and Trisha looked like a bomb had been dropped on her, which it had. Mike had a lot of reassuring to do before he got to his planned conversation about the pros and cons.

The setting. Sometimes a conversation can be affected, negatively or positively, by the location you choose. A noisy room is not conducive to a serious conversation. A public place may not be the place to discuss a very personal concern. Doing something else (even the dishes) while talking can be distracting for both speaker and listener.

Bonnie's Story

When I was a single parent, my teenage daughter and I always had our best conversations when we went out to dinner. I learned more about my daughter's life over simple meals in inexpensive restaurants than at home. It seemed the atmosphere was more congenial and there were fewer distractions. One of her complaints was that I never listened when we were at home. I was always doing dishes, cleaning up, or making a meal rather than giving her the full attention she needed.

I found the same to be true with my husband. We seem to linger over coffee and talk about important issues in more depth in restaurants than in our own kitchen. Part of the reason is the telephone is not constantly interrupting us. We now have a rule about letting the answering machine take all calls when we are having dinner.

Now that we've reviewed the best ways to express the message, let's look at the listener's responsibilities.

Active Listening

God gave us two ears and one mouth so we could listen more than we speak.

Folk saying

Good listening is the backbone of successful communication. A good listener looks at the speaker. The listener waits until the speaker is finished before responding. Active listening includes the responsibility to clarify that the message you have received is the message the speaker intended. This means paraphrasing the thoughts and feelings expressed by the speaker, implicitly (by the speaker's body language) or explicitly, in your own words. You don't have to get it right the first time. Each attempt will help the speaker clarify his or her message.

Most of us don't regularly do any of these things. We will repeat back a phone or credit card number to make sure it is right, but not a complicated message or thought where the chances of misunderstanding are even greater! Why don't we listen? What gets in the way? Good listening requires discipline. If you haven't learned that discipline earlier in your life, it may take some practice to develop it as an adult. It takes energy and concentration to listen well. We're so busy that we often just don't take the time. If you take the time to actively listen, however, you'll prevent many disagreements, saving you time and aggravation in the long run. The benefits of active listening are numerous.

Active Listening[4]

- Allows the other person to clarify his or her message by speaking directly to the specific misunderstanding you have revealed.
- Demonstrates that you want to understand what the other person is saying. It conveys interest in and respect for the other person.
- Increases the accuracy of communication and the degree of mutual understanding.
- Satisfies the other person that you really do understand his or her point. She or he will then probably be more willing to attempt to understand your views.
- Gives the other person a chance to vent negative feelings, which then allows you to work on the problem at hand.
- Can result in highly productive, creative outcomes (problem solving) when all participants in a discussion clearly understand various positions that people hold with regard to problems.
- Allows movement from a superficial conflict to the basic underlying problem.

Practice active listening with co-workers, friends and family members. Using the following statements or your own, practice what questions or responses you would use to really understand the intended communication. Play both roles, the speaker and the listener.

"I can't get anyone to help me."

"I feel guilty going to work when my child is sick."

"Mommy, I want you to stay home."

Open-ended questions. Part of active listening requires questioning. Asking good clarifying questions requires creativity and thought. For example, it's easy to say "why" but more difficult to ask a specific question, perhaps incorporating some of the speaker's language to help the speaker clarify his or her message. An open-ended question will always give you more information than a closed question, which can generally be answered in one word.

Open-Ended	*Closed*
What's bothering you?	Do you like being angry?
Can you explain what you mean?	Do you want to be punished?

The response needn't be a question. There are open and closed responses as well.

Open Response	Closed Response
Tell me more.	So what.
You're really upset.	Because.
Something is wrong.	Stop complaining.

The more caring and understanding you can be while asking questions, the more success you will have helping the speaker clarify the question. Judging, blaming, or criticizing will only harm the conversation. In all likelihood, the speaker will get defensive or just shut down. Similarly, denying the communication will only frustrate your listener. An extreme statement may not be an accurate message, but it is an opening gambit for a conversation about the topic. Let's look at some of the typical responses you probably give to or hear from members of your family.

	Bad Response	Good Response
"I hate school!"	No, you don't.	It sounds like you had a bad day. What's wrong?
"You're so insensitive."	No, I'm not.	What triggered that? Was there something I did (or didn't do) that bothered you?
"You never come to see me."	That's not true.	I come to see you once a week. Would you like me to come or call more often?

Here's another example of the power of open-ended questions. Joan and Syd are discussing the schedule for the weekend. Joan repeatedly says no to every suggestion Syd makes. Syd keeps asking why, and Joan continues to say because. Soon, they are at a dead end. Syd takes a deep breath and applies active listening.

Syd:
Joan, it's unlike you to be so negative. What's wrong?

Joan:
I'm sick and tired of being responsible for all the work around here.

Syd:
So you feel you are responsible for everything?

Joan:
Well . . . yes.

Syd:

I'm not sure I understand. Can you be more specific?

Joan:

Well, I appreciate that you help out. But the burden of organizing and making sure the details are worked out is always on my shoulders.

Syd:

So, you don't want to assign and supervise the chores anymore. Is that what you are saying?

Joan:

I guess so. I'm just tired of disciplining the kids if they don't help out and having to tell you what has to be done.

Syd:

Well, I'm not sure I can be the supervisor of the house responsibilities, but I would be willing to try. I can make sure the kids do their jobs.

Joan:

That would be great!

Syd:

But don't complain if I do things differently. Can you live with that?

Joan:

You bet!

Syd listened to key words and used them in open-ended questions to clarify Joan's responses. Not all situations are this easily resolved, but it is a model of the type of effective communication we all should try to achieve.

Keep the following points in mind to enhance your listening skills:

- Make eye contact; look at the speaker.
- Show interest (even if you're tired and even if you're not really interested).
- Avoid doing other things while listening; give your full attention.
- Clarify; ask questions until you are sure you understand the message.
- Don't talk; allow silence while the speaker is gathering thoughts.

- Stay relaxed; try not to jump to conclusions.
- Recognize and get past your immediate emotional response (anger, upset, irritation).
- Paraphrase; summarize points of agreement and disagreement in your own words.

Effective Confrontation

Effective communication is essential when the behavior of another person is unacceptable or displeasing to you. When confronted with such a situation you have three constructive options:

- Leave the scene.
- Change yourself (i.e., redefine what is acceptable to you) to remove the conflict.
- Confront the other person and attempt to change their behavior.

If you choose the first option, the behavior might be repeated. Most of us will react to the repeated behavior with anger, even though we know it is unfair to direct anger at the other person when you never told them the behavior was troublesome the first time.

The second option, changing yourself, is a difficult but very valid choice. We should always consider whether it would have less effect on *us* to change than on the other person whose behavior we want to change.

The third option, confrontation, often just provokes an unproductive fight. It needn't if effective communication skills are used. An effective confrontation can be accomplished by use of an "I" message.

Going through the exercise of creating an "I" message can clarify the situation for you as well as for the other person. If you can't determine the tangible effects the behavior has on you, maybe you need to reevaluate your reaction. Perhaps you just need to accept that your reaction is unwarranted. Maybe you don't like the behavior because of a personal preference. Once you recognize your reaction in this light, you can accept it or negotiate a compromise, a swap of preferences, such as, "I'll put the lid down if you put your clothes away" rather than a confrontation.

"I" Message Confrontation[5]

- Focuses on your feelings rather than on a critical judgment of the other person.
- Includes active listening to handle defensive reactions.
- Refrains from telling the other person what to do (either by instruction, suggestion, or demand), leaving the decision whether or not to change up to that person.
- Lets the other person know the effect of the behavior on you.

An "I" message confrontation is made up of three elements:

1. A nonblameful and specific description of the problematic behavior.
2. A description of the concrete effects the behavior has on you.
3. An expression of the negative feelings the behavior caused you to feel.

The following examples illustrate good "I" message confrontations:

Behavior	Effects	Feelings
When you don't do the chores you say you'll do,	I have to do them myself,	Which makes me over-tired and stressed.
When you contradict me in front of the children,	it makes it harder for me to get them to do what I say,	which makes me angry at them and at you.
When you assume I know what I did that annoyed you,	I have to guess at what I did wrong,	which frustrates me and makes me angry.

Mary's Story

Mary and Ken have been married for five years. They share household chores. Ken is responsible for laundry. Over the years, they have had a number of arguments over Ken's leaving the washing machine lid up. Mary asks him to keep it closed. Ken always leaves it up. Having learned about "I" messages, Mary decides to have an effective confrontation. She knows the behavior (leaving the lid up) and her feelings (annoyed, displeased), but try as she might she could not come up with a plausible effect the behavior had on her. She simply prefers the lid down. Now, if she sees it up she closes it. She no longer seeks a behavior change from Ken.

When you initially start to use "I" messages, you are likely to encounter the same defensive reactions you got when you demanded change. But if you stay in the "I" message mode, eventually it becomes uncomfortable for the other person to ignore you.

The "I" message confrontation in action. (In this example, the "I" messages are in bold print; active listening is in italics.)

Kate and Tom have a three-year-old daughter, Cindy, who attends a day-care center near their home. Kate and Tom share drop-off and pick-up duties by alternating weeks. On many occasions, Tom has called Kate at work at the last minute and told her she has to pick up Cindy because he has to work late. Invariably, Kate has to frantically rearrange her schedule and/or arrange a backup either at work or to pick up Cindy. To no avail, she has yelled, begged, nagged, and cajoled to get Tom to be more conscientious. She has told him to either give her more notice or, better yet, prevent the problem or arrange a backup himself. Nothing has worked. She has decided to try the "I" message approach. Rather than confronting the issue the minute Tom walked in the door, as she has in the past, Kate waits until after dinner, when they are relaxing over dessert and Cindy is watching TV.

Kate:

Tom, I know we've talked about this before, but I'm not sure I've made myself clear about what effect your failure to pick up Cindy has on me.

Tom:

Oh, not this again. Do you just want a fight?

Kate:

No. I want to see if we can resolve this problem once and for all in a way that works for both of us. **When you don't pick Cindy up when you have agreed, I have to juggle my schedule at work, which upsets me and the people I work with and makes me feel that you don't believe my work is important.**

Tom:

That's not true; I know your work is important to you. I don't want to interfere with your job. But things come up.

Kate:

Do you mean unexpected things happen?

Tom:

Yes, things you don't plan.

Kate:

I understand that unplanned things happen. **But when you don't handle the unplanned things yourself, it throws the full responsibility back on my shoulders, and I resent it and feel that the burden is all on me.**

Tom:

Have you been watching "Oprah" again?

Kate:

Tom, I'm serious. **When you tell me to handle picking Cindy up at the last minute, I have to juggle my schedule or quickly arrange for a backup, and it makes me stressed out and angry with you.**

Tom:

What do you want me to do about it?

Kate:

I don't want to tell you what to do. What do you think you can do?

Tom:

Can I have another copy of the list of phone numbers of the other parents who can pick Cindy up? I'll put it on my work computer so I won't lose it.

Kate:

Sure. *So you will handle getting backup rather than asking me to do it?*

Tom:

Yes. But maybe we could agree on days at the beginning of the week based on our work schedules instead of alternating weeks, so the problem won't happen so often.

Kate:

Good idea. What does next week look like for you?

All of the factors of communication we have discussed played a part in this successful resolution. Kate, the speaker, thought out her words. She chose her time and setting to be appropriate for the conversation. She maintained a positive attitude and a calm, rational tone of voice. Tom listened and was defensive at first. But by restating her "I" message and refusing to let the behavior be put back on her, Kate enabled Tom to come up with a solution that would work for him.

Effective confrontation takes practice. But it works. Tell your family members about the technique and ask that they work with you to raise the level of effective communication in your house.

COMMUNICATING WITH CHILDREN

For working parents, being away from the child's day can be a constant source of stress. You want to feel in touch with your child's interests, friends, and behavior. You want to be a good parent. How can you keep in close touch with your child daily when you are working? Or if you are home and your child attends school all day? You guessed it—communication!

Probably the most neglected element of adult communication is listening. Although it can be difficult for the harried parent to listen, it is the best way to keep channels open and to encourage and teach the child to listen.

Remember to pay attention to body language. It can be a great help in communicating with young children. Ask good questions. With children, that may mean choosing words that get their attention. You also need to understand their development level so that the words you choose are those they understand. If you have the opportunity to attend your child's preschool or daycare center, listen to the professional teachers. Observe how they speak and relate with the children. You will probably hear them speak in direct, uncluttered language. We have included charts of a child's development levels and of the development of language skills at the end of this chapter. For more information, read some of the books listed in Resources.

Repetition is also part of the process. Repeating the same messages slowly and clearly in different ways will clarify any misunderstanding on the child's part. For example, "This is an outside toy (ball). When we go to the park, we take the outside toy. Let's see if we can find an inside toy. Can you think of any?"

The timing of the conversation can also be important. Trying to talk to a tired or hungry child can be a frustrating experience for you both.

Jan's Story

Jan is the working parent of a three-year-old. She believes she won't be a good parent unless she knows the details of her son's life at day care. When she picks him up, she immediately wants to know everything about the day. He is often tired, hungry, and not communicative. Jan usually feels frustrated. However, once they are home and after dinner, he is usually relaxed while he's taking a bath. At that time, he often brings up things that happened during his day. Jan finally picked up on the cues and let things drift until bath time when she asks questions gently and gets a sense of what he did, who he played with, what he was leaning, and how he felt.

Young children often talk about things at the most unpredictable times. Something will remind them of things they have done during the day, and then they talk. Your ability to be patient, probe gently, and listen well will promote conversation with young children.

Tom's Story

Tom was helping his four-year-old son get dressed. Tom was running late and was worried about missing his train. His son was whining about his socks. Tom wasn't listening and continued to put on the clothes he had chosen. Soon the situation was out of hand and the child was on the floor screaming. "No. I don't want those!" Tom got angry and was yelling at the child for being uncooperative. Tom missed his train, the child went to school upset, and the day started badly for everyone. What Tom didn't do was listen. The words weren't clear, and Tom didn't try to understand what was going on. Tom's child was asserting his independence and simply wanted to wear a different pair of socks. A few good, understanding questions could have prevented the whole incident.

Early-morning conflicts between parents and their children are common. These situations cause stress and can get everyone off on the wrong foot. It's important for parents to be as calm as possible and let children know that getting to work on time is important. Avoiding lengthy explanations but still dealing with the issues at hand is a delicate balance for a parent.

The following example is of a three-year-old child and her parent. The child has been in a day-care center for two years. In general, the child has been cooperative in the mornings except for an occasional incident of not wanting to getting dressed immediately. This morning, however, she is particularly upset about going and refuses to eat or get dressed. Her mother is starting to get upset about being late for work but realizes she must stay calm if she is going to get cooperation from her child. The child is sitting in front of the TV as the mother walks into the room to talk with her.

Mother:

Alice, you aren't eating or getting dressed. What's the matter?

(Open-ended question)

Child:

Don't want to.

(Dead-end response)

Mother:

Let's turn this TV off now. Remember it's a school day not a play day. Please get dressed.

Child:

No. (Whines and rolls on floor.)

Mother:

But today is a workday for mom and a school day for you. Let's have a race back to your room and I'll help you to get dressed.

(Encourages the child to understand the circumstances.)

Child:

Don't want to. (Pulls legs up to knees and pouts.)

Mother:

Can you tell me why you don't want
to?

(Speaks patiently and
calmly. Rubs child's back
while talking.)

Child:

I hate dumb, old school.

Mother:

It sounds like you're really unhappy
about school. What don't you like
about it?

(Active listening—para-
phrase) (Open-ended
question)

Child:

(No response.)

Mother:

Could it be Ms. Miller (teacher)? Did
she say something that made you upset?

(More specific probe;
open-ended question)

Child:

No.

Mother:

Could it be nap time . . . or snacks?

(More specific probe)

Child:

No.

Mother:

Alice, you'll have to help me. I don't
know why you are so unhappy about
school.

(Gets closer to child and
offers her lap to sit on.)

Child:

Amy says she won't ever play with me
again.

Mother:

Tell me about Amy while we get your
clothes on.

(Gently lifts child to her
feet and walks toward
room.)

Child:

(Doesn't resist and begins talking.)
She said I'm stupid and she doesn't
want to be my friend.

Mother:

That must feel very bad.   (Acknowledges feelings.)

Why did Amy call you stupid?   (Probe)

Child:

Because I didn't want to play dress
up.

Mother:

Could you play something else with
Amy? You told me last week that you
played puppets with her. Maybe you
could do that again.

Child:

(Unenthusiastic) Maybe . . . but she
always takes the best puppets.

Mother:

I bet you could ask her to share. While
we are driving in the car, let's talk
about how you could get Amy to
share puppets with you today.

Child:

OK.

When Alice and her mom got to school, Alice didn't want to go in
and face Amy. In a sympathetic but firm manner, the mother explained to Alice that she was going to have to leave for work and
that she was confident Alice was going to figure out how to get
Amy to share. The mother spoke with the teacher to let her know
what had happened. The teacher agreed to help the two children
work out their differences. The mother was only a few minutes
late to work, and she explained to her supervisor what had occurred. She offered to take a few minutes off her lunch hour to
make up the time.

General hints for handling emotional outbreaks follow:

- Look for causes. Don't try to reason a child out of an emotional situation. Most conflicts are caused by feelings of
  frustration and anger. Acknowledge and respect these feelings. Accept that the feelings are real.
- Do your homework. Investigate what might be the cause.
  Get as much information as possible from the child who is

having the conflict. Talk to others who might have insight, such as caregivers or other parents.

- When the conflict arises when you are on your way to work or at other inconvenient times, remain calm and try to gather information quickly so you can resolve it, at least temporarily. Don't throw a tantrum yourself. It will only escalate the problem. You need to be in control. This is your strength.
- Stand firm and be clear on what the choices and consequences are if the child doesn't cooperate.
- If the child regains control, praise him or her.
- When you have resolved the conflict, allow some time for yourself. It takes a lot of energy to stay in control when these emotional outbreaks occur. If you're on your way to work, take some deep breaths to help you relax. Give yourself a pat on the back. You deserve it.
- Prevent the problem from occurring by developing ways to assist a child to handle frustration and anger. Show, not only tell, the child what you mean. You're the role model.

Keep in mind that when a child's behavior gets out of control frequently, professional help may be needed to identify and resolve the problem. Services like the Capable Kid Centers in Illinois can help you with discipline and behavioral problems when they occur. Your knowledge of your child and the circumstances will help you determine when things have gotten out of hand. Then you'll know if counseling is necessary.

Finally, while we cannot talk or listen to a child the same way we would to another adult, neither should we talk down to a child. Each child is a person, entitled to respect. Treat your child the way you would want to be treated.

Play

Free time when you just play with your children is important time, and very valuable to good communication. Whether your children are young or teenagers, finding the time to go to dinner, dance, play a game, go hiking, or work a puzzle with them is important for many reasons. First, it is fun. It is the stuff that fond memories are made of. During those informal moments, you will probably learn more about your child than at any other time. Your communication is relaxed and playful. Your children will respond in the same way and probably discuss things that they want to share with you. Many parents have told us that bedtime, after the story when the lights were low, was when they had the most meaningful conversations with their children. The children felt safe, warm, loved, and ready to share.

COMMUNICATING WITH ADOLESCENTS

Developing understanding between you and your teen is one of the most challenging aspects of parenting. Using the skills of effective communication, instead of focusing on the emotion of the moment, will save you many exasperating experiences as your teen goes through the typical stages of adolescence.

When your teen is moody and quiet, use good probing questions and observation skills to start a dialogue. "Tom, you look very unhappy today? Want to talk about it?" Unless you detect something serious is going on with your teenager, silence and an expressed need for privacy may be the norm for this stage of development. You may not get the same willingness to respond from your teenager that you got when she or he was eight years old. When that happens, be patient and understanding. But if you think a problem exists, be persistent.

Dan's Story

Dan is a single parent of a teenage daughter, Leslie. Like many teenagers, Leslie is sometimes moody and difficult to reach, but she had always been a good student and active in social events. Then Dan learned from school that Leslie had been absent several times from one of her classes. Dan tried to discuss it, but Leslie refused to talk about it.

Dan was frustrated but determined to find out what had caused the behavior change and why she was cutting the one class. He brought the subject up again. Leslie just stared and answered his questions in monosyllables. However, Dan noticed her nervously running her hands through her hair and tapping her foot whenever he mentioned the teacher of the class she was skipping. Her nervous actions weren't congruent with her words, which said everything was OK. He kept probing and finally discovered the teacher had said something sexually suggestive to her. She was embarrassed and frightened to talk about it. She thought it was her fault. They eventually got the situation resolved, but it might have never come out if Dan hadn't noticed the inconsistency between her words and actions.

Bonnie's Story

When my 17-year-old daughter came to breakfast with seven earrings on, it was most difficult for me to control my feelings and words. I wanted to say, "You look like a gypsy. Take those off." Although the observation was probably true, the response was negative and judgmental and would have immediately started an argument. Instead, I held my temper and tried a probe. "Is there something special going on at school today?" Her response was short. "No, this is what is 'in,' Mom!"

I asked her another question to get her to think about how she might be viewed by others. "What do you think others think when they see you dressed that way?" She responded by saying, "They probably think I'm weird." I asked, "Do you want to be weird?" She was silent and then got up abruptly to leave for school. I made one final comment as she walked out the door. "You might want to think about how other people judge you because of your clothes and jewelry. If you want to make a certain impression on others, you might want to change your appearance to match that." I never said another word after that.

On the first day of her summer clerical job, she walked into the kitchen wearing a lovely blouse, skirt, low pumps, and only two pearl earrings. I felt I had made some impression on her from our earlier nonjudgmental conversation. By choosing words and taking an attitude that encouraged her to evaluate her behavior herself, I was able to get my point across constructively.

Not all situations will work out like these. Many variables affect how adolescents behave. But good communication skills along with a sense of humor will help you through some trying moments.

- Pick up on body language.
- Be a good detective and investigate other ways of finding out information. Teachers, friends, and neighbors may be able to fill in the gaps. Many parents have told us that when they chauffeur their young teens to events, they learn all sorts of things about their children's lives from the kids' conversations. Because their parents aren't allowed to talk, the kids forget they're there!
- Avoid judgmental and negative comments; this will assist you and your adolescent to have mutual respect. Young people are particularly sensitive about the way they express themselves in dress, music, and words. Their self-esteem can be affected by negative comments.
- Don't deny their feelings. Adolescent feelings are just as real as yours or ours, maybe more so.

The following scenarios can help you practice dealing with typical situations that cause conflict between parents and adolescents. Think about how you will respond if it happens with your child.

1. You have set an 11:30 P.M. curfew for your 16-year-old daughter to return from her evening out with friends. She arrives at 1:00 A.M., her third late arrival in four outings.
2. You have let your 16-year-old son borrow the car on Saturday morning. You told him to return it by 2:00 P.M. because you have errands to run. It's now 3:00 P.M. and he is just pulling into the driveway.
3. Your 15-year-old daughter calls you at work to discuss borrowing money. She is argumentative and pushing your guilt button.
4. Your 14-year-old son has been told not to bring friends home until his homework is done. You have arrived home early from work to find his friends there. His homework isn't done.

Discuss the scenarios with your teen and let him or her participate in determining the consequences. By allowing the teen to participate, you encourage good communication and let the child figure out his or her own solution within the boundaries you have set. Preset, agreed on punishments, which escalate for repeated rule breaking, might help avoid fights. "I" message confrontations may also work. Remember, if there is no effect (either on you or their safety), is there a need for the rule? If there is, continue the discussion until your teen understands. Try not to retreat to that old standby "Because I said so." We know it is easier than explaining, but recall how frustrated you were when you received that response from an adult. Take a deep breath and explain again. When they do understand, obtain their commitment. The communication skills you use now will help them communicate better—now and as adults.

COMMUNICATING WITH ELDERS

There are many pervasive myths about the effects of aging. One of the most common is that elders become childlike. In fact, there is no evidence that the elderly have minds like children. Therefore, treating an elder like a child will only get in the way of healthy conversations. Similarly, many individuals assume the elderly are rigid and irrational or overly emotional. Elders are likely to have the same personality traits and characteristics that they have exhibited their whole lives.

As elders age, however, their patterns of communication may change. New health problems and fears can alter the way they relate to you. Suddenly you are faced with a new communication challenge. Finding out what is really going on can be difficult. We all find it hard to admit we need help, but it is particularly difficult when you need help with things you've been able to do all of your life. Try putting yourself in your elder's place, and it might be easier to empathize with the difficult changes that person is experiencing. Many of our elders never felt free or permitted to talk about personal things. It may be especially hard for them to open up to you. Don't let denials or evasions, theirs or yours, get in the way of identifying and dealing with changing circumstances.

Carrie's Story

Carrie's mother is a very quiet 76-year-old woman who lives alone. It is difficult for Carrie to know how to help her because her mother rarely asks for help, even when she really needs it. Her mother always says everything is all right. Carrie found out from a neighbor that this isn't always true. The last time Carrie visited her mother she noticed a change in her mother's facial gestures. Whenever they talked about things that were giving her mother problems, her mother's mouth began to move forward and back. When she saw that signal, Carrie knew her mother needed help but she couldn't say it with words. Carrie would then gently probe and find ways to help.

Be patient and look for the key words and phrases that will give you hints. Keep in mind the times in which your elders grew up (Depression, war, and so on) and how those factors may be affecting their perceptions and communication with you. In many instances, they just need to hear some reassuring words from you. Understanding their frustrations and acknowledging their feelings should be key elements in your exchange.

Try to listen for the messages and feelings behind the words. Be aware, too, that you may be distracted or overwhelmed by your own feelings.

Mary's Story

Mary has a part-time housekeeper who stays with her mother while she is at work. Mary's mother isn't an invalid, and her understanding and communication are fair. However, she gets frustrated when she needs assistance. Sometimes her frustrations get in the way of good communication. While Mary was in a meeting at work, she was called out by her secretary who said there was an emergency call from her mother. When she got to the phone, her mother was very upset because she wasn't getting what she needed from the housekeeper. She began to cry and tell Mary she shouldn't leave her with "that awful woman."

> Mary got angry for being called at work and didn't really listen or ask questions. She left work and her meeting to go home and check on the problem. When she got there, her mother calmly asked her why she had returned from work. Mary was confused and angry. After some discussion with the housekeeper, she discovered her mother and the housekeeper had already worked out their misunderstanding. Mary went back to work feeling frustrated and more angry. All in all, it was a very unproductive day.

This was not an easy situation. However, a few simple questions like, "Mom, you sound upset. What's going on?" or "Mom, I'm not sure I understand. Are you saying that you want to use the stove and Hilda won't let you?" or "Mom, can we have a long talk about it tonight when I get home?" might have prevented Mary from leaving her meeting and her workplace.

If you keep in mind that you can't alter their situation (age, health, and so on), you will feel less frustrated. You can assist your elders through difficult times by reassuring them you understand and you are there for them, even though you may not be able to solve all of their problems.

The two major objectives in communicating with our elders are:

- Identifying and helping them get what they need.
- Achieving understanding, trust, and respect.

To accomplish those objectives, you will have to rely on good probing questions, active listening, and observations of body language, voice quality, gestures, and messages under the words.

Here's a typical phone exchange between an elder mother and daughter.

Daughter:

Hello, Mom.

Mother:

Hi. So you finally called. I haven't heard from you in a long time.

Daughter:

Mom, I talked to you two days ago.   (Clarifying)

Mother:

That was a long time ago.

Daughter:

I know it must seem like a long time to you. Next time it feels too long, you call me, OK?   (Confirming feelings)

Mother:

I can't find your number.

Daughter:

OK. How about if we get you a programmable phone so you just have to push a button?

Mother:

That would be good.

Daughter:

What's new?   (Open probe)

Mother:

Nothing, same old thing.

Daughter:

Sounds like you could use something new in your routine.   (Probing)

Mother:

I'm too old to change . . . and besides my legs are too weak to go anywhere.

Daughter:

I'm sorry you're feeling that way.   (Acknowledging feelings)
Would you like me and the kids to   (Concrete suggestion)
take you out for lunch?

Mother:

Maybe . . . we'll see.

Daughter:

Mom, I know it must be hard for you some days. I wish I could make it easier for you. I'll call you tomorrow and you can tell me then if you'd like to go to lunch this weekend. OK?

Mother:

OK.

Your communication may also be hindered by old patterns left from when you were a child. Too many of us never establish adult-to-adult relationships with our parents. If you haven't, you're operating under a communication handicap. If you had difficulty communicating in the past, you probably still will—unless you change those old patterns. You'll have to work at changing destructive patterns of behavior. (There are a lot of good suggestions about how to deal with destructive behaviors in *How To Survive Your Aging Parents*, a resource listed at the end of the chapter.)

Here are some general guidelines to follow when communicating with your elders:

1. Listen.
2. Paraphrase.
3. Use "I" messages.
4. Be prepared for resistance.
5. Do your homework; offer solutions.
6. Don't judge or blame.
7. Look for underlying, hidden messages and feelings.
8. Respect your elder(s) wishes, values, feelings.
9. Acknowledge when you need to consult a professional for guidance.

Martha's Story

Martha is one of those individuals in the "sandwich generation." She has children at home, and she helps her 70-year-old widowed mother who lives alone. Martha works full time and travels occasionally. During their frequent visits, her mother often said she had adjusted to living alone. Recently, because of her travel schedule, Martha was unable to see her mother regularly for a while. She kept in contact by daily phone calls. Suddenly, her mother complained that Martha never came to visit her. Martha reacted with feelings of guilt, sure she was not being a good daughter. Through subsequent conversations, Martha determined her mother was lonely. Even though it was painful for Martha to discover, it clarified the issue. Martha was then able to make suggestions and help her mother get involved in group activities.

For Martha and her mom, there was a concrete solution. Not all situations will work out as easily.

Paul's Story

Paul is an only child and has had a very close relationship with his parents. Both of his parents are in their 80s. In the past year, his father became fearful of traveling or going out to social events. Paul tried to reason his dad out of the fear. Their conversations always ended in shouting matches. Paul's wife observed the situation and suggested she talk to his dad. She was able to get Paul's dad to talk about the reasons for his fears—bouts of confusion and disorientation. She was able to get Paul's dad to admit things to her he was unwilling to admit directly to his son. These conversations went on for several months. In the end, Paul's dad maintained his fears, but he began to make small attempts to go out more as they found ways to provide transportation and other things that made him feel more secure outside of his home. There were no easy solutions to the problems, but there was better understanding and less tension between father and son.

COMMUNICATING WITH SPOUSE/SIGNIFICANT OTHER

For real communication to be achieved, there must be some enthusiasm on both sides, a kind of preliminary communion.

George Gusdorf, *Speaking*[6]

Setting up and maintaining good communication with your partner is crucial. It affects all family members. Being able to successfully negotiate, compromise, and understand each other's point of view will contribute immeasurably to a healthy family system. Your communication with your partner also serves as a role model for your children.

Try some of the following techniques suggested in Jane P. Jones's "Healthy Conflict" workshops:

- Approach conflicts with curiosity rather than a negative attitude.
- Make good eye contact and use "I" statements rather than "you." Don't blame or judge.
- Allow your partner to finish without interrupting.
- Ask for what you want.
- Use words and phrases that show you care about the individual even though you are in conflict.
- Be ready to compromise.
- When you are finished, reaffirm your appreciation for each other and do something fun.

In Virginia Satir's book, *Making Contact*, she emphasizes that being honest with feelings is an important part of communication and being able to change. She says, "Being emotionally honest is the heart of making contact."[7] Gayle Kimball writes in *The 50-50 Marriage*, "Couples with successful marriages in which both feel nurtured realize that communication is the lifeblood of their marriages and that time must be specifically carved out to talk about their feelings."[8] Feelings must be shared even if they are unpleasant. Sharing feelings and expectations can lead to greater intimacy.

How well do you and your partner work together for common goals? Fill out this assessment sheet out with your partner to find out the areas of strength and weakness.

Healthy Relationship Communication Assessment

	Myself			My Partner		
	Always	Sometimes	Never	Always	Sometimes	Never
Listens	1	2	3	1	2	3
Doesn't interrupt	1	2	3	1	2	3
Compromises willingly	1	2	3	1	2	3
Expresses feelings	1	2	3	1	2	3
Accepts feelings of other partner	1	2	3	1	2	3

Maintains an atmo- sphere of cooperation	1	2	3	1	2	3
Is willing to resolve conflicts	1	2	3	1	2	3
Is willing to talk through resentments	1	2	3	1	2	3

Talk about areas where you could improve and how you could help each other to better understand. Each partner has responsibility to shape the nature of the relationship through communication. Recognizing uncomfortable situations and then approaching the conflict with curiosity (instead of anger) may help you discover something about yourself and your partner that you haven't known before. When you get stuck, get help from a professional counselor. Choose someone who will assist you to develop a healthy communication style.

Here are some guidelines to help you in your role as a partner:

1. Know what is important to your partner. Ask good questions, listen, clarify.
2. Don't take anything for granted. Communicate daily. Your partner's needs may change and your assumptions may be wrong.
3. Be creative in finding new ways to be more available, supportive.
4. Learn to compromise and negotiate.
5. Gather information from other couples on how they are managing.

Healthy problem solving and negotiating can preserve sanity and save energy. Move away from the emotion of the situation and try to look at it objectively. Here is a problem-solving formula to assist you when you are faced with difficult situations.

Problem-solving formula.

1. Define the issue(s). What is causing the conflict(s)?
2. Identify any underlying feelings that affect the issue(s), such as guilt, fear of losing elders, losing contact with children, etc.

3. Identify individual needs.
   • My needs—to see my parents regularly.
   • My spouse/partner's needs—to see his children or grandchildren regularly.
4. Identify what you will do to compromise and what is your bottom line.
   If you do . . . then I will do . . . .
5. Use "I" message confrontation to express your problem.
6. Find ways to alleviate tension between you (humor, hugs, etc.).
7. Be flexible and open. You may not get all your needs met at once.
8. Get counseling, if needed.

A common issue that causes conflict between spouses is lack of time for each other. Even in situations when children are grown, there is a constant juggling act. For example, Jane and Joe have been happily married now for three years. Both have jobs that require regular travel. Their children (from previous marriages) are out of school and live on their own. Jane and Joe have elder parents still living. Their dilemma is how to schedule their business travel and visits with children and parents and still have time for each other.

Using creative problem solving, here is how they worked it out.

1. The issue(s):
   • Time for each other on the weekend because of family commitments.
2. Underlying feelings:
   • Strong desire to keep in contact with each child.
   • Strong desire to make sure elders are taken care of.
   • Guilt—not having had enough time for children or elders in the past.
3. Individual needs:
   • Jane wants to have elderly parents stay overnight on weekends frequently; also wants to visit with her children.
   • Joe wants to see elderly parents on occasion; also wants to visit with his children.

- They both want some extended time together.

4. Jane and Joe discussed compromises and solved their problems by first consulting their calendars and planning carefully.
   - Jane compromised by not having frequent visits but rather several lengthy visits going into the week; she planned weekend visits when Joe was traveling.
   - Joe planned some of his visits with children and elders during the week when Jane was traveling.
   - They agreed that time earmarked for each other was inviolate.

5. They agreed after each planning session to go out for coffee or ice cream to break the tension.

6. They both agreed they would reevaluate the situation as needed and keep the communication open. As they talked, they grew to truly understand each other's personal needs and feelings. Their problem solving brought them closer as a couple.

In situations like Jane and Joe's, each person must remember the commitment to the relationship is primary. However, within that relationship there are values that are dear to heart. Respecting those values and negotiating in a healthy manner can eliminate resentment that can ultimately hurt the relationship.

Finally, it has long been clear to most of us that men and women talk (and listen) differently. Deborah Tannen calls it "genderlect."[9] Neither style is bad or good. They are just different. Just acknowledging gender differences can assist a couple's communication. Reading about it can help even more and give you an understanding of where breakdowns in communication may be coming from. The process of achieving true understanding is an expression of your love and respect for each other.

COMMUNICATING WITH YOUR SUPERVISOR

Applying the techniques and skills we have discussed in this chapter will help you negotiate time off for family responsibilities more effectively. However, your ability to successfully negotiate flexibility with your supervisor will depend on your company's philosophy as it relates to employees with family responsibilities. Be realistic. You know the corporate culture in which both you and your supervisor work. There may be limitations to the degree of flexibility possible under the guidelines set by upper management.

If your corporation has not started a work/family initiative and permitted flexible management styles, consider looking for a different employer. Corporations in general are becoming more conducive to employees with family responsibilities, striving to become "family friendly." Or try helping your company catch up (see Chapter 10). In the meantime, focus your energies on working with your supervisor to get the flexibility you need to manage your family responsibilities. Try the following suggestions:

1. Plan ahead. If you know you will need to take time off for a conference or child-related event, talk to your supervisor ahead of time, giving him or her time to plan your replacement or work load reassignments.

2. Find a proper time for the conversation. Choose a setting where your supervisor can concentrate on what you are saying.

3. Rehearse what you will say before your meeting. Anticipate the effect the request will have on your supervisor. Put yourself in the supervisor's place. Prepare responses to all questions and concerns your supervisor may express. Prepare possible solutions and ways to handle resistance.

4. Start your conversation with your objective—what you want to accomplish.

5. Outline the plan you have prepared by suggesting ways you can make up the time and/or work. For example, if you need to take a few hours off on Friday afternoon, suggest you work through your lunch hours during the rest of the week. Or plan to come in early or stay late a half hour each day. If your job responsibilities can be done at home, suggest you will complete tasks at night or over the weekend. Make sure you do what you say you will.

6. Use good listening and observation skills to handle any resistance to your plan. Remember to focus on nonjudgmental phrases. Your goal is to keep the conversation aimed at a win/win solution.

Use the accompanying checklist to get a feel for how your supervisor perceives you as an employee.

Flexibility Assessment

		Never	Rarely	Sometimes	Frequently	Always
1.	I get/make personal calls during work time.	1	2	3	4	5
2.	I am late.	1	2	3	4	5
3.	I call in sick.	1	2	3	4	5
4.	I am distracted and less productive than my peers.	1	2	3	4	5
5.	Co-workers must assist with my work load.	1	2	3	4	5
6.	I refuse to work overtime because of family issues.	1	2	3	4	5
7.	I don't travel because of family issues.	1	2	3	4	5
8.	I refuse additional or special assignments.	1	2	3	4	5
9.	My performance reviews have been poor to unsatisfactory.	1	2	3	4	5
10.	I ask for accommodations or special treatment.	1	2	3	4	5

Add up your points.

Less than 20 Your boss would be crazy to lose you. Your work record entitles you to flexibility.

21–30 You are a good and valuable employee, likely to get some flexibility.

31–40 Your supervisor may be somewhat resistant. Have a good plan for how the work will get done.

41–50 Make sure you demonstrate to your supervisor how the accommodation will result directly in improved work performance. Consider ways to improve your work performance before asking for special accommodations. For example, if you are chronically late because you wait to put your kids on the school bus, ask if you can take a shorter lunch or work longer to eliminate the tardiness issue.

Be prepared for the possibility of not getting the time you need. Many variables affect negotiating time off. The department's work load or deadlines may not allow it. Your supervisor may not want to show favoritism in the department, or she or he may not understand the importance of your needing the time off. If that situation occurs, talk to someone in human resources for support and suggestions.

Handling Telephone Calls

Getting phone calls at work from lonesome children, elders, or other members of the family can be frustrating and time consuming. To avoid lengthy calls that can interfere with performance and cause conflict between you and your supervisor, try the following hints:

- Don't get emotionally tied into the conversation. Stick to the basics.
- Ask good questions to find out why the person is calling.
- Because you can't see the individual who is calling, you'll have to decode by listening to pauses and voice quality to pick up feelings. Pick up on key words and phrases to help you to detect what is really going on.
- Respond to those feelings by acknowledging and accepting that they are real. However, explain you are at work and it's not an appropriate time to have a lengthy conversation. Transmit your empathy but suggest to the individual that you can continue discussing the topic in the evening when you can give your full attention. Let the individual know you are really interested in hearing what she or he has to say, but not while you are at work.

For example, "It sounds like you've had a bad day at school. I'd really like to hear more about it in person instead of over the phone so let's talk about it when I get home." Or, "Mom, you sound frustrated. I'd like to be able to help you solve this problem. Can I call you when I get home this evening?"

Getting lengthy or frequent telephone calls is a reason many supervisors cite for low productivity. Solving the problem of phone calls at work will assist in promoting your professional image. You want to create a good working relationship with your supervisor so that when you need to negotiate time off for a family member, your record of performance will be viewed as excellent. You don't want to give your supervisor any reason for turning you down when you need time off.

Many individuals feel very guilty when they hear a child's voice at the other end of the phone saying: "I really miss you, Daddy!" or "Why do you have to work? Johnny's mom stays home," or "You love work more than you love me."

These phrases often set off feelings of guilt and neglect, that you aren't a good parent. This leads to more unproductive time at work while you are feeling guilty. When this occurs, focus on the positive aspects of working. Reflect on why you have chosen to work (see Chapter 3).

Then, respond in a positive manner. "It sounds like you are feeling a little lonesome. Well, I miss you too. But I'll be home in a few hours and then we can spend some time together. In the meantime, why don't you plan something special that we can do together when I get there." By responding positively, you are acknowledging the feelings and yet not allowing guilt to manipulate you.

By following these simple guidelines, you are also being a role model for your children. They see and hear how you solve your problems daily. By setting clear guidelines for phone calls to you at work, you are creating a model of behavior for your children to follow.

It helps to practice. What would you say to the following calls?

1. "Dad, I'm sick and tired of going to the baby-sitter. Why do you have to work?"
2. (Latchkey child) "Mom, I'm scared. Can't you come home early?"
3. (Young child) "I'm really sick. Can you come home now?"
4. (Young teen) "You never have time to talk to me. You're always too busy working."
5. (Elder) "I need my medication. Can you come home and take me to the drugstore?"

Communication Review

What do you need to practice?

As a speaker, I:	Yes	No
Clarify the message (words)	☐	☐
Use repetition when necessary	☐	☐

Am aware of my body language   ☐   ☐
Maintain a productive attitude and tone   ☐   ☐
Have good voice quality   ☐   ☐
Am empathetic   ☐   ☐
Get feedback   ☐   ☐
Choose the time for significant communications   ☐   ☐
Choose appropriate settings   ☐   ☐
Use "I" messages   ☐   ☐

As a listener, I:
  Actively listen   ☐   ☐
    Paraphrase   ☐   ☐
    Probe/ask questions   ☐   ☐
    Ask open-ended questions   ☐   ☐
    Clarify that the message received is the
        message intended   ☐   ☐
  Don't interrupt   ☐   ☐
  Show interest   ☐   ☐
  Encourage trust   ☐   ☐
  Maintain eye contact with the speaker   ☐   ☐

Practice all of your communication skills and watch your relationships improve.

RESOURCES

General

Satir, Virginia. *Making Contact*. Berkeley, Calif.: Celestial Arts, 1976.

Gusdor, Georges. *Speaking (La Parole)*. Evanston, Ill.: Northwestern University Press, 1966.

Children

Dinkmeyer, Don, and Gary D. McKay. *The Parent's Guide: Systematic Training for Effective Parenting*. Circle Pines, Minn.: American Guidance Services, Inc., 1976.

Dinkmeyer, Don, Gary D. McKay, and James S. Dinkmeyer. *Parenting Young Children*. New York: Avon Books, 1969.

Faber, Adele, and Elaine Mazlish. *How to Talk So Kids Will Listen and Listen So Kids Will Talk.* New York: Avon Books, 1980.

Ginott, Haim G. *Between Parent and Child: New Solutions to Old Problems.* New York: Macmillan, 1969.

Adolescents

Dinkmeyer, Don, and Gary D. McKay. *The Parent's Handbook: Systematic Training for Effective Parenting of Teens.* Circle Press, Minn.: American Guidance Services, Inc., 1982.

Ginott, Haim. *Between Parent and Teenager.* New York: Macmillan, 1969.

Elders

Edinberg, Mark A. *Talking with Your Aging Parents.* Boston: Shambhala Publications, Inc., 1987.

Shulman, Bernard H., M.D. and Raenann Berman. *How to Survive Your Aging Parents.* Chicago: Surrey Books, 1988.

Spouse/Significant Other

Kimball, Gayle, Ph.D. *The 50/50 Marriage.* Boston: Beacon Press, 1983.

Tannen, Deborah. *You Just Don't Understand: Women and Men in Conversation.* New York: Ballantine Books, 1990.

Tannen, Deborah. *That's Not What I Meant: How Conversational Style Makes or Breaks Relationships.* New York: Morrow, 1986.

Supervisor

Germer, Jim G. *How to Make Your Boss Work for You: More Than 200 Hard-Hitting Strategies, Tips, and Tactics to Keep Your Career on the Fast-Track.* Homewood, Ill.: Richard D. Irwin, Inc., 1991.

NOTES

1. Montaigne, Essays, III. 9.
2. Robert Fulghum, *Uh-Oh* (New York: Villard Books, 1991), pp. 26–27.

3. *Webster's Ninth New Collegiate Dictionary* (Springfield, Mass.: Merriam-Webster, Inc., 1983), p. 407.
4. Adapted from *Active Listening* and reprinted with the permission of Malinak McCarty, Inc.
5. Adapted from *I-Messages* and reprinted with the permission of Malinak McCarty, Inc.
6. Georges Gusdorf, *Speaking (La Parole)* (Evanston, Ill.: Northwestern University Press, 1965), p. 85.
7. Virginia Satir, *Making Contact* (Berkeley, Calif.: Celestial Arts, 1976).
8. Gayle Kimball, Ph.D., *The 50/50 Marriage* (Boston: Beacon Press, 1983), p. 156.
9. Deborah Tannen, Ph.D., *You Just Don't Understand: Men and Women in Conversation* (New York: Ballantine Books, 1990), p. 297.

A CHILD'S DEVELOPMENT

Much is known about the stages of a child's physical development of language skills. Your pediatrician can, of course, tell you how your child is doing. There are also many books that can help you measure your child's progress. Some are listed at the end of this chapter. The chart below, based on Piaget's work, can help as an overall guide.

Language Skills		*Stages of Development*
Responds to different pitches. Cries.	Newborn	Natural (unlearned) reflexes become more efficient.
Distinguishes human voice and develops different cries for pain, hunger, discomfort. Coos and makes other sounds in syllables.	1–4 months	Sucking, opening and closing fist, and other behaviors become repetitious. Reacts to voices and smiles.
Listens. Varies sounds to express pleasure, displeasure. Imitates sounds. Differentiates voices (familiar versus unfamiliar; male versus female).	4–8 months	Repeats chance behaviors. Looks for stimulus.
Says Mama, Dada. Sounds start to sound like words. Understands gestures like bye-bye and some names, words. May say one or more words. Can repeat words. Responds to "No."	8–12 months	Solves simple problems. Demonstrates intentional behavior. Can point to objects.
Vocabulary increases to 20+ words. Answers simple questions.	12–18 months	Begins to alter behavior based on past learning (trial and error).
Names objects or points them out (nose, dog in picture). Carries out instructions. Starts to combine words into phrases.	18–24 months	Starts to experiment with new ways to solve problems. Develops ability to describe objects and actions in general ways.
Repeats sentences. Vocabulary increases to 800–1,000+ words. Recognizes signs and symbols (can name objects in a picture).	2–4 years	Express himself or herself verbally. Speech patterns are repetitious. Egocentric monologues are common.

Language Skills		*Stages of Development*
Vocabulary increases to 15–20,000 words by about age 6 and 40,000 words by age 12. Learns to write and to read, with proficiency increasing over time.	5 and up	After the age of about 4, a child begins to reason. Initially, the child can solve problems but cannot tell you how she or he did it. Concrete problem-solving begins about age 7, when the child begins to think logically and reversibly and starts to put information into categories. At about 11, a child begins to think abstractly and is able to evaluate information and reason deductively.

Keep in mind that each child develops differently. Your child may be slower in one area of development and faster in others. For example, David was slow to develop language skills because of a slight hearing impairment due to constant ear infections. However his motor and coordination skills were exceptional. At 3, he could skip, hop, and put a ball through a hoop. David's parents worked very hard to help him with verbal skills and provided as many social activities as possible. They also made up stories together, sang songs, and recorded poems on an audio tape. David's ear infections have ceased, and at age 4 his language skills are now age appropriate.

You know your child better than anyone else. Get all the information you need, and then have fun helping your child develop to his or her full potential.

Chapter Five:

Organizing for Life Management

Time is life. It is irreversible. To waste your time is to waste your life, but to master your time is to master your life and make the most of it.[1]

Alan Lakein, *How To Get Control of Your Time and Your Life*

One portion of a minister's lot concerns the dying and the dead. The hospital room, the mortuary, the funeral service, the cemetery. What I know of such things shapes my life elsewhere in particular ways. What I know of such things explains why I don't waste much life time mowing grass or washing cars or raking leaves or making beds or shining shoes or washing dishes. It explains why I don't honk at people who are slow to move at green lights. And why I don't kill spiders. There isn't time or need for all this.[2]

Robert Fulghum, *All I Really Need to Know I Learned in Kindergarten*

I t is a simple fact of life that there isn't enough time to do all of the things we want to do. But we know that if we plan and organize our time well, we can fit in more than if we don't. Nevertheless, most people don't organize their personal lives. Even those of you who have been trained in time management probably don't take those skills home with you. You may never have thought about transferring those skills to your home life. Even if you did, you may never have taken the time or devoted the energy to construct a plan for you and your family.

For example, John wants to be on the fast track at work; he wants to be a high-level manager before he is 40. At the same time, he wants to be a good spouse and parent. His father was an executive who didn't spend much time with John. John remembers feeling hurt and disappointed by what he took to be a lack of interest by his father and wants to be more involved in his own children's lives. He thinks he spends too much time at work and not enough time with his family, although he has never decided how much time with his family would satisfy his parenting goals. Nor has he talked about it with his wife. Because he has never planned his time, he feels caught in a constant state of turmoil and guilt.

Do you feel like John? To resolve role and time conflicts, you need to identify your priorities and then plan your time to accomplish the things that are most important to you. Maybe you've heard it before, but what have you actually done about it? Take time now to reflect on what is really important to you. Ask yourself, what's missing? What do you long for? What can you do about it?

IDENTIFYING YOUR PRIORITIES

Refer back to the values, family norms, and goals you identified in Chapter Two, especially your action plan. Let's compare them to what you are currently doing. What things that are important to you are you accomplishing now?

1.	6.
2.	7.
3.	8.
4.	9.
5.	10.

What things that are important to you are you not doing now?

1.	6.
2.	7.
3.	8.
4.	9.
5.	10.

Which of those things could you be doing? Don't eliminate anything at this point. Be daring—translate your dreams into reality!

You may not be able to accomplish everything, but if you are creative and willing to ask for help, you can do more than you ever thought possible.

In order of their importance to you (see the hint below to help you prioritize), list at least 10 things you want to accomplish every week, whether or not you are doing them now.

1.
2.
3.
4.
5.
6.
7.
8.
9.
10.

Now when you plan your week, put as many of those things in as possible, starting from the top of this list.

Hint: On a separate sheet, list the things you want to accomplish. To prioritize them, compare each item to every other item (1 to 2, 1 to 3, 1 to 4, etc. then 2 to 3, 2 to 4, 2 to 5, etc.). After each comparison, write down the number of the item that is more important to you. Do the same for each item. When you are finished, you can rank or prioritize each item by the number of times you wrote it down.

Example:
1. Get exercise 3 times per week
2. Eat nutritious meals
3. Read one novel every 2 weeks
4. Set up tickler system at office
5. Have a date with Jim every other week

Comparisons:

1:2	1	2:3	2	3:4	4	4:5	5
1:3	1	2:4	4	3:5	5		
1:4	1	2:5	5				
1:5	5						

1 was more important—3 times
2 was more important—1 time
3 was more important—0 time

4 was more important—2 times
5 was more important—4 times

So the goals by priority would be:
1. Have a date with Jim every other week
2. Get exercise 3 times per week
3. Set up tickler system at office
4. Eat nutritious meals
5. Read one novel every 2 weeks

The Status Quo—Where Does Your Time Go Now?

We often don't have an accurate perception of how our time is actually spent. Let's find out if you know how you spend your time, and then replan (if necessary) to achieve what you want to do.

On the accompanying chart, indicate in different colors or styles (x's for work, //// for sleep, \\\ for home chores, etc.) where your time goes during the average week. If you prefer to plan by the month, use a monthly planner (we've included one at the end of the chapter). Be sure to include hours at work, commute time, sleep, chores, work done at home, child care, exercise, and any other regular activity. Don't worry about being exact or specific, but do try to cover all of your regular activities. (Look ahead to the section on putting priorities and organization into action for an example of what a completed weekly planner can look like.) Extra weekly planners are included at the end of the chapter if your partner or other family members want to do the exercise with you.

Let's look at the overall results. There are *168* hours in a week. How many hours a week do you spend on the following activities? Add to the list things that are unique to you and cross out those that don't apply.

I work an average of _____ hours a week at work.

I work an average of _____ hours a week at home.

I spend an average of _____ hours a week commuting.

I sleep an average of _____ hours a week.

I spend an average of _____ hours a week with my spouse or significant other.

Weekly Planner

Time	Monday	Tuesday	Wednesday	Thursday	Friday	Saturday	Sunday
6 A.M.							
7 A.M.							
8 A.M.							
9 A.M.							
10 A.M.							
11 A.M.							
12 P.M.							
1 P.M.							
2 P.M							
3 P.M.							
4 P.M.							
5 P.M.							
6 P.M.							
7 P.M.							
8 P.M.							
9 P.M.							
10 P.M.							
11 P.M.							
12–5 A.M.							

I spend an average of _____ hours a week with my children.

I spend an average of _____ hours a week with elders in my life.

I spend an average of _____ hours a week doing something just for me.

I spend an average of _____ hours a week with my friends or socializing.

I volunteer or participate in a community activity _____ hours a week.

I exercise an average of _____ hours a week.

I spend an average of _____ hours a week on household chores.

Are the total of hours a week you spend on each activity consistent with your priorities? If not, are there changes you can make to better reflect your values and priorities and make yourself happier and more content in the process? There probably isn't much you can do about the number of hours you work or sleep. But what about all those other hours?

MAKING TIME

Obviously, you need to shop for food, mow the lawn, take out the garbage, cook, do the laundry, help your mom, take the kids to the park, and take care of all life's other necessities. Though all of these activities demand our time, we can use a number of techniques to make time for ourselves or time that could be better spent on things more important to us.

Major changes might be appropriate. Could you live closer to work and eliminate or significantly lessen your commute? Or would you prefer to live in a small town, even if your commute increases or your new job would pay less? Should you reduce your work hours or change jobs to have more time?

Most of us don't have major lifestyle changes to make. Smaller changes can make a big difference as well. Let's look at some practical ways to make it happen.

Look at your weekly planner (and the accompanying chart) and fill in/cross out the jobs that need to be done each week. Keep them in mind as we go through ways to eliminate or reduce the time spent on each job. You can fill in the "Action to Be Taken" column as we go through the options. Over time, you'll need to go through the same process with seasonal/annual chores such as finding child and/or elder care, washing windows, putting on storm windows, painting and decorating, financial planning, and, everyone's favorite, tax return preparation!

Who Is Doing It Now?

	Days per Week It Needs to Be Done							Every 2 weeks	Who Is Doing It Now? (Use initials or code*)	Time Spent (Hours per week)	Action to Be Taken (Write in option or use abbreviations)†
	M	T	W	T	F	S	S				
Grocery shopping											
Making list											
Weekly											
Staples											
Putting Away											
Laundry											
Washing											
Drying											
Folding											
Putting away											
Ironing											
Housekeeping											
Dusting											
Vacuuming											
Bathroom											
Kitchen											
Change linens											
Refrigerator											
Stove/Oven											
Yard work											
Home maintenance											
Pet care											

Who Is Doing It Now?

	Days per Week It Needs to Be Done							Every 2 weeks	Who Is Doing It Now? (Use initials or code*)	Time Spent (Hours per week)	Action to Be Taken (Write in option or use abbreviations)†
	M	T	W	T	F	S	S				
Making beds											
Preparing meals											
Breakfast											
Lunch											
Dinner											
Setting the table											
Breakfast											
Lunch											
Dinner											
Meal cleanup											
Breakfast											
Lunch											
Dinner											
Empty dishwasher											
Sewing/mending											
Water plants											
Take out garbage											
Picking up											
Clothes shopping											
Woman											
Man											

Who Is Doing It Now?

	Days per Week It Needs to Be Done								Who Is Doing It Now? (Use initials or code*)	Time Spent (Hours per week)	Action to Be Taken (Write in option or use abbreviations)[†]
	M	T	W	T	F	S	S	Every 2 weeks			
Children											
Shopping for gifts and cards											
Planning personal entertainment											
Car maintenance											
Pay bills											
Handle investments											
Child care											
Pick up											
Drop off											
Appointments											
Extracurricular activities											
Getting baby-sitters											

*Who is doing it now?
(M) Mom
(D) Dad
(G) Grandma/grandpa
(F) Friend/neighbor
(H) Hired help
(A) Child A (or use initials)
(B) Child B (or use initials)
(C) Child C (or use initials)

†Action to be taken
(C) Choose not to do it
(D) Delegate
(P) Postpone
(R) Reduce time/do it better
(B) Barter
(H) Hire help

Option 1: Choose Not to Do It

What a concept—don't do it! Give yourself permission not be perfect. What is the worst thing that would happen if you vacuumed every other week instead of every week? Would your family starve if you had a sandwich night once a week? Would your five-year-old son be scarred for life if he didn't get that dog until he was actually old enough to care for it? Would the world come to an end if you bought bakery cookies for the school bake sale rather than baked them yourself—or made brownies that didn't have to rolled, cut, baked, iced, and decorated?

Make a list of things that you could give up, permanently or just once in while, so that you could have more time. Refer to the chore chart for ideas. Then write in the consequences of that action and the results (the time you will save). This step will help you accept that the consequences may not be as severe as you might imagine, particularly when compared with the rewards (found time). Many things you could give up are probably "shoulds" you grew up with that may not be appropriate for your adult life. Remember to keep in mind what you've already said is important to you. Go back to your values and that fantasy plan.

Elimination List

I can give up the following things to have more time for what's *really* important to me and my family.

Action	Consequences	Time Saved (hours/week)
Example: Weekly cleaning	House dirtier in week 2	6 hours/week
1.		
2.		
3.		
4.		
5.		
6.		
7.		
8.		
9.		
10.		

Starting with the three actions with the least painful consequences, don't do them for at least two weeks. Pay attention to
whether anyone even notices that the job did not get done. Then
don't do the other chores on your list. Make adjustments if necessary to make "not doing" work for you. And keep an eye out
for more things you could choose not to do.

Saying No

One variation of choosing not to do it is not agreeing to do it in
the first place. Just say no. It is harder than it sounds because we
all want to help. Lots of "shoulds" and guilt may come up the
first few times. But really evaluating whether or not you want to
do something allows you to stay in control of where your time
goes. If you don't want to do it or would have to give up something more important to you, say no.

Joy's Story

Joy was very active as a volunteer in community organizations.
She was a member of the PTA, worked on a committee to establish
a child-care center for homeless children, and assisted in her
daughter's classroom once a week. When Joy went back to work
full time, she had to say no to most of her volunteering activities.
Her best friend called her frequently and criticized her lack of in-
volvement. It was difficult for Joy to hold to her decision, but she
knows that someday she will return to her volunteering role. She
is using the "whole life approach" by postponing community and
volunteer commitments until her parenting responsibilities lessen.

Option 2: Postpone Responsibilities

This technique is simple to use and often avoids the guilt feelings
that may come with choosing not to do it at all. When you make
a list of tasks to be accomplished in a week's time, carefully

prioritize those that *really* have to be done that week. Postpone some to next week. Example: Clean kitchen weekly. Postponing until next week saves one hour.

Option 3: Delegate

Children who are old enough to mess up are old enough to clean up.[3]

Dr. Dan's Prescriptions

Delegation, the art of getting someone else to do it, is rarely used to its potential. Often we are uncomfortable asking for help. We may be too proud to admit we need help. Have you ever thought of asking someone to do something you were going to do but were stopped by a "should" (I "should" to do it myself)? Sometimes, too, it is easier to do it yourself than negotiate with a spouse or argue with your children. That may be true the first or even the fifth time, but once delegation takes effect, the task is off your plate.

Some people avoid delegating because they feel guilty. They already believe their children are "put upon" because the parents work, so they don't give them chores. Guilt is a particularly big issue for single parents, who may avoid asking their children to help around the house because they think the kids are having a hard enough time adjusting to divorce and/or life without the other parent. This selflessness can backfire. Remember, the patterns you set when your children are young will persist as they get older. A young child who has no chores will resist assignments as a teenager. A child who does no chores also doesn't learn much about work or develop a work ethic that will aid him or her as an adult.

Similarly, guilt can stop us from asking for help from elders who live with us. But if the elder is a member of the household, she or he should pitch in where possible just like everyone else. Everyone needs to believe they are a valuable, contributing part of the whole.

You've decided to delegate. Identify the chores you can delegate and the person you're going to delegate the task to.

Now you know what and to whom. How can you go about it without causing World War III at home? Try the following techniques.

Chore/Task	Person
1.	
2.	
3.	
4.	
5.	
6.	
7.	
8.	
9.	
10.	

Accept that others can do the job. If you are going to be successful at delegating, you need to accept that others can do the job. Not everyone will do the task the same way you do. But remember, your objective is to have more time. You're going to have to let go of some of your convictions about the way things "should" be done and trust that the other person will get the same (or sufficient) result. This attitude is extremely important to get results from family members, particularly spouses and other adults. If you don't believe it, it will show. You'll always be checking up on others and not letting them take on the challenge by themselves.

Susan's Story

Susan and Al had been married for three years during which Susan had done 95 percent of the household chores. One week, after a particularly hard week at work, Susan came home to a dirty house, no dinner, no food to make it with, and a complaining husband. After the fight, Susan explained how difficult it was to run the house and work full time. Al said he had always been willing to help, but she never asked. He thought she wanted to do it all. They divided up the home chores, giving each to the person who minded doing it least.

After a month, Al called a meeting. He said he was tired of being criticized for the way he emptied the dishwasher (nothing was put away right), cleaned the bathroom (he used Windex on everything), and did the laundry (the clothes weren't folded right). Susan wanted everything done her way. They talked it out. Al agreed not to use Windex on everything, and Susan let go of her rigid laundry-folding and dish-placement requirements, accepting that dishes in the cupboards and clean clothes were the point.

Remember the previous exercise you did that stated actions and consequences? Well, ask yourself if there are serious consequences to having someone else dust, mow the lawn, or prepare a meal differently than you?

Diana's Story

Diana and Jeff take turns cooking dinner, with the other one cleaning up afterward. One night, Diana cooked. She followed Jeff into the kitchen to talk while Jeff cleaned up. In the middle of their conversation, Jeff asked "What are you doing?" Confused, Diana said, "What? I am just talking to you." Then, looking down, she realized she had been rearranging the dishes in the dishwasher. Jeff had done the dishes for months with no problem, but he did it differently than Diana. The result? She stayed away from the dishwasher on Jeff's cleanup nights.

Compare your role to that of a manager. Can you remember a time when a manager let you handle an assignment with complete trust, just told you what she or he wanted and let you do it on your own? It probably was a very motivating experience. Most likely, you wanted to do the best job you've ever done. Family members are no different. Give them a task they can do and then trust them to do a good job.

Sally's Story

Sally decided to delegate shopping for weekly groceries. Sally is a single parent and keeping staples (milk, bread, lettuce) in the house was always difficult. Her 10-year-old daughter, Mary, is dropped off at the corner store when her after-school program is over. Sally took her into the store, introduced her to the shop-keeper, and demonstrated the steps of grocery shopping. Every Monday morning, Sally gives Mary a list of the items Mary is re-sponsible for buying that week and enough money in an envelope. She writes down the brand of each item she wants and substitutes. Mary is delighted with her new responsibility and has taken her job very seriously. She is proud that she can handle the money and help her mother. Sally lets Mary know how much she appreciates her contribution to the family and has promised to give her more responsibilities as she gets older.

No-nonsense attitude. If you take on an attitude that others are expected to participate, you will be on your way to get-ting action from others. In other words, "no nonsense"—no ex-planations are needed or given. It's just the way it is.

If you have already set up a family system that doesn't include delegation, you'll have to do some work to revise it. A democratic household is fine, but at some point a working parent has to make decisions that members of the family may not like. Have a family meeting and simply explain that you feel overburdened and that chores aren't getting done well. Tell them you need their support. Don't spend too much time on the why. Come prepared with a list of chores and assignments. Don't allow a lot of bar-gaining or complaining.

Communicate expectations clearly. Your skills in being able to communicate effectively (see Chapter Four) will be in-valuable when it comes to getting cooperation. The better you communicate your expectations, the more likely it is you will get what you need. Establish the task and break it down carefully. A demonstration may help. Keep in mind that this may be the first time your child (or spouse) has ever attempted this task. Set standards as to time frame, quality, and quantity. If you are vague, the task may not be accomplished in the time frame or with the quality you expect. There's a big difference between saying "Clean your room" and "Pick up your clothes, make your bed, dust your dresser, and take out the trash by bedtime today."

Marge's Story

Marge was tired of trying to get her young teenager to clean up his room properly. He always said he didn't understand what she meant. One day, Marge cleaned the room herself and then took a Polaroid picture of what it should look like. She posted the picture on his door as a reminder of what the result should be. The job was done satisfactorily after that. (She used notes on the refrigerator to remind him to walk the dog after school.)

Punishment for tasks not done should be outlined in advance. If the chore is not done, the child knows what the consquences will be. Try more chores next week. Save rewards for extra achievements. Children should be expected to participate without them. Or use natural consequences if the job doesn't get done correctly. If someone forgets to set the table or there are no forks, sit down to eat and see what happens.

Paul and Karen's Story

Paul had agreed to do the laundry on weekends but never got around to it. For weeks, Karen reminded, pleaded, nagged, and finally did it herself, getting more resentful of the extra burden every week! Finally, she had had it. She let it sit. On Monday, Paul didn't have any clean shirts to pack for his business trip. He became a good deal more conscientious about getting the laundry done after that.

Motivate others. Getting others to help often depends on your ability to motivate them. Do you know what your family's hot buttons are? Have you thought about the techniques you use to get people to help you? Do you beg and plead, demand and threaten? Or do you entice, motivate, encourage, and thank? Positive reinforcement is a much better motivation technique than a negative or punitive approach. Even if the job isn't done exactly the way you had in mind, let the individual know you appreciate the effort. Use positive language to give any feedback.

Supervision. If it's difficult for you to give up control of the household chores, supervision is for you. It allows you some quality control, but the chore is still someone else's responsibility. To be an effective supervisor, keep in mind the ways you can motivate others. Be positive! Reflect on role models who have successfully supervised you in the past. Use their techniques as a guide when you supervise others.

Take turns. If a task is unappealing, take turns to distribute the chores no one wants to do so no one ends up feeling dumped on. A chart on the refrigerator with basic tasks, such as walking the dog, taking out the garbage, getting milk, and changing the kitty litter can be posted and the task can be rotated among family members.

The element of choice. When possible, give the other person some say in how or when the chore gets done. Does it really matter whether the garbage is taken out right after dinner or an hour later? Get a commitment on when, but let them choose. This technique often avoids power struggles.

Make it fun. Young children often can be encouraged to help if the tasks are presented like a game. For example, give the task at hand a name such as the dusting game, the folding napkins game, or sorting colored socks game. One working mother in a hospital told us about a "Cookie Jar of Jobs" she created for her three-year-old. She put slips of colored paper in a cookie jar, describing different tasks such as "dust living room furniture," "pick up toys," "polish shoes," or "brush the dog." Her child would choose one and her mom would read her the task. When it was done, the child was praised for both the work and contribution to the family. A variation is a spinner (or colored index cards in a box) that has tasks written in like "wash dishes," "put away dishes from dishwasher," "set the table," and so on. The child spins the spinner and wherever it lands determines the task for that day.

Young children also like colored stars. When a child finishes a task such as making a bed or picking up toys, a colored star can be applied to a chart that has a list of their chores. That way your child can see his or her accomplishment concretely. You can give a diploma for difficult tasks or consistently good performance. Or create a point system (two for dusting, five for vacuuming) with accumulated points redeemable for a special treat.

Some children can be enticed through competition. A young child will get the mail or newspaper while you count to see how fast she or he gets it. One father we know created a chore race. Whoever got the most leaves picked up (or whatever the Sunday project was) got to choose a videocassette for the evening's entertainment.

You can enter into a written contract with an older child. This is a more "adult" way to describe the job responsibilities and also the rewards/consequences. If the child is involved in drafting the contract, it can be an educational experience that promotes commitment and prepares the child for the real world of work.

As a general rule, the more that chores can be made fun, the more likely you'll have voluntary participation. Also, keep your sense of humor. Remember, these are only chores.

Spouses/significant others. Motivating your spouse to help out can be accomplished with many of the same techniques. Games may not work, but natural consequences, humor, and rewards may. Couples often spend unfulfilling time arguing about chores. If couples can work together to help each other, they are not only sharing fairly but also being excellent role models for their children. Rotate and divide jobs on the basis of preference and performance rather than gender stereotypes. Try not to nag, reprimand, or monitor chores. Nor should you do (or redo) the chore yourself and then complain that your partner didn't do it. This only causes bad feelings.

In Deborah Tannen's book, *You Just Don't Understand*, she points out that gender differences play a role in chore assignments.

> Women are inclined to do what is asked of them and many men are inclined to resist even the slightest hint that anyone, especially a woman, is telling them what to do. A woman will be inclined to repeat a request that doesn't get a response because she is convinced that her husband would do what she asks, if he only understood that she really wants him to do it. But a man who wants to avoid feeling that he is following orders may instinctively wait before doing what she asked, in order to imagine that he is doing it of his own free will.[4]

If this happens in your relationship, try talking it out. Try to determine whether gender differences are the cause and find more cooperative methods of getting chores done. If arguments over chores persist, consider a few visits to a counselor. It might help to establish realistic expectations and effective communication.

Pass on the manager role. You know your family member better than anyone. Identify a motivation technique you think will work for each of them and give it a try! Finally, pass on your responsibility of being the manager. Take turns with your partner or teenager weekly or monthly. Let other members of the family be responsible for organizing.

Option 4: Do It Better (and Reduce Time Spent)

Sharing responsibilities helps to make a long task a shorter one. Two hands really are better than one. Actually, families or couples who do chores together also find time to talk while they work. For example, for busy couples who have hungry families at the end of the day, sharing meal preparation and cleanup is an effective way to make the task a family affair.

Carol and Fred's Story

Carol is usually home before Fred and begins the meal. Her children use the spinner game on the refrigerator to decide who will set the table, who will feed the cat, and who will empty the dishwasher. Fred arrives sometime during this process and joins in after changing clothes. They all chat while this preparation is going on and catch up on the day's events. After dinner, Fred cleans up while the children begin their homework and Carol reads or relaxes in front of the TV.

Find a better way to do the chores in less time. Here are some useful ideas to save some time and do it better.

- Prepare meals on weekends; expect everyone to help. Make extra and reheat leftovers during the week or freeze for later.
- Keep a calendar and message center in a central area.
- Put a grocery list and pen on the refrigerator door. Write down what you need from the store as it is used up.
- Shop once and at one store.
- Shop for two weeks.
- Shop on your way home from work.
- Dust the whole house, then vacuum all rugs.
- Exercise after work as a transition to home.
- Do all mirrors and glass surfaces at once.
- Send clothes that need ironing to the cleaners.
- Take clothes out of the dryer immediately.
- Buy permanent press.
- Find a dry cleaner that picks up and/or delivers.
- Find a supermarket that takes phoned-in orders and/or delivers.
- Buy nonperishables in large amounts. Store in garage or basement.
- Use a crockpot.
- Prepare weekly menus. Let family members participate. Shop for those meals. Post the menu on the refrigerator. Others will know what to do to help. It may result in more nutritious meals.
- Get a microwave.
- Make chore and shopping lists.

- Put out children's (and your) clothes the night before.
- Put all cleaning supplies in a bucket or carryall that you can take with you from room to room.
- Set the table for breakfast the night before.
- Set up the coffeepot the night before. Get a coffeepot with a timer (or a timer for your present coffeepot).
- Put a clock in the bathroom.
- Clean the shower and tub while you are taking a shower.
- Make lunches the night before.
- Get children to set their own alarms.
- Make "to do" lists. Use a planner.
- Rethink pets; fish are easier than dogs.
- Buy gifts and cards in advance (when you're shopping for something else).
- Speed clean—set a time limit within which the cleaning will be done. If you eliminate distractions and procrastination, the chore will get done faster. What you don't get to doesn't get done.
- Pay bills twice a month.
- Use your lunch hour for things other than eating (i.e., have a sandwich from home while you pay your bills).

There are many ways to do it better. Look through some of the Resources at the end of this chapter. Use your and your family's creativity and imagination.

Option 5: Barter

Bartering for services is a great way to get chores done without spending a lot of money. This method is excellent for single parents who often don't have another parent with whom to share responsibilities.

The first step in bartering is to belive that "it's OK." Because bartering hasn't been practiced widely in many years, you may never have seen it in action. You'll have to take the lead. Don't expect others to initiate a barter arrangement. You know what you need and it's up to you to find others who can help you get it. Be creative. You can barter with anyone—neighbors, other single parents, friends, family, and so on. Discuss what you need and what you can do in trade.

Option 6: Hire Help

Hiring help is a wonderful choice. Figure out which jobs you would like to farm out. Start with those that are most time consuming (housecleaning, yard work). Investigate where help might be found and how much it will cost. Even if you don't think you can afford to hire help, explore the possibility anyway. You may be pleasantly surprised at the price of the service. Or you may be able to juggle the budget to cover the expense, particularly if it means less work and more time for you. If you can't afford a maid every week, then do small cleaning jobs between visits. Or hire a service twice a year for the heavy cleaning.

To find help, check the following:

- Friends' recommendations.
- Neighbors' recommendations.
- Retired people.
- Grocery store bulletin boards.
- Want ads in neighborhood newspapers.
- A local high school or college placement or job office.

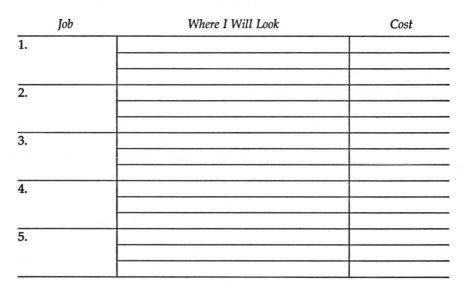

Job	Where I Will Look	Cost
1.		
2.		
3.		
4.		
5.		

Once you've defined your options, hire someone.

Whether you hire a professional service, an individual, or a student, the following tips will help you make it successful.

- Don't take anything for granted. Outline all responsibilities and expectations as well as what you will pay.
- Determine what you will provide (meals, telephone, equipment, transportation, etc.) and communicate clearly.
- Clarify the time alloted. Do you want them for an hour or a day? Weekly or every other week? How much time should be spent on certain chores?
- Clarify the schedule—hours and days.

Make sure you get what you need:

- Observe the job done.
- Provide feedback, positive and negative.
- If the work doesn't get done, don't hesitate to find someone else.

Revised Weekly Planner

Now that you have made time for yourself by eliminating or delegating chores and have eliminated activities that are inconsistent with your goals, you may want to redo your weekly planner (or monthly planner) to give you a visual reminder of your new schedule. There are extra weekly planners at the end of this chapter.

PUTTING PRIORITIES AND ORGANIZATION INTO ACTION

Still not convinced that all this can make a difference for you? Here's what a hard look at priorities and planning did for one couple.

Celia and Jim's Story

Celia and Jim were dissatisfied with their work/family balance. They always felt rushed and vaguely unhappy. They decided to assess their priorities and replan their week to accomplish those priorities. They started by taking a hard look at where their time was going on their present schedules.

Weekly Routines

Celia and Jim have been married for 10 years. Celia is a claims manager for an insurance company located about 20 minutes from their home. Jim is an engineer, in charge of maintenance at his plant, which is 30 minutes from home. They have two children, Sharon, age three, and Tommy, age five. Sharon is in family day care at a neighbor's home. Tommy is in half-day kindergarten. He goes to the same caregiver before and after school.

Celia's weekday begins at 6:30 A.M., when Jim leaves for work. She gets ready for work, wakes the children, helps them dress, and prepares breakfast. She drops the kids off at the caregiver's home at 7:45 A.M. and is at work by 8:00 A.M. She leaves work at 4:30 P.M., picks the kids up, and is home by 5:00 P.M. She talks to the kids about their days while she fixes dinner.

Jim gets home about 6:00 P.M. He finishes work officially at 3:30 P.M. but generally works until at least 4:30 P.M. At least three times a week, Jim goes to his health club before going home. The family has dinner together. Celia usually bathes the kids while Jim does the dishes. Sharon then plays until her bedtime at 8:00 P.M., when she gets a bedtime story from one of her parents. Tommy watches TV or reads after his bath, until his bedtime at 8:30 P.M. Celia or Jim usually read or tell Tommy a story as well. By 9:00 P.M. both children are asleep. Celia is usually not far behind, after picking up the house and getting things ready for the next morning. Jim reads, watches TV, or works until about 10:00 P.M., when he turns in.

Weekends are a marathon of chores, with an occasional family outing. On Saturday mornings, Jim usually works. Celia cleans the house and does the laundry. When Jim gets home, he watches the kids, mows the lawn, and does other household chores while Celia shops for groceries and other weekly needs. Sunday is the day to catch up on what has not yet been done or to recuperate from the week.

When put into a planner, Celia's present schedule looks like this:

Time	Mon.	Tues.	Wed.	Thurs.	Fri.	Sat.	Sun.
6 A.M.	Breakfast / getting kids ready						
7 A.M.	C o m m u t e					Breakfast	
8 A.M.						Clean house	Read paper
9 A.M.			Work				
10 A.M.							
11 A.M.							Rest
12 P.M.							
1 P.M.						Lunch	Lunch
2 P.M.						Grocery shopping	Chores
3 P.M.							
4 P.M.	C o m m u t e						Play time
5 P.M.	Dinner preparation and meal						
6 P.M.	Clean up/chores						
7 P.M.	Bathe kids					TV/occasional outing	
8 P.M.	Put them to bed						
9 P.M.	Try to read a little						
10 P.M.							
11 P.M.			Sleep				
12-5 A.M.							

Celia was distressed to see that she spent virtually no time alone with her husband. She also was surprised at how little time she spent with her children when she was not doing something else (cooking, dishes, bathing them) as well. She had long realized she took very little time out of her week to do something for herself. She had often envied Jim's workout schedule—the fact of it as well as the results—and she missed reading, an activity that had given her a lot of pleasure in the past.

When Jim filled out his weekly planner, it looked like the one on the next page.

Jim was most startled by how little time he spent with his children. He had known he did not spend as much time with his wife as he would like. He wanted to move up in his company and realized he would need additional business courses to be qualified for promotion, but he didn't know how he could fit it all in.

New and Reaffirmed Priorities

After completing their individual Values Clarification Exercise and discussing their own and family goals, Celia and Jim agreed family dinner time was something they wanted to keep, but it didn't have to happen seven nights a week. They also agreed that, given their career aspirations and the reality of their jobs, the time spent on work was appropriate for both of them. They still believed their home was in a convenient location. Finally, they decided not to decrease the amount they were putting away for retirement, college educations, vacations, and the like, which meant they had to stay within their present budget. They then came up with the following priority lists.

Celia's Top Five Priorities	Jim's Top Five Priorities
1. Spend time with Jim.	1. Spend more time with children.
2. Spend quality time with the children.	2. Spend time with Celia.
3. Exercise (time for self).	3. Take a management class.
4. Join a book club (for self).	4. Eat better balanced meals.
5. Give up weekly housecleaning.	5. Spend less time on chores.

Time	Mon.	Tues.	Wed.	Thurs.	Fri.	Sat.	Sun.
6 A.M.	Commute						
7 A.M.							Breakfast
8 A.M.							Read
9 A.M.							paper
10 A.M.		Work					
11 A.M.							Rest
12 P.M.							
1 P.M.							Lunch
2 P.M.						Mow	Work
3 P.M.						lawn	around
4 P.M.							house,
5 P.M.	Workout/Home					Work	watch
6 P.M.	Dinner &					around	sports
7 P.M.		dishes					
8 P.M.	Spend a little time with					house	
9 P.M.	kids/tell story/work/						TV
10 P.M.				TV			
11 P.M.	Sleep						
12-5 A.M.							

Making It Happen

Given the realities of the time they had left after work and sleep, they planned accordingly. Jim takes a business class one night a week. He studies on his lunch hours and, if he needs to, before bed instead of watching television. He also has taken over meal planning and makes up the shopping list he gives to Celia. Celia joined a friend's book club, which meets one night a month. Jim picks up the children and handles dinner that night. (He has informed his co-workers this night is off limits for meetings and has arranged for his backup to be on call for emergencies.) Celia does grocery shopping for staples on her way home (and has found that it goes faster because the store is less crowded). She goes to the health club three nights a week after work, picking up the kid's at the caregiver's an hour later (time that was paid for anyway in their weekly fee). Jim has bartered with a neighbor to cut both lawns every other week, giving both of them a week off, time Jim spends playing with his kids. Both children were assigned small chores to help with housework. They hired a maid, who comes every two weeks to do general housecleaning. Both Celia and Jim take lunch to work most days and use the savings to pay for the maid. Laundry is now a joint morning effort. (Jim puts a load in the washer and Celia puts it in the dryer on her way out.) They also take turns with the weekly grocery shopping. Last but not least, Celia and Jim have made every other Saturday night "date night." They have a standing order with a neighborhood baby-sitter. They also make an effort to plan one family outing a week—dinner at McDonald's, a movie, a trip to the zoo, a park, or a museum, or a visit to grandma's.

Now more conscious and organized about their use of time, Celia and Jim are amazed at how much more in control they feel. They are doing things that make them happy. After some initial grumbling about the changes, the children have commented that they see their parents more and do "neat stuff." While not every day or week goes as planned, the net result is that both Jim and Celia are enjoying their lives more than before. They have agreed to go through the exercise annually.

SUMMARY

In summarizing this chapter, see which areas you need to practice, review, or spend more time researching.

1. Setting my priorities

| Needs work | OK | Very satisfied |

2. Making time.
   a. Choose not to do it

| Needs work | OK | Very satisfied |

   b. Postpone

| Needs work | OK | Very satisfied |

   c. Delegate

| Needs work | OK | Very satisfied |

   d. Reduce time spent

| Needs work | OK | Very satisfied |

   e. Barter

| Needs work | OK | Very satisfied |

   f. Hire help

| Needs work | OK | Very satisfied |

Check some of the following books listed in Resources to see if
they can help you find more ways to make time for the important
things in life.

RESOURCES

Barret, Patti. *Too Busy to Clean: Over 500 Tips and Techniques to Make Housecleaning Easier.* Pownal, Vt: Storey Communications, 1990.

Bliss, Edwin. *Getting Things Done: The ABC's of Time Management.* New York: Scribner, 1976.

Campbell, Jeff. *Speedcleaning.* New York: Dell Publishing, 1985.

Fulghum, Robert. *All I Really Need to Know I Learned in Kindergarten.* New York: Ballantine Books, 1986.

Kanter, Rosabeth Moss. *Men and Women of the Corporation.* New York: Basic Books, 1977.

Kiley, Dan. *Dr. Dan's Prescriptions.* New York: Coward, McCann and Geoghegan Publishers, 1982.

Lakein, Alan. *How to Get Control of Your Time and Life*. New York: P.H. Wyden, 1973.

McCullough, Bonnie Runyan. *401 Ways to Get Your Kids to Work at Home*. New York: St. Martin's Press, 1981.

McCullough, Bonnie Runyan. *Bonnie's Household Organizer*. New York: St. Martin's Press, 1980.

Mitchell, Susan E., and Jill Fox. *30-Minute Meals*. San Francisco: California Culinary Academy, 1986.

Olds, Sally Wendkos. *The Working Parents' Survival Guide*. Toronto and New York: Bantam Books, 1983.

Shell, Adeline Garner, and Kay Reynolds. *Working Parent Food Book*. New York: Cornerstone Library, 1979.

Tannen, Deborah. *You Just Don't Understand: Men and Women in Conversation*. New York: Ballantine Books, 1990.

NOTES

1. Alan Lakein, *How to Get Control of Your Time and Your Life* (New York: P.H. Wyden, 1973), p. 1.
2. Robert Fulghum, *All I Really Need to Know I Learned in Kindergarten* (New York: Ballantine Books, 1986), p. 123.
3. Dan Kiley, *Dr. Dan's Prescriptions* (New York: Coward, McCann and Geoghegan Publishers, 1982), p. 236.
4. Deborah Tannen, *You Just Don't Understand: Men and Women in Conversation* (New York: Ballantine Books, 1990), p. 31.

Monthly Planner

	Monday	Tuesday	Wednesday	Thursday	Friday	Saturday	Sunday
A.M.							
P.M.							
Evening							
A.M.							
P.M.							
Evening							
A.M.							
P.M.							
Evening							
A.M.							
P.M.							
Evening							

Weekly Planner

Time	Monday	Tuesday	Wednesday	Thursday	Friday	Saturday	Sunday
6 A.M.							
7 A.M.							
8 A.M.							
9 A.M.							
10 A.M.							
11 A.M.							
12 P.M.							
1 P.M.							
2 P.M							
3 P.M.							
4 P.M.							
5 P.M.							
6 P.M.							
7 P.M.							
8 P.M.							
9 P.M.							
10 P.M.							
11 P.M.							
12–5 A.M.							

Weekly Planner

Time	Monday	Tuesday	Wednesday	Thursday	Friday	Saturday	Sunday
6 A.M.							
7 A.M.							
8 A.M.							
9 A.M.							
10 A.M.							
11 A.M.							
12 P.M.							
1 P.M.							
2 P.M							
3 P.M.							
4 P.M.							
5 P.M.							
6 P.M.							
7 P.M.							
8 P.M.							
9 P.M.							
10 P.M.							
11 P.M.							
12–5 A.M.							

Weekly Planner

Time	Monday	Tuesday	Wednesday	Thursday	Friday	Saturday	Sunday
6 A.M.							
7 A.M.							
8 A.M.							
9 A.M.							
10 A.M.							
11 A.M.							
12 P.M.							
1 P.M.							
2 P.M							
3 P.M.							
4 P.M.							
5 P.M.							
6 P.M.							
7 P.M.							
8 P.M.							
9 P.M.							
10 P.M.							
11 P.M.							
12–5 A.M.							

Weekly Planner

Time	Monday	Tuesday	Wednesday	Thursday	Friday	Saturday	Sunday
6 A.M.							
7 A.M.							
8 A.M.							
9 A.M.							
10 A.M.							
11 A.M.							
12 P.M.							
1 P.M.							
2 P.M							
3 P.M.							
4 P.M.							
5 P.M.							
6 P.M.							
7 P.M.							
8 P.M.							
9 P.M.							
10 P.M.							
11 P.M.							
12–5 A.M.							

Chapter Six

Beginning a Family . . . While Having a Career

I discovered that I always have choices and sometimes it's only a choice of attitude.[1]

Judith M. Knowlton

DECIDING TO HAVE A FAMILY

Deciding when to have a family is often a difficult decision. The need to work combined with a desire to have a family creates a conflict for many couples. Not working while raising children is not a real option for many parents-to-be; income and lifestyle choices require two incomes. Economics isn't the only conflict couples face when planning to have children, however. The desire to maintain a career while raising children can also be a major factor. The dedication it takes to maintain a career is a major commitment. Most couples worry about how their careers will be affected once there is a child in their lives. On the other hand, many couples also worry that children will suffer if both parents pursue their careers.

Other factors weigh on couples as well. The fact that 50 percent of marriages end in divorce is a reality. It could happen to any of us. Raising a child as a single parent is a difficult task for which most of us are unprepared. Knowing you could be a single parent at some time during your life is disquieting.

These are just a few factors you will consider in deciding whether or not to have a (or another) child. What can you do to help you through the decision-making process?

ASSESSING YOUR CAREER AND FAMILY VALUES

Begin by examining your values and desires related to work and family. Discuss the similarities and the differences between your values and those of your spouse or partner. It is important that each partner clarify what is really important to him or her. Have a conversation with your partner about each of your values. Talk about what adjustments you can make to eliminate problematic differences. Be honest about what you want from your careers and your family life. Create a vision of what you and your partner want your life to look like when you combine careers and family. This process may not happen in one conversation but may evolve over time.

To help you through this process, work on the accompanying Career and Family Life Values Assessment individually. Then share your thoughts with your partner.

Career and Family Life Values Assessment

The following questions will help clarify your feelings and beliefs about combining your career and family and the issues that may arise. Write in answers if your choice isn't there. The exercise should spark an in-depth discussion with your spouse or partner. (You may also want to fill out the Values Clarification Exercise in Chapter Two, if you haven't already done so.) Answer the following questions honestly.

1. My work is:
   _____ very important   _____ important to me   _____ not important to
   to me   me

2. My job requires me to work late and on weekends:
   _____ routinely   _____ sometimes   _____ rarely

3. My job requires me to travel:
   _____ routinely   _____ sometimes   _____ rarely

4. I do work at home:
   _____ routinely   _____ sometimes   _____ rarely

5. My employer has:
   _____ supportive   _____ no or limited   _____ work/family
   work/family   work/family   policies that are
   policies   policies   a mystery to me

6. My work hours are:
_____ flexible   _____ predetermined   _____ sometimes
                                                      variable

7. A woman who works and has children:
_____ cannot be a   _____ cannot be a   _____ cannot be both
      good mother   good worker
_____ can be a good
      mother and a
      good worker

8. If I decide to work part time after my child is born, my career will be:
_____ temporarily on   _____ ruined   _____ the same
      hold

9. If I decide to work fewer hours after my child is born, my career will be:
_____ temporarily on   _____ ruined   _____ the same
      hold

10. If I decide to take extended time off, my career will be:
_____ temporarily on   _____ ruined   _____ the same
      hold

11. A man who takes time off to take care of his children is:
_____ a wimp   _____ a good father   _____ undecided

12. I will expect my partner to stay home when our child is sick.
_____ Always   _____ Sometimes   _____ Never

13. If my child is sick, it is my responsibility to stay at home to care for him
    or her.
_____ Always   _____ Sometimes   _____ Never

14. A child who is cared for by people other than its parents will:
_____ prosper   _____ be unhappy   _____ not be as well
                                                      adjusted as a
                                                      child cared for
                                                      by its parents

15. My mother:
_____ was at home   _____ worked full   _____ worked part
                              time   time

16. My mother was:
_____ a good parent   _____ a bad parent   _____ an OK parent

17. My father was:
_____ a good parent   _____ a bad parent   _____ an OK parent

18. My partner and I have discussed:
how to discipline a
child.   _____ Yes   _____ No

the importance of
quality child care.   _____ Yes   _____ No

how we will pay for quality care.	_____ Yes	_____ No
what kind of parents we each had.	_____ Yes	_____ No
what kind of parents we want to be.	_____ Yes	_____ No
how we will pay the baby's expenses.	_____ Yes	_____ No
how we will handle child care responsibilities.	_____ Yes	_____ No
how we will handle disagreements about parenting.	_____ Yes	_____ No
religious upbringing.	_____ Yes	_____ No
other issues we think will come up when we have a child.	_____ Yes	_____ No

19. I am comfortable with the idea of having my child cared for by a qualified caregiver and not by me or my partner:

    _____ 4 hours/day   _____ 6 hours/day

    _____ 10 hours/day   _____ Not at all

20. To me, making money is:

    _____ very important   _____ somewhat important   _____ not very important

21. My partner and I have discussed what we want our lifestyle to be.

    _____ True   _____ False

22. Finding and choosing child care is the responsibility of:

    _____ the mother   _____ the father   _____ both parents

23. My partner and I have discussed how we will handle our finances.

    _____ True   _____ False

24. A reasonable child-care expense for our new baby will be:

    _____ $75/week   _____ $100/week   _____ $125/week

    _____ $150/week   _____ $175/week   _____ $200/week

25. I know all of the benefits and policies my employer has relating to leave of absences and child care.

    _____ True   _____ False   _____ Not sure

26. I have spoken to other new parents and know what to expect.

    _____ True   _____ False   _____ Not sure

27. My spouse and I both want to have a baby:

    _____ True   _____ False   _____ Not sure

28. If a conflict arises between work and family, I will:
_____ put work first   _____ put family first   _____ it depends
                                                                       on the circum-
                                                                       stances

29. I believe that a person must:
_____ keep work and   _____ devote equal   _____ find their own
        family separate   time to work   balance between
                                      and family   work and family

30. Name three things you would have to give up if you chose to stay home
    with your baby.
    1.
    2.
    3.

31. Name three sources of support you can draw on if you choose to have a
    family and continue a career.
    1.
    2.
    3.

32. What are your most important family norms or how do you think fami-
    lies should behave and what you would want to happen in your family?
    (e.g., a family should have dinner together every night. A child should
    have at least one home-cooked meal a day.)
    1.
    2.
    3.
    4.
    5.

33. Name three lifestyle changes you would have to make if you had a child
    (e.g., would not eat out as often, couldn't go away on short notice).
    1.
    2.
    3.

34. Name three things you won't change, even when you have a child (e.g.,
    my exercise schedule, weekly night out).
    1.
    2.
    3.

35. Name three other subjects you think you need to discuss with your part-
    ner to be prepared to have a baby.
    1.
    2.
    3.

Once you've completed the assessment, share your answers with your partner. Do your answers conflict or coincide? Are your expectations regarding life after your baby's arrival compatible? For those positions that are important to you, discuss how you could achieve them. For example, if one of you wants to stay home for an extended period, outline a financial plan. What areas need further discussion? What additional information do you need? Are you ready to combine career and family?

PLANNING YOUR LEAVE OF ABSENCE

Once you have decided to combine working and a family (or find that you must whether you consciously decided or not!), you need to plan your leave of absence. Many companies have a paid and/or unpaid leave of absence policy for childbirth or adoption. Some companies make this leave of absence available to either parent. The leave is designed to help you and your family recover and adjust to the changes associated with the arrival of a baby. Contact your human resources department for your employers' specific policies on leaves of absence. Make sure you are clear on what benefits are covered, what conditions apply, what is required of you, and the procedure to apply for your leave. If you don't think the formal leave plan will work for you, explore the option of creating your own leave. Maybe you could phase-in and extend your leave by coming back sooner but at a reduced commitment.

Working Out Your Leave with Your Partner and Family

To successfully plan your leave, work out an action plan with your partner. Answer the following family-leave questions:

1. What is your employer's leave policy (available from the human resources or personnel department)? What other child-care benefits are in place?
2. What will you need during your leave from your partner? Discuss your expectations.

3. What will you need from other members of your family? For example, do you want your mother and/or your mother-in-law to help after the birth? Discuss your expectations with them.

4. What financial arrangements need to be considered? How long will your benefits last? Will the time off from work be paid or unpaid?

5. What child-care arrangements need to be made and when? (See Chapter Seven.)

6. Are you going back to work? If so, will you return full-time or on a flexible work alternative? If you don't go back to work or you go back to work less than full-time, how will you manage financially?

For many of you, working out a plan is primarily between you and your partner. However, because of divorce and remarriages, you may be part of a blended family that includes children from a previous marriage. If you have waited to have children until later in life, you may also have an elder relative living with you or for whom you are responsible. All these family members may need to be part of the process of working out aspects of your plan.

The following points should be part of your discussions with your partner and/or other family members.

1. Be specific and clear about what is going to happen and when—preparing space for the child, looking for child care, leaving your job, returning to work, and so on.

2. Clarify roles before the baby is born and again after the baby is born. If you have other children, prepare them for the new addition to the family to avert sibling jealousy. For blended families, a new baby may cause some tension with children from other marriages. Be prepared for some resentment. Decide what you will do to prepare them and handle problems.

3. Avoid being defensive. Consider all viewpoints and everyone's responsibilities.

4. Do what you and your partner want to do about work schedules, day-care schedules, and so on. Try not to be pressured into living up to someone else's expectations.

5. Be flexible. Your feelings or plans may change after the baby arrives or after you return to work.

6. Keep the lines of communication open. The more you discuss the changes that will occur, the more likely you are to get the cooperation you need. Don't be afraid to ask for what you need.

7. Keep a sense of humor. Change is difficult for everyone. And preparing for a new child is both exciting and frightening.

8. Get all of the information and help that you can—forewarned is forearmed. Read books and articles about welcoming a new baby. Attend an expectant parents' workshop.

Getting Support from Your Supervisor

Communication is one of the most important factors in making a smooth transition to and from a leave of absence. Effective communication with your supervisor will ensure your work is covered during your absence and that things progress smoothly for you, your supervisor, and your co-workers. You need to start by telling your supervisor that you are pregnant (many women prefer to wait until after the first trimester) and will be taking a leave.

The following steps will help you achieve success when communicating with your supervisor:

- If you're nervous or have a difficult supervisor, you may want to rehearse with your partner or a friend.

- Choose a time and setting for your discussion that are conducive to a good discussion.

- Do some homework. Know your employer's policies. Talk to other women who have taken a leave from similar positions or the same supervisor and get a feel for the do's and don'ts.

- Talk to your supervisor as openly and candidly as possible. Maintain a positive attitude. Don't be surprised if your supervisor is distressed rather than excited by your good news.

- Reassure him or her of your commitment to your job by taking all of his or her concerns seriously.

- Be sensitive that she or he may feel upset or inconvenienced by your need to take a leave. Reassure the supervisor that you will do everything you can to minimize his or her burden.

- Be prepared to answer your supervisor's questions, such as:

  - When you plan to begin your leave (paid or unpaid).
  - How long you plan to be on leave.
  - Whether you are going to add your vacation and/or accrued sick time to the leave. (Try not to use your sick days. You may need those later.)
  - Whether you'll be available for questions by telephone.
  - How your work will be done while you're on leave. Options may include:
    - Splitting your work load among your co-workers.
    - Temporary replacement from within the company.
    - Temporary replacement from outside the company (the most widely used option; some companies turn to retired employees).
    - Urgent work is reassigned, the balance is held for you.
    - Work sent home.
    - Permanent replacement with you reassigned to another job.

  - Those parts of your job that will require cross-training (teaching someone else to do things only you know how to do).
  - Any restrictions on your work before you begin your leave (travel, overtime, etc.).
  - Whether or not you are coming back (if your employer doesn't give you paid maternity leave if you are not coming back, you may not feel you have much choice but to say you will be back; in any event, you may not be absolutely sure what you will want to do). You don't need to discuss uncertainty with your supervisor. Do what you need to do to keep your options open).
  - How you plan to return to work (full time, phased-in, part time, voluntary reduced hours and pay for a set period, flextime, job sharing, etc.).

- Identify the issues on which you are prepared to compromise.
- Adopt a collaborative approach by setting mutual priorities with your supervisor.
- Confirm your agreement in a memo. Send a copy to the human resources department if required or you think it advisable.

If you plan to return to work less than full time, you will need to develop a plan for how the option you choose will work for your employer. If your company does not yet offer flexible working options formally (see Chapter Two), be creative. Develop a plan to present to your supervisor and the human resources department. If you are well prepared, your supervisor will be more willing to work things out with you. Gather data and case studies from other companies on successful flexible work options to help you sell the idea (see Chapter Ten).

Planning for Your Replacement at Work

It's important to have backup plans before you leave your job. Begin planning early because it is sometimes difficult to predict with certainty the date you will need to begin your leave.

The following steps should facilitate the transition to your leave of absence:

- Organize your paperwork, desk drawers, files, and other work-related materials.
- Keep your supervisor informed about the status of each project assigned to you. Ask him or her to assign the projects to others in advance. Keep up-to-date transition memos that will allow your replacement to pick up and run with each project or duty. Provide a list of relevant phone numbers and other important information that may be needed in your absence.
- Have periodic meetings with co-workers to update them on projects that will be assigned to them.
- Accept offers of help when you need it! Reject it tactfully when you don't.

- If you are unsure of the exact date on which you will begin your leave, take a few minutes at the end of each day to straighten up your work area as if it were the last day before your leave.

During your last week at work, have a conversation with your supervisor and the co-workers who will be filling in for you. Be patient and sympathetic about their concerns and sensitive to their needs. Review your plan and tell them how you're going to keep in touch with what's going on. Expect that everyone will feel some anxiety about your leaving. You may even want to give the people who are helping out a special little gift to thank them for their efforts. Doing this preparation will give you one less thing to worry about. The time you spend in planning will be one of the best investments you'll ever make.

MATERNITY LEAVE

Maternity leaves (usually a six- to eight-week paid leave for a normal vaginal delivery covered under an employer's sickness and disability leave policy, with or without job protection) have been offered by most employers for a while now. While they may not be happy about losing you, even for six weeks, your co-workers and supervisor generally will not question your right to the time off. If you work with them and plan the leave well, your leave can be a happy, productive one for everyone affected by it.

Patti's Story

Patti is a legal secretary. She has job shared, working three full days a week, since the birth of her first child, Angela. When Angela was five, Patti and her husband, Rick, decided to have another baby. After her first trimester, Patti told the lawyers she worked for and the firm's personnel department she would need a leave. Fortunately, her baby was due in May and her job-share partner, a student, offered to work full time for the summer. (When Patti's previous job-share partner had her second child, a temporary secretary took over her two days). Although Patti gets no paid maternity leave (a benefit not available to part-time employees), she was able to take a three-month unpaid leave. She took her accrued vacation time as well. Always organized, Patti made sure her job-share partner was fully up to speed on those parts of the job only Patti did and that all filing and projects were up to date before she left. Her leave went smoothly, and she is back at work part time.

Barbara's Story

Barbara is an associate lawyer at a large law firm. When she became pregnant, she waited until her fifth month to tell her department head, after her annual performance review. "I was afraid the partners would perceive me differently. And they did." Comments were made questioning her continued commitment, and she even overheard one partner moan about losing another good lawyer to "Mommy-dom." Barbara found such comments very hard to take and to overcome. As her due date approached, she felt like a lame duck, unsure of how much authority she had or how much work she should do on her cases. For those cases that had to be reassigned in her absence (only about 10 percent of her caseload), she kept up to date transition and fact memos and kept the associates assigned to cover them briefed on the cases' progress.

The leave itself went smoothly. She received a few calls from co-workers and was able to give them the information they needed, although from their comments, they seemed to think she was home eating bonbons! Barbara is now back at work, and the partners are again starting to see her as a regular lawyer.

Both Patti and Barbara enjoyed their maternity leaves, and the leaves went well for their employers as well. Both women noted they loved the time at home with their baby, in part because they knew the time was finite.

Many women have told us that the transition from work to being home, especially before the baby is born, is a difficult one. You are likely to be physically uncomfortable. You're busy work pace comes to a halt. Most of them report that if they had it to do again, they would have enjoyed "doing nothing" and rested more. Once the baby arrives, your life is his or hers. The first few months are exhausting and stressful. Get help if you can.

PATERNITY LEAVE

In *The Woman Who Works, The Parent Who Cares,* Dr. Sirgay Sanger describes the rewards that come with being an active father:

> Often, when a man becomes . . . deeply involved in his child's life . . . , he is responding not only to what he sees, hears, and is told but to what he remembers. Part of the deep satisfaction of succoring a hurt, confused, or upset child is that a part of us remembers how good it felt when, at three or four and in distress or pain, we were held and comforted by a loving parent.[2]

The Paper Organization, an opinion survey firm, reports that most men have long believed in taking on a larger share of house-keeping and child-rearing duties. Now some are actually doing it.[3] U.S. Department of Labor statistics show that 20 percent of medium to large companies offer a paternity or parental leave, a formal policy for fathers who want to take some time off when the child is born and/or extended time after the birth. In some companies, an informal or personal leave is possible. Check with your human resources department or your supervisor if you or your partner want to take some time off when the baby is born.

Dale and Anita's Story

Dale and Anita had been married seven years and each had a career. When Dale and Anita decided to have their first child, they both agreed they didn't want a caregiver to raise the baby during its infancy. Dale's work as a photojournalist was more flexible than Anita's corporate job. Dale felt his career would not be in jeopardy if he took off six months to be with their newborn child. So when their first child was born, Anita stayed home for six weeks (her mom helped for the first month). From that point on Dale stayed home to care for his daughter. After six months, Dale decided to continue in his role as full-time caregiver.

A year later, their second child was born. Dale felt very comfortable in his role of at-home dad, so they continued the arrangement. After three and a half years, he's still at home and enjoying his role. Dale is comfortable with children. "I've always liked kids." He notes that raising his children has been the hardest job he's ever had.

When we asked him about his motivations for continuing his at-home role, he commented that he wanted to be involved full time as a parent. He said he wanted to "give his children the tools to be involved in life." Dale's father was unavailable when he was growing up. He felt his childhood was unhappy and he wanted a better start for his children.

For Dale and Anita, the role reversal was easy. They had common values, strong egos, and no role conflicts. Anita's salary provided the necessary finances for the family, and her career goals are being met. Dale can get back into his profession when the children are ready for kindergarten. Most importantly, they feel fulfilled in their goals for family life. Each of them is achieving the values that are important to them.

For men who work in corporations and have less flexibility than Dale, the decision to take time off is colored by two often conflicting factors—their own values and those of the corporate culture where they work. Many organizations measure your job performance by how much time you are *at the job* ("face time") or how many hours you put in more than by the quality or quantity of work you produce. If you believe family is as important as work and you want to spend more than accrued vacation time with your family after the birth of your baby be prepared to do the following:

- Sell the idea to your supervisor as well as the organization.
- Look for other individuals who can give you case studies of successful paternity leaves.
- Gather as much data as possible to promote your idea.
- Cite the fact that the organization will get positive public relations for initiating a leave for fathers.
- Decide how you will handle unfavorable comments from peers.

When deciding to take a leave, you are setting new standards for men, their employers, and their families. It is an opportunity to change the culture to view family and work with equal importance. It's a challenge! It's also a wonderful opportunity to be actively involved in the raising of your child from birth. It can have a very positive effect on a baby to have both mother and father rearing it.

Charlie's Story

Charlie is a computer professional who works for a health-care organization. He and his wife discussed the importance of sharing the responsibility of raising a child as part of their decision to have a baby. Charlie wanted to participate right from the start. He believed he had been cheated by his own father who was never home or available for him. Soon after his wife became pregnant, Charlie went to his supervisor to discuss time off for the birth and a new flexible work schedule. Charlie's organization does not have a formal paid paternity leave, but it did have an unpaid family leave policy. Charlie and his wife agreed they could not afford more than two weeks of unpaid leave. Charlie proposed a two-week family leave to his boss. Together with his accrued vacation time, he would be gone for five weeks. He had carefully worked out a plan of cross-training with co-workers as well as some work at home to make sure all aspects of his job would be covered. Charlie explained the importance of helping with the new baby and wanting to be an active parent.

Charlie's traditional supervisor (his wife never worked outside the home) was surprised at Charlie's request and initially resistant. He became more supportive, however, after Charlie showed him the schedule he had worked out. Charlie cited a case study from another department and described that successful story. Charlie also used statistics he had gathered from other companies that had implemented time-off policies for fathers. Those companies showed high morale and improved productivity because of the policies, as well as increased visibility as a family-friendly company. Charlie's strong beliefs about the importance of family and his carefully designed plan persuaded his supervisor to approve his leave.

Because the first part of his proposal went well, the second part was easier. Charlie explained he wanted to continue active parenting after his two-week family leave, but he also wanted to keep doing his job well. Charlie suggested a flexible work plan where he would come in at 3:30 P.M. and work until midnight. He explained that he could accomplish more on the computer because most personnel would be off it after 5:00 P.M. He also volunteered to cover the phones, explaining the department's ability to service its West Coast and international customers would be enhanced by the extended hours. His supervisor said he would think it over. In the meantime, Charlie worked through more details with the human resources department and accumulated more success stories to back up his plan.

Two weeks later, Charlie again met with his boss to work out details. His supervisor agreed to try it for a short time, with the option to change back if it didn't work. Charlie agreed to make some calls from home before 3:30 P.M. when necessary and to be available once a week for midmorning staff meetings. He and his supervisor explained the proposed flexible work arrangement to his department and ironed out some other details that would affect co-workers.

Charlie worked hard on every detail, and 18 months after coming back from his leave, he is still on the flexible schedule. Charlie's wife, a nurse, went back to work after 10 weeks and works an earlier shift (7 A.M. to 3 P.M.) so she can be home before Charlie leaves.

Both Charlie and his wife feel good about their choice of raising a child together and yet continuing with their careers. They got the support they needed from each other (weekends are their only couple time) as well as from their employers. They are both valued employees, and their employers did not want to lose them. At this point, Charlie's career has not been hurt. In fact, his situation has been used as an example for other departments to follow.

Not all paternity leaves turn into flexible work arrangements. Just taking two to four weeks off right after the baby is born to help your partner or after your partner's leave is up to extend the infant's time at home can be a tremendous opportunity to bond with your new child.

CHILD-CARE ARRANGEMENTS

It is never too early to start looking for child care. Some child-care centers have waiting lists so long that parents sign up before the baby is born! Different forms of child care require different lead times. As a guide, consider the accompanying table.

Child Care—When to Start Looking

Type of Child Care	When to Start Looking
Nurse, in your home	Four months before child is due
Day-care center for infants	Nine months to a year before you return to work
Family day care	Six to eight weeks before you return to work
In-home care	Six to eight weeks before you return to work
Live-in child care	Twelve weeks before you return to work
Au pairs	One year before you need them to start

Specific factors you should consider in choosing the form of child care best suited to you and your family are discussed in Chapter Seven.

PLANNING YOUR RETURN TO WORK

When you are on leave, you need to plan your return to work. To prepare yourself for your return, consider the following:

- Stay aware of what's happening at work while you're away. It will be easier to go back if you do not feel out of the information loop. Ask that intraoffice memos, mail, newsletters, and reading you may need to keep up in your field be sent to you at home.
- Begin to prepare yourself mentally several weeks before you return. Visualize how your life will be different once you're working and parenting.
- Do what you and your supervisor agreed you would do. Return precisely on the day you're supposed to. One day's delay may mean a lot to your co-workers.
- Make sure your child-care arrangements are in place. It is a good idea to start with your new caregiver a week or two

before you are due to return to work so that you and your baby can ease into the new routine. It will also give you time to see how your baby and caregiver interact and time to make adjustments, if necessary.

- Minimize any work-related problems that may have occurred while you were gone. Give your co-workers the benefit of the doubt.
- Be aware that your co-workers and supervisor may treat you differently now that you're a new parent. People are probably just trying to be considerate of your new demands. If this happens, reassure everyone that you're capable and eager to work.
- Expect to experience conflicting emotions (glad to go back to work but sorry to leave the baby). The first few weeks may be tiring and draining. Any new lifestyle requires time for adjustment.

Reentry Shock

Getting back into the workplace may be a shock after the rhythms of home and child care. The fact that life went on at work in your absence, despite this wonderful event that occurred in your family, may also be a difficult adjustment. If you anticipate these temporary changes, they will be easier to cope with.

SUMMARY

- Identify and assess work/family issues with your partner.
- Plan your family leave with your partner, supervisor, and other family members.
- Consider alternative leave plans with your partner.
- Plan for your replacement at work.
- Plan for your return to work.
- Enjoy your new baby!

RESOURCES

Abraham, Danielson; Eberle; Green; Rosenberg; and Stone. *Reinventing Home: Six Working Women Look at Their Home Lives*. New York: Plume, 1990.

Barrett, Nina. *I Wish Someone Had Told Me: Comfort, Support & Advice for New Moms from More Than 60 Real-life Mothers*. New York: Simon & Schuster, 1990.

Block, Joyce. *Motherhood as Metamorphosis*. New York: Penguin Books, 1990.

Boston Children's Hospital. *New Child Health Encyclopedia: A Complete Guide for Parents*. New York: Delacorte Press/Merloyd Lawrence, 1987.

Canape, Charlene. *Part-Time Solution: The New Strategy for Managing Your Career While Managing Motherhood*. New York: Harper & Row, 1990.

Cuozzo, Jane Hershey. *Power Partners: How Two-Career Couples Can Play to Win*. New York: Master Media Ltd., 1990.

Gillspie, Clark. *Prime Life Pregnancy: All You Need To Know About Pregnancy after 35*. New York: Perennial Library, 1987.

Leinberger, Paul, and Bruce Tucker. *The New Individualists*. New York: Harper Collins Publishers, 1991.

Lewin, Elizabeth. *Financial Fitness for New Families: A Guide for Newlyweds and Parents of Young Children*. New York: Facts on File, Inc., 1989.

Marzolla, Jean. *Your Maternity Leave: How to Leave Work, Have a Baby, and Go Back to Work Without Getting Lost, Trapped or Sandbagged Along the Way*. New York: Poseidon Press/Simon & Schuster, 1989.

McKaughan, Molly. *Biological Clock: Balancing Marriage, Motherhood and Career*. New York: Penguin Books, 1987.

Sangar, Sirgay, M.D. and John Kelly. *The Woman Who Works, The Parent Who Cares*. New York: Harper & Row, 1987.

Shapiro, Jerold Lee. *When Men Are Pregnant: Needs and Concerns of Expectant Fathers*. San Luis Obispo, Calif.: Impact, 1987.

Wheatley, Meg, and Marcie Schorr Hirsch. *Managing Your Maternity Leave*. Boston: Houghton Mifflin Company, 1983.

NOTES

1. Judith Knowlton, *Meditations for Women Who Do Too Much* (San Francisco: Harper & Row, 1990).
2. Sirgay Sanger, M.D. and John Kelly, *The Woman Who Works, The Parent Who Cares* (New York: Harper & Row, 1987), p. 198.
3. "Mr. Mom," *Training Development*, August 1991, p. 62.

Chapter Seven

Finding and Managing Quality Child Care

When it comes to raising children, labor before birth doesn't compare to labor after.

Gayle Kimball

F inding and choosing quality child care is a challenge for every working parent. Some of the most important decisions you'll make as a parent are associated with finding child care. You may find yourself questioning your decision to return to work and experiencing conflicting emotions. It takes a lot of courage to leave your child with someone else, even if it's a family member. But recent research into child development and working parents has shown:

- Child care outside the home seems to speed up the development of a child's social skills, though children who stay at home catch up quickly once they enter school.
- Some studies show that mothers who work outside the home spend as much time with their children, on average, as mothers who are at home.
- Husbands in two-income homes tend to be more involved with their children than husbands of nonemployed wives.

To reduce your fears, do your homework. Make yourself knowledgeable about every child-care option that may be available. Familiarize yourself with the pros and cons of each type of child care. Then choose the one that is best for your child and family.

CHILD-CARE OPTIONS

We've divided the various types of child care into three major categories:

- Child care in your home.
- Family day care.
- Day-care centers and preschools.

Child Care in Your Home

Child care in your home can be provided at no charge by a friend or family member or by someone you employ. About a third of working parents choose in-home care for their preschool children. It is the most popular form of child care for infants under six months of age. It is also a popular option for before- and/or after-school care for grade school children.

The caregiver's responsibilities depend on your assessment of their training, experience, and skills. A wide variety of arrangements, with a consequent variation in cost, is possible. With most, you become an employer and are responsible for complying with federal and state compensation and benefit laws. Some of the most common forms of in-home care are the following:

Nannies. A nanny is a child-care specialist who lives in your home. Often, nannies are professionally trained and certified by a licensed nanny college. Other nannies are qualified through years of experience in caring for young children. In 1987, there were nearly 200 nanny agencies and 100 nanny training programs in the United States. Usually, agencies place nannies with families that pay their agency fees.

Generally, nannies don't do work around the home that doesn't relate to the children. Full-time nannies assume full responsibility for child rearing. Part-time nannies help parents with child rearing but in a secondary role. Nannies offer very personalized services and receive higher salaries than other in-home caregivers.

A nanny usually will require his or her own room. Days, weekends off, and vacations are negotiable. Nannies can be a viable alternative when:

- A young child needs individualized care.
- You want a committed caregiver to provide long-term care.
- You work late or irregular hours or travel extensively.
- You have enough room in your house and are willing to lose some family privacy.
- You can afford a nanny's fees and associated costs (food, insurance, and so on).

Au pairs.   An au pair is usually a young domestic worker who provides child care on a live-in basis. Many au pairs are foreign students, giving children a chance to learn a foreign language or about another culture. The au pair bathes, dresses, feeds, watches, and is a companion to your family's children. She or he may also run errands, wait for the plumber, and shop for groceries. This arrangement is convenient in families with school-age children who still need supervision and can benefit from the cultural exchange aspects of having an au pair live in the home. The prime disadvantage of using au pairs is that they tend to be available only for a limited time, typically a year. This can present a problem in the care of infants and toddlers who need to establish a stable relationship with their caregivers.

If you consider using an au pair, be aware of the legal requirements (such as visas and work permits) required of individuals who aren't U.S. citizens. There are organizations that make arrangements for au pairs in accordance with U.S. immigration requirements (see Resources at the end of this chapter). Au pairs are usually entitled to a room of their own, meals with the family, a weekly allowance, and a day and a half off every week. They're guaranteed one free weekend per month and two weeks off during the first 10 months of their stay. At the end of their one-year assignment, their visa allows them to tour the United States on their own for one month.

Parents consider using an au pair when:

- They have adequate space for a live-in.
- They have school-age children or children with a broad range of ages.
- Their work demands flexibility in child care, such as during the evening, or weekends, or because of frequent business travel.

- They can afford to pay, feed, and house an au pair.

Baby-sitter. It is also possible to find a caregiver who will come to your home daily, and not live-in, on either a full- or part-time basis. The baby-sitter's responsibilities will depend on how you assess the sitter's training, experience, and skills. Working parents typically use baby-sitters when:

- They have an infant or preschool child(ren).
- They need after school care for an older child(ren).
- They need flexibility in caregiver hours due to their work schedules.
- You can afford in-home care.

In addition to daytime baby-sitters, most parents supplement their child-care arrangements with part-time baby-sitters who watch their children in the evening or on weekends.

Housekeepers. Housekeepers are available full- or part-time and can live in or out of the home. They usually take care of children and do household chores and cooking. However, because they take care of household duties and care for the children, one or the other of these responsibilities may suffer.

Shared care. If in-home child care is appealing but the costs are too high, consider a shared care arrangement in which several families, often in the same neighborhood, hire one child-care provider. One home can be used regularly as the child-care site, or the site can be rotated. This option allows families to have the personalized services of in-home care while keeping the costs down. Parents who use shared care often feel they have more control over the kind of care their children receive. They also have the ability to design their own program and include activities that are important to them. If you choose this option, be sure to clearly spell out, preferably in writing, what each family will provide (money, space, resources) and what the caregiver's duties are.

Relatives and friends. Relatives, family friends, or neighbors are a much-used source of free or low-cost child care in the home. Having people you know care for your children reduces some of the discomfort parents experience leaving their children with a caregiver. This arrangement is particularly helpful when family resources don't permit more expensive forms of child care.

You may want to consider having your relatives and family friends provide child care when:

- Your work requires flexible child care.
- You're uncomfortable leaving your child with caregivers you don't know well.
- You have several children with different child-care needs.
- Your financial situation does not permit other child-care options.

However, be aware of the negatives that can be associated with using family members or friends as caregivers for your child. Ask yourself:

- Will my relative/friend accept direction, and even criticism, from me graciously?
- Over the long term, will my relative/friend feel imposed upon, despite initial excitement about being with my child?
- How compatible are my relative/friend's child-rearing practices with mine?
- Do my relative/friend and I work out our conflicts well?

Care for the Child at Work

A variation of caring for your child in your home is caring for your child at your place of work. Sound fantastic? Approximately 9 percent of parents are doing it, particularly with infants.

Family Day-Care Homes

Most working parents (approximately 36 percent) take their preschool children to family day-care homes. Group care is provided in the home of the caregiver. Often while caring for his or her own children, the caregiver takes care of up to 12 children (depending on the state). Home-based child care may be the most popular arrangement for the care of preschool children because it's one of the most affordable options.

Day-Care Centers and Preschools

Approximately 24 percent of working parents use day-care centers and nursery schools for their preschool children. Most centers provide group care for a number of children of different ages in a facility designed or adapted especially for child-care use. Centers and preschools are open all day and all year to meet the needs of working parents. Some have extended hours and overnight-care options.

Day-care centers are generally supervised by a trained professional with a staff of caregivers. Most accommodate children ages two to five years old. Some are designed specifically for infants, while others take infants through preschoolers. Some offer kindergarten programs as well. Preschools are for children aged three to five.

Centers and preschools are licensed by the state to ensure compliance with health and safety standards, staff ratios, and space requirements. Check with your state's Department of Human Services or Department of Child and Family Services for a list of preschools, day-care centers, and family day-care homes available in your area. Also check newspaper ads, community bulletin boards, and your friends and relatives who use child care.

BE FLEXIBLE . . . BE PATIENT!

You'll find that creativity and flexibility are required in arranging for child care, particularly if you have children of different ages. In addition, you'll need lots of patience and perseverance as you set about your quest for *quality* child care.

Karen's Story

Karen is a single parent. When her daughter, Jody, was an infant, Karen worked at home part-time until her daughter was a year old. A neighbor watched Jody while Karen worked at home. Because she needed to make more money, Karen got a full-time job as a secretary. Her neighbor was unable to continue baby-sitting because she was expecting a second child.

Karen began looking for child care by researching the local not-for-profit agencies in the city that provided lists of child-care providers licensed by the state. Karen preferred an in-home caregiver because she wanted a home-like situation with fewer children. Cost, quality, nearby public transportation, and hours were all considerations for Karen. After interviewing seven in-home caregivers, she found one who was highly recommended by a friend. She enrolled Jody and the arrangement worked well. After six months, however, the caregiver gave notice that she was moving to another state.

Another search began. This time Karen also checked the local papers for ads. She interviewed many caregivers but couldn't find a situation that met her needs. She decided to try a nanny service. The service was expensive and she had to take a loan from her family to pay for the service charge. She interviewed several nannies and found one that met her standards. This arrangement worked well for three months until the summer ended and the caregiver decided to go back to school. By this time, Jody was toilet trained and ready for a child-care center.

Karen went back to the local not-for-profit agency for a list of licensed child-care centers in her area. She was able to locate one within walking distance and close to public transportation to work. The philosophy was good, and she could afford it. Jody was enrolled.

This story is typical of many parents who find and then lose care. The next challenge for Karen will be to make before- and after-school arrangements when Jody gets into kindergarten.

Child care for your family may include several types of the caregivers described above. For example, if you have an infant, a preschooler, and a school-age child, your child-care arrangements can include all of the following:

- Infant day-care center.
- Part-time baby-sitter for evening or weekend obligations.
- Preschool.
- School.
- Neighbor for before- and after-school care of the school-age child.

After looking at the options, identify those choices that might be most suitable for your particular family's needs.

WHAT IS A GOOD CHILD-CARE PROGRAM?

Let's start by looking at the American Academy of Pediatrics' definition of a good child-care program. The academy says a child-care program should:

1. Provide a safe, clean setting.
2. Use trained personnel who are warm and responsive.
3. Promote good health habits.
4. Offer a stimulating environment to help children master cognitive (thinking) and communication skills.
5. Encourage children to develop at their own rate.
6. Nurture children's self-confidence, curiosity, creativity, and self-discipline.
7. Stimulate children to ask questions, solve problems, make decisions, and engage in a variety of activities.
8. Foster children's social skills, self-esteem, and respect for other children and adults.
9. Help parents improve their child-raising skills.
10. Promote cooperation between parents, teachers, public and private schools, and the community.

You may want to consider these factors when evaluating your child-care options.

Characteristics of Child-Care Programs

It's helpful to consider the characteristics of each type of child care and then determine which options best meet your needs and desires. As you consider each option, you may want to think about the factors described below.

Flexibility. If your work schedule is unpredictable, you'll need child-care arrangements that are flexible. Family day care, in-home care, and shared care tend to be more flexible than day-care centers or preschools.

Reliability. The reliability of your child-care provider is an important factor to consider. Imagine the impact on your stress level if your caregiver is frequently late in the morning when you need to catch a train or leave the house to get to work on time! Generally, baby-sitters tend to be among the least reliable caregivers, but the reliability of an in-home or family-care provider depends on the individual. Day-care centers and preschools will be the most reliable. No matter how reliable you think your caregiver is, plan a backup for when she or he is unavailable.

Licensing. While licensing is not required of all types of care providers, some types are regulated by state law. Generally, family day-care homes, day-care centers, and preschools are licensed. Licensing assures you only that the caregiver meets the state's minimum standards, not necessarily the high standards you may have. It's best to rely on your own judgment in selecting child care.

Accreditation. An accredited program meets the standards of quality set by an organization like the National Association for the Education of Young Children (NAEYC), which has an accreditation program for day-care centers. The National Academy of Early Childhood Programs (NAECP) accredits preschool programs. Again, while accreditation is a factor to consider, rely on your own judgment and investigation when selecting a child-care provider.

Staff/child ratio. The number of children that each caregiver is responsible for is critical when assessing the quality of care your child will receive. When caregivers are responsible for fewer children, they're more likely to have a close, personal relationship with your child.

Each state has different guidelines for the maximum number of children per adult. Typically, in family day-care homes, 6 to 12 children can be watched per adult, no more than 2 of whom can be infants.

For child-care centers accredited by NAEYC, the typical required ratios are one adult for every:

Four infants, 0 to 15 months.
Four infants, 16 months to two years old.
Six two-year-olds.
Eight three-year-olds.
Nine four-year-olds.
Ten five-year-olds through kindergarten.

Programs offered. Quality child-care programs offer structured, yet fun, activities. Although day-care centers and preschools usually provide more structured activities, many family day-care homes offer informal learning activities, such as building block houses and finger painting. An in-home caregiver can just let the child play or can plan activities for the week. The quality of the program generally depends on the caregiver's training and experience.

One advantage to the day-care center or preschool may be workshops and support groups for parents. This can be especially helpful for first-time parents.

Staff qualifications. The skills, training, and experience of the child-care provider affect their job performance. Research indicates the key factor in a caregiver's qualifications is child-related training. Day-care centers and preschools tend to have more formally trained caregivers than do family day-care homes. Nearly 75 percent of states have no training requirements for family day-care providers. Nannies can be very highly trained. Au pairs and baby-sitters generally have little or no formal training. A caregiver who is credentialed as a child development associate (CDA) has proven his or her competence in working with young children through a national assessment system.

In addition, you may want to ask yourself about the characteristics of the caregiver and his or her compatibility with your own values and expectations. This is particularly important in family day-care homes and in-home care situations. How important are the following factors in your choice of a caregiver?

- Age.
- Education/training.
- Experience in caring for children.
- Being a parent.
- Motivation for caregiving.
- Religious, ethnic, or cultural affiliation.
- Parenting and discipline philosophies.

Stability. A key to high-quality child care is consistency. Children thrive on consistency and will be less upset by child-care arrangements if they are cared for by the same caregiver for extended periods. When choosing a day-care center, ask about turnover among the staff. How long has the staff member who will teach your child been working at that center? When choosing an in-home or family caregiver, get a commitment as to how long the person will care for your child.

Cost. When selecting child care, cost is an important consideration. On average, child care is the single biggest expense after housing, taxes, and food in the working parent's budget. The typical dual-income family spends between 10 percent and 25 percent of gross income on child care. Single parents generally spend between 18 and 25 percent. The costs for full-time child care vary considerably across the country, depending on the age of the child and the type of arrangement. The accompanying chart lists expenses you can expect to pay for different types of child care. Dollar amounts are based on caring for one child 40 to 50 hours per week.

There are other financial considerations when budgeting for child care. Find out exactly what you're getting for your money. Are there additional fees for registration, deposits, meals, transportation, or materials? Are there overtime fees if you're late picking up your child? Will you be charged for days when your child is out sick or on vacation? Be sure to ask these questions.

If you're using in-home care, consult your accountant for social security, unemployment, and federal and state income tax requirements.

Cost of Child-Care Options

Type of Care	Average Costs
Nannies	$10,500–$24,000/year, plus room and board
Au pair	$100–$200/week plus room, board, and airfare
Baby-sitters	$4–$8/hour
Family day-care home	$90–$150/week for infants $65–$125/week for preschoolers
Day-care center or preschool	$95–$195 : infants $90–$150 : toddlers $70–$140 : 2 and 3-year-olds $60–$140 : 4 and 5-year-olds Plus class fees, late charges, and materials costs
Montessori school	$90–$150/week
Government, employer, or university subsidized day-care center	$50–$100/week

Assistance in Paying for Child Care. As an employed parent, you're entitled to a dependent care tax credit if you have someone take care of your child (for a fee) while you work. The dependent care tax credit also includes a deduction for a placement fee paid to an agency that helps you find a child-care provider. You may qualify for the federal credit, claimed on your personal income tax form, if you pay for child care for children aged 12 or younger to maintain your employment and you are:

- A two-parent family, both employed full or part time, filing a joint tax return.
- A two-parent family with one parent working full or part time and the other a full-time student, filing a joint tax return.
- A single parent, working full or part time.

The tax credit can't be more than you actually paid for child care. Wages paid to a housekeeper may also be included if his or her work includes duties related to caring for a child under age 15.

The maximum amount you can claim is a percentage of your actual child-care costs. That percentage depends on your earnings. You must keep records of all costs incurred in using an in-home caregiver, a family day-care home, a day-care center, or a nursery school. Be sure to get your caregiver's social security or other tax identification number as it's required for you to take your deduction. Talk to your accountant for further details or questions.

Your employer may have a program in place (Dependent Care Assistance Program) that may allow you to pay for child care with pretax dollars, depending on the type of provider. Consult your employer's human resources or benefits department. Other child-care benefits may also be available through your employer, such as reimbursement for child care incurred due to overtime or business travel, child-care subsidies, sick-child-care subsidies or services, discounts at select providers, and financial assistance with child care and child care resources and provider referrals.

Scholarships and local government funding may be available for your child. Federal Social Service Block Grant funds (Title XX) are administered by the state and provide child-care assistance for low-income families. The Resources section provides information on where to apply for these subsidies.

DETERMINING YOUR CHILD-CARE NEEDS

The need for child care can become a primary consideration of family life when both parents work outside the home. Each family situation has its own special child-care requirements. Each child is different. Some children need one-on-one in care; others seem to be happier in a larger day-care setting. Making a good child-care decision requires that you look at the characteristics of each child-care option and compare them to your child's and your family's needs.

The best place to begin narrowing down available child-care options to those that most closely meet your needs is to prioritize your own child-care needs and preferences. What are your needs and time constraints? Do you require care for more than one child?

Look at the accompanying list. Circle the degree to which each factor is important to you. Discuss them with your family.

Prioritizing Child-Care Needs

	Not Important	Somewhat Important	Important	Moderately Important	Very Important
Child care in your home	1	2	3	4	5
Having someone live in your home	1	2	3	4	5
Child care in someone else's home	1	2	3	4	5
Privacy	1	2	3	4	5
Housekeeping services	1	2	3	4	5
Reliability	1	2	3	4	5
Cost of care	1	2	3	4	5
Taking child out of his/her home	1	2	3	4	5
Ease of transportation from home	1	2	3	4	5
Being in neighborhood/ near home/near school	1	2	3	4	5
Hours of care available	1	2	3	4	5
Flexibility in hours of care	1	2	3	4	5
Availability of extended hours	1	2	3	4	5
Care for sick child	1	2	3	4	5
Number of children in the setting	1	2	3	4	5
Ages of children in the setting	1	2	3	4	5
Experience of caregiver	1	2	3	4	5
Personality of caregiver	1	2	3	4	5
Discipline	1	2	3	4	5
Philosophy of the program	1	2	3	4	5
Learning materials and activities	1	2	3	4	5
Structured programs	1	2	3	4	5
Field trips and special outings	1	2	3	4	5
Special services (like dance or music classes)	1	2	3	4	5
Staff turnover/time commitment	1	2	3	4	5
Your control over the child's activities	1	2	3	4	5

Ethnic/cultural diversity	1	2	3	4	5
Religious affiliation/ training	1	2	3	4	5
Atmosphere (e.g., friendly, quiet, organized)	1	2	3	4	5
Having all your children in the same setting	1	2	3	4	5
Using a licensed facility	1	2	3	4	5
Using an accredited facility	1	2	3	4	5
Becoming an employer/ dealing with the paperwork	1	2	3	4	5
Parent workshops, seminars, or support groups	1	2	3	4	5

Compare your most important requirements with the characteristics of the types of care and identify which options you want to pursue.

SELECTING A CHILD-CARE PROVIDER

Once you've determined the type of care setting and provider you and your family prefer, the next step is to find a specific caregiver.

Step One: Get Started Early

First, recognize that there's a shortage of quality child-care providers, particularly for infants and toddlers. Some care settings have long waiting lists. Also, choosing child care involves making emotional decisions. Therefore, give yourself ample time to investigate available providers. Allow at least one month.

Be sure to investigate any child-care services or benefits your employer may provide (educational workshops, support groups, resource and referral, voucher or pretax payment programs, financial assistance, discounts or reserved slots in child-care centers, employer-sponsored on- or near-site child care centers).

Step Two: Narrow the Field of Choices

Next, select several potential care providers. Many companies provide a resource and referral service that you can call for assistance. If your organization doesn't, here's a list of resources to help you get started:

- Your local DCFS.
- National Association of Resource and Referral.
- Religious organizations.
- NAEYC.
- Social service or family agencies.
- YMCA or YWCA.
- Yellow Pages.
- Local schools.

Use your networks. Talk to other parents, friends, neighbors, and relatives. Review community newspaper ads, parent/women's groups newsletters, and bulletin boards at your grocery store, church, or doctor's office for information on the available care in your area.

If you're hiring someone to provide child care in your home, you can:

- Place an ad in the classified section of the newspaper.
- Place a listing in college placement offices.
- Contact an agency or nanny school that arranges for nannies and au pairs.
- Advertise with working parents' networks.

When placing an ad, clearly state the number and ages of your children and your requirements. Advertise on Fridays, Saturdays, and Sundays. Limit the hours during which you welcome telephone inquires. A sample ad is provided below:

Caregiver wanted for energetic 2-year-old boy. Daily 7:00A.M.–5:00 P.M. Oak Park Area. Nonsmoker. Light housekeeping. Experience and early childhood education preferred. Must have references and own transportation. Call (555) 555-5555 between 6:00 and 8:00 P.M.

Step Three: Screen Providers by Telephone

Screening providers by telephone can save you a lot of time. Use some of the sample questions provided in the accompanying list of interview questions. Modify them as necessary to get all of the information you need. Keep careful notes during the conversation so you can remember details if you decide to conduct an in-person interview.

Sample Telephone Interview Questions

Tell me about yourself.
How old are you?
Do you have children? What ages?
How would you get here? (transportation: car, bus, train)
Are you working now?
How many children do you care for?
How old are they?
Who was your last employer?
May I have his/her phone number and call him/her as a reference?
How long did you work there?
Why did you decide to change jobs?
How long have you been caring for children?
Why did you decide to care for children?
What other child-care experiences have you had?
What is your educational background and training?
Are you registered or certified? What credentials do you have?
How many children will you care for?
For what hours are you available?
What happens if I'm late leaving work and get home after we agreed?
What's your favorite children's book?
What do you hope my child will learn?
What happens if you are sick?
How often were you sick last year?
What happens if your children are sick? Do you have backup help?
Will you take the child out in a car for any reason, like field trips?
Are you willing to take the child to appointments?
Will you care for my child if she or he is sick?
What are your plans for the future?
What do you see yourself doing in five years?

(If the applicant is an immigrant) Are you a U.S. citizen? Do you have
  a visa or work papers?
What would you do if . . .
  my child cries?
  my child continues to cry?
  my child hits another child?
  my child refuses to do what you asked?
  my child refuses to eat lunch?
  my child cries when we leave for work?
  you and I disagree about something?
Are you willing to enforce our rules and work with us on discipline,
  food, routines, etc.?
May I have the names and telephone numbers of people you have worked
  for before?

After you get answers to your basic questions, describe your
needs in detail. Mention what you think is most important and
listen to the caregiver's reactions or comments. Be sure to include
specifics about the amount you're willing to pay, work hours, vacations, and other working conditions for in-home providers. If
you would like the caregiver to help with housekeeping or errands, see if the person is willing to do so. If you are both interested, let the caregiver know when you will call if you decide to
arrange a personal interview (or to tell the person a personal interview will not be needed), which will be after you have completed your telephone screening.

Step Four: Check References

Be sure to ask the care provider for references. For in-home providers, ask for the name and telephone number of one or more
former employers and, if possible, the parents who use the caregiver now.

Ask family day-care and day-care center providers to give you
references of current parents who use their service. You may also
want to ask for the names of parents who don't use the facility
any longer to find out why they left.

References do no good unless you actually follow up by calling. Make a list of questions to ask the references about the provider's past work experience and effect on their children. You may want to ask some of the following questions.

Sample Questions to Ask References

Introduce yourself and your reason for calling. Then ask:
   Were you satisfied with his or her services?
   What specific services did she or he provide?
   How much did you pay?
   Did you check references?
   How did your children like him or her?
   Why did the employment terminate?
   Does she or he communicate well with children?
   How did she or he respond in emergency situations?
   Did she or he react appropriately to children needing assistance, guidance,
      or discipline?
   Do you trust him or her?
   Did you have any problems with him or her that could have been avoided
      with advance preparation?
   What were the caregiver's strong points?
   What were the caregiver's weak points?
   Would you use this caregiver again?
   Is there anything else you think I should know?

Step Five: Interview and Observe

Make an appointment to visit and observe those caregivers you like best and who had good references. It may be uncomfortable at first, especially if you are not used to interviewing and hiring. Just remember you are the employer and a good parent and have a right and need to know as much as possible about the person who will be entrusted with your child. Remember, though, you are also being interviewed by the caregiver, particularly for an in-home or family day-care situation. For the arrangement to work, you must both be comfortable and be able to relate well to each other.

For your first visit to a family day-care home, allow at least an hour. Allow more time for a day-care center or school. While you're visiting, collect handbooks, brochures, and other printed materials offered to help you make your decision. Use the checklists at the end of this section to record your observations and impressions.

You will interview and observe in-home caregivers in your home. If they don't show up promptly, consider crossing them off your list unless they have a *very* good reason for being late. Provide an opportunity for the caregiver to interact with your child so you can observe them together. Try to have two interviews, with both parents present if at all possible. If this is the first time you have chosen a child-care provider, consider asking a friend who has hired a child caregiver to sit in on an interview. Consult the checklists at the end of this section for questions to ask.

Step Six: Revisit with Your Child

Once you've narrowed the field, make a second appointment and take your child along. Your child's reaction to the provider can be a sign of future success or failure. How does the caregiver interact with your child? If other children are around, what are they doing while your child is getting the attention of the caregiver? How does your child interact with other children? Many family day-care homes and day-care centers offer a free "get-acquainted" day. If you are interviewing an in-home caregiver, hire them for a full or half day. Observe how the caregiver handles the child. If it seems appropriate, leave for a few hours.

After this experience, talk to your child. Did she or he enjoy the day? Was the child comfortable with the caregiver, environment, and/or other children? Would she or he like to try it again? For nonverbal children, look for behavioral changes. Is the child clean and fed? Do you notice bruises or a rash? Does the child cry more than usual or for no reason?

Step Seven: Establish a Professional Relationship

After all of your investigation is complete, you must choose the caregiver who seems best suited for your child and your needs. Call the providers you did not choose and let them know you have made other arrangements at this time. Be pleasant and friendly. You may need to go back to your list if your first choice doesn't work out.

It's important to establish a businesslike relationship with your new caregiver from the start and to maintain the same standards of professionalism you would expect at work. Day-care centers and schools will most likely ask you to sign a contract for service. For family day care and in-home care, you may want to write an agreement. You can use the accompanying form as a guide. Go over the agreement with the caregiver in detail. Outline the hours, duties, and privileges clearly. Clarify what will happen when your caregiver is unable to take care of your child due to illness or other personal reasons. State the rate of pay and a schedule for a salary and performance review. Consider a probationary period before the agreement is formalized. Decide how you will handle income tax and social security payments.

Sample Employment Agreement for In-Home Child-Care Providers

Employer _____   Employee _____
Address _____   Address _____
Phone _____   Phone _____
Employee's: Social security number: _____
                   Driver's license number: _____
                   Work permit/visa number: _____
Salary will be paid every other Friday week by personal check.
Salary: $_____/day   Room?   Yes/No
                   $_____/week   Meals?   Breakfast/Lunch/Dinner
Overtime Rates: $_____/hour   Overtime Policy: _____

Work schedule: Hours
                                                     A.M.–P.M.

Monday

Tuesday

Wednesday

Thursday

Friday

Saturday

Sunday

Rules: No smoking
        No guests
Job responsibilities (describe in detail):
    Child care:
    Housekeeping:
    Food preparation:
Paid holidays: _____ _____ _____
Unpaid holidays: _____ _____ _____
Paid vacation: Days _____   Paid sick days: _____
                     Weeks _____   Unpaid sick days: _____
Unpaid vacation: Days _____
                     Weeks _____
Notice requested: _____ Approval required for vacation days? Yes/No
Employer will pay the following:
$_____ $_____ $_____
    Social Security   Unemployment   Worker's Compensation
        Taxes   Tax   Insurance
Employee's share of social security taxes will be deducted from each
    paycheck.
Employee is responsible for payment of his or her own federal and state
    income taxes.
Salary review will be on: _____
Performance review will be on: _____
Employment is on an at-will basis and can be terminated by employer with
no notice/ _____ days/weeks notice. Employee will give _____ weeks
of quitting.
Employee's signature _____ Date _____
Employer's signature _____ Date _____

Part of a professional relationship is a regular performance review. You will want to meet frequently to talk about the chil-
d(ren), but you should also set aside some time to discuss what
changes you would like to see in the caregiver's performance and
if there are changes you could make that would make the caregiver's job easier or be better for your child. Try to work out problems through compromise. Make sure your expectations are
realistic. If you cannot get the situation to work, you will have to
end the relationship. If may be difficult for you, especially with
an in-home provider, and for your child who will not like the

changes. But it is your child (and your money) and your requirements must be met.

Step Eight: Time Together

After you have found the caregiver that best fits your needs, it is a good idea for your child and the caregiver to spend some time together when you are not working. It could be for just a day or two or for a couple of weeks. This will help them get acquainted with each other, and it will give you a chance to evaluate the relationship and the arrangements before it affects your work. Your child will have some familiarity with the caregiver and the surroundings before the arrangement becomes permanent. This will also make the transition of your child being cared for during the day as well as your return to work much easier.

CHILD-CARE CHECKLISTS

These checklists are designed to assist you in deciding about a child-care provider. First, underline the factors that are most important to you (filling in additional factors in the lines provided). Then, use the checklists as you interview care providers and visit family day-care homes and day-care centers to record your impressions. Finally, compare them to each other, especially on the underlined items, to help you make your decision.

The Caregiver

The Caregiver: (Name) _____	Yes	No
Appears to be warm and friendly	☐	☐
Has a sense of humor	☐	☐
Seems to be someone my child will enjoy being with	☐	☐
Has child-care training/education	☐	☐
Has child-care experience	☐	☐
Has a compatible child-care philosophy to mine	☐	☐
Is requesting a salary within my budget	☐	☐
Is someone I can talk with about my child	☐	☐
Has time to look after all the children in his/her care	☐	☐

Is intelligent

☐ ☐

Appears to be in good health and energetic

☐ ☐

Expresses himself/herself well/is articulate

☐ ☐

Exhibits self-esteem (for example, good eye contact and a
    positive attitude)

☐ ☐

Has a good command of the English language

☐ ☐

Listens to and accepts my family's values

☐ ☐

Has own transportation

☐ ☐

Has excellent references

☐ ☐

_____

☐ ☐

_____

☐ ☐

Comments: _____

_____

_____

In-Home Care

The Applicant: (Name) _____	Yes	No
Does not smoke	☐	☐
Has had first aid instruction	☐	☐
Has a good attendance record	☐	☐
Can comply with my policies on use of the telephone, meals, and visitors	☐	☐
Can commit for the time period needed	☐	☐
_____	☐	☐
_____	☐	☐

Infant Care:	Yes	No
Has experience caring for an infant	☐	☐
Will pick up the baby when she or he cries	☐	☐
Knows how to prepare a baby for a nap	☐	☐
Knows infant CPR	☐	☐
_____	☐	☐
_____	☐	☐

Toddlers:	Yes	No
Will handle toilet training in a way I approve	☐	☐
Will respond to temper tantrums as I'd like	☐	☐
Will respond appropriately in an emergency	☐	☐
Enjoys playing with children	☐	☐
_____	☐	☐
_____	☐	☐

Older Children:	Yes	No
Will enforce my rules about television and homework	☐	☐
Responds to misbehavior in an appropriate way	☐	☐
Plays appropriate games	☐	☐
Is relaxed with older children	☐	☐
_____	☐	☐
_____	☐	☐

Comments: _____

_____

_____

_____

Day-Care Centers and Family Day-Care Homes

The Home or Facility: (Name) _____	Yes	No
A convenient location	☐	☐
A current license	☐	☐
Accreditation	☐	☐
Written policies regarding:		
Fees	☐	☐
Extra charges	☐	☐
Hours	☐	☐
Overtime/late payments	☐	☐
Illness/sick days	☐	☐
Accidents	☐	☐
Vacation	☐	☐
Meals	☐	☐
An open-door policy regarding parent visits	☐	☐
Proper liability insurance	☐	☐
An acceptable contract	☐	☐
Fees within my budget	☐	☐
Been in operation for at least one year has experience in managing groups of children	☐	☐
_____	☐	☐
_____		

Comments: _____

_____

_____

_____

Environment	*Yes*	*No*
Enough furniture and equipment for all children	☐	☐
Is proportioned for children	☐	☐
Is safe (toddler-proof)	☐	☐
Clean and comfortable facilities	☐	☐
Is big enough for all children	☐	☐
Is bright and colorful	☐	☐
An organized/not chaotic play area	☐	☐
A rest/nap area	☐	☐
A safe outdoor area for play	☐	☐
Facilities and equipment are in good repair	☐	☐
Lots of toys and books (enough for all)	☐	☐
Enough clean bathrooms for all the children	☐	☐
_____	☐	☐
_____	☐	☐

Comments:_____

_____

_____

_____

Programs	*Yes*	*No*
Participation by parents	☐	☐
Children of compatible ages	☐	☐
A schedule of activities, routines, and play periods	☐	☐
Children are interested in activities	☐	☐
Children seem to get along	☐	☐
Learning materials suitable for the ages of the children	☐	☐
Learning material that reflect diverse cultures	☐	☐
Programs/workshops for parents	☐	☐
Provides regular reports to parents	☐	☐
Program is not sexist or racially biased	☐	☐
Program is evaluated and changed	☐	☐
Regular parent/teacher conferences	☐	☐
Music/art supplies and program	☐	☐
_____	☐	☐
_____	☐	☐

Comments: _____

_____

_____

_____

Staff	Yes	No
Proper staff/child ratio	☐	☐
Background checks are done	☐	☐
Little turnover	☐	☐
A training program/trained staff	☐	☐
Substitute teachers are infrequently used	☐	☐
Evaluation procedure	☐	☐
	☐	☐
	☐	☐

Safety	Yes	No
Toxic substances accessible to children	☐	☐
Emergency numbers posted near the telephone	☐	☐
An emergency exit plan	☐	☐
Regular fire drills	☐	☐
Smoke alarms	☐	☐
Covered electrical outlets	☐	☐
Arrangements for medical emergencies/accidents	☐	☐
A first aid kit	☐	☐
A low/no accident record	☐	☐
	☐	☐
	☐	☐

Health and Nutrition	Yes	No
A sensible method for handling sick children	☐	☐
A policy of giving medicines only with parent's permission	☐	☐
A no smoking policy	☐	☐
Nutritious meals and snacks	☐	☐
A cot or mat for each child	☐	☐
	☐	☐
	☐	☐

PREPARING FOR CHILD CARE

Leaving your child in the hands of a caregiver to go to work can be a smooth transition for you and your family. All that's required is preparation. Below are guidelines for preparing yourself, your child, and your caregiver for a positive child-care relationship.

Preparing Yourself

Child development researchers suggest the following guidelines for juggling work and family life.

- Learn to compartmentalize. When you're at work, be there. When you're at home, be home.
- Prepare yourself for separating each day. Then prepare your child. Accompany him or her to the caregiver initially.
- Don't be too hard on yourself. Avoid guilt. You're doing the best you can. Avoid superparent fantasies.
- Talk to other working parents and share your concerns and stress. Join a lunchtime support group.
- Put energy into the coming-home ritual. Many parents have found that working out is the perfect transition period, giving them energy for the people at home. Let your child know you're happy to see him or her. Gather the whole family together to spend 30 minutes catching up. Try to eat together.
- Expect your children to want to spend time with you when you get home; they've saved up all their strongest feelings for you all day.
- Include your children as you do your household chores.
- Spend a special time alone with each child as often as possible.

Preparing Your Child for Child Care

A young child may be distressed when she or he is left with caregivers. This is a normal reaction. Do whatever you can to assure your child that when you leave him or her with the caregiver, you will be back. Emphasize the fun your child will have while with the caregiver. Even if your child is so young she or he doesn't understand the words you use, the child will understand the tone of your voice and the expression on your face.

Consider the following hints to help your child adjust well:

- Accept your child's distress and be confident that it'll pass. (If it doesn't, investigate.)

- Before making the commitment full time, visit the caregiver several times with your child. Play there and then come home and talk about how much fun it was.
- Talk with your child about what you do at work. If possible, show your child the building you work in.
- On the first few days of day care, stay with your child and the caregiver for a while in the morning and in the evening.
- Save other big changes for after your child has adjusted to child care. For example, wait to redecorate your child's room.
- Try to have your child meet at least one other child from the day-care center or preschool ahead of time.
- Ask your child to tell you how she or he feels about the new situation. Talk about what you'll do together on the weekend or after work.
- Create routines for your child. Don't rush wakeup and departure. Drop-off and pickup times should be as consistent as possible.

Preparing Your Caregiver

It's important to communicate regularly with your caregiver. Having good communication with the people who take care of family members while you work will clarify roles, expectations, and provide valuable feedback to you.

One of the pitfalls when working with caregivers is that you often think the caregiver knows everything you want done. Don't take anything for granted. Imagine that this person knows nothing and you are training him or her for the first time. By clarifying every aspect of the caregiver's role, you will be assured of getting what you really want. To assist the new caregiver in understanding your child, provide a list of words the child uses, favorite foods, games, toys, and medical information. In addition, you must clue your child-care provider in to the unique aspects of your child, his or her likes and dislikes, and so on. Add your own preferences about menus, snacks, watching television, and disciplinary procedures. Help devise a schedule for walks, meals, naps, and play.

My Child's Day

	Activities	Snacks/Meals	Events
Monday Morning			
Afternoon			
Tuesday Morning			
Afternoon			
Wednesday Morning			
Afternoon			
Thursday Morning			
Afternoon			
Friday Morning			
Afternoon			

Provide a list of who to call in case of an emergency. Talk about when the caregiver and child should call you at work (rarely). Make sure your secretary, receptionist, or co-workers know the name of your caregiver and will put him or her through. It may be advisable to give your caregiver written permission to get medical care for your child in an emergency in your absence. Also make sure your caregiver has your doctor's number, preferred hospital, and insurance information.

Make sure the caregiver knows about any changes in your child's emotional or physical development. When changes occur in your home, such as a move, new baby, divorce, job change, and so on, be sure to inform the caregiver. Spend a few minutes at the end of each day to find out about your child's day from the caregiver—activities, playmates, appetite, nap time, changes in development. If your caregiver doesn't take formal notes, provide copies of the accompanying sheet for him or her to record the day's activities.

Drop-off and pickup times may be good for a quick chat about how your child is doing. Keep in mind that the provider has other obligations, so don't expect an extended conversation. Instead, arrange in advance for a time when you can talk away from your child.

When problems arise, address them immediately. Even though the caregiver may have experience with his or her own or other people's children, explain clearly how you want your child handled. Be specific when giving instructions.

WHAT ABOUT CHILD ABUSE?

Stories about children being abused or mistreated in day-care arrangements are very frightening to all of us, but especially to parents. Fortunately, such situations are not the norm. Most childcare providers are professionals who respect and enjoy children. Don't choose a day-care center or family day-care provider who discourages you from dropping in unannounced. A caregiver who's unwilling to discuss any concern you may have about your child should be avoided.

Look for any unusual signs from your child:

- Repeated unwillingness to be left with caregiver. Even babies will act out their fear of going somewhere where they are not comfortable.
- Signs of unusual or intense anxiety.
- Physical signs, such as bruises, cuts, hair loss.
- Extreme hunger or thirst.

Talk to your children about what they do everyday. Be a critical observer of your child's words and behaviors. If you suspect unprofessional conduct, calmly ask your child to talk about it. Listen to what your child says about the caregiver. Respond calmly to whatever your child says in order to avoid frightening him or her. Begin your investigation, if necessary, by speaking with other parents who use the caregiver. Drop in on the caregiver unannounced. A visit to your child's pediatrician may be a good idea.

MEETING SPECIAL CHILD-CARE NEEDS

Care of Sick Children

For the working parent, having adequate backups for sick children, emergencies, and holidays is a must. Children under five get sick an average of 12 days a year. When children are ill, the usual care arrangements may not work. Unless you have backup arrangements, you can find yourself in a bind with conflicting work and family responsibilities.

The timing is always bad. Today's your busiest day in the week, yet the most important person in the world needs your attention. Having a backup child-care plan for those days when your child's ailment is contagious and the child can't participate in the usual child-care arrangement is essential. Your plan should also include backups to the backup.

If your child feels very sick, or the illness is just beginning, she or he will probably want you there. When there are two partners, you can take turns being home with a sick child, using vacation days and personal time. Consider asking family members (grandparents, aunts) to help out.

As your child begins to get better, or if the illness isn't serious, consider asking neighbors or baby-sitters to provide temporary in-home care. Find out whether your local hospital has a sick child-care center in its pediatrics department. Some hospitals offer sick-child-care services. Also, some nanny services will provide nannies to care for sick children. Similarly, some nursing services will send a nurse to your home.

Some day-care centers and family day-care homes have programs for helping you with sick children. However, many don't. Be sure to ask about your provider's sick-child policy.

Emergencies

If you receive an emergency phone call about your child while you're at work, stay calm. Urge the caregiver to be calm, too. Ask questions about what happened. Ascertain how your child got hurt or ill and exactly what his or her condition is. After you have enough information, you can decide whether your child needs your personal attention immediately. If you can't get there, who can? Your spouse, mother, father, a neighbor?

Holidays

School/day-care center holidays, parent-teacher conference days, snow days, and the like can be a parent's nightmare. If you know about them in advance, you can try to take the day off and spend a special day with your child. If you can't take care of the child yourself, you'll need to find someone who can if your regular caregiver is not available. For unplanned days, your backups may be the same people you rely on for sick care (spouse, family member, neighbor, nanny service).

Overnight

Overnight care generally arises in connection with business travel. Again, you may need backup. If you are married or live with another adult, that person may be able to take over. You may need intermediate care if your partner does not get home as early as you do. If you are a single parent, you will need to find backups.

Backup Care

To ensure you are well prepared, complete the accompanying worksheet. Put one in your office and one in your home. Have at least four names for each category.

Who Will I Call?

Name	Telephone Number	Availability*	Cost
Sick care			
1.			
2.			
3.			
4.			
Emergencies			
1			
2.			
3.			
4.			
Holidays			
1.			
2			
3			
4.			
Overnight			
1.			
2.			
3.			
4.			

*Specify the days of the week this person is available. For example, can your mother or neighbor take care of your child on Monday, Wednesday, and Friday but not on Tuesday or Thursday due to other commitments?

Children with Special Needs

Special needs are defined as any disability, emotional, behavioral, intellectual, or physical condition that significantly impairs a child's ability to learn or to develop effective relationships with peers.

Children with special needs share the same needs as all others, plus some additional ones. Some family day-care homes and day-care centers are designed for children with special needs, or your child may be able to attend a regular family home day care or preschool program. When evaluating care for a child with special needs, consider:

- Does this program have other children with special needs?
- Does the program communicate a caring and sensitive feeling?
- Does the provider have high expectations for special needs children?
- Has the environment been adapted to the special needs of your child?
- Does the program support you, as a parent, in dealing with your child's special needs?
- Are there necessary support services available that your child needs (i.e., physical therapists, speech therapists, nurses)?
- Has the caregiver had specialized training?

Your special-needs child may be eligible for programs provided or paid for by the public school system. Contact your local school district for more information.

CARE FOR SCHOOL-AGED CHILDREN

More than 6 million children are routinely left to care for themselves before or after school while their parents work. They're called "latchkey kids" because they often wear a house key on a string or chain around their necks. Besides being alone after school, many youngsters get themselves off to school in the morning after their parents have left for work.

When Can Children Take Care of Themselves?

Many experts say the earliest age at which it's appropriate to leave a child unsupervised is 10. Others say 12 or 14. Children under 10 generally are not mature enough to make responsible decisions about their own welfare. In many states, it's illegal to leave a child under a certain age home alone. You and your child must judge when the child is sufficiently responsible to take care of himself or herself.

The Benefits of Self-Care

For the child who's mature enough to be alone for an hour or more a day, the benefits can include:

- Enjoying independence from the structured routine at school; in fact, children ages 10 through 13 who perform self-care mature faster and learn how to take care of themselves earlier.
- An opportunity to make decisions for themselves; latchkey children are likely to develop resourcefulness and a sense of responsibility.
- Developing new home management skills, including those needed to do household chores and meal preparation.

The Risks of Self-Care

While many of the risks of self-care can be minimized if you plan for them in advance, you may want to consider the following issues:

- Emotions—How does your child feel about staying alone? Is she or he afraid of the dark or storms? Will the child be lonely? Encourage your child to share his or her feelings about self-care.
- Safety—You may fear for your child's safety while alone. Children aren't always prepared to handle emergency situations such as fire or accidents. You can help your child by teaching him or her survival skills.
- School—Unsupervised children sometimes neglect to do their homework. That might not be a problem if there's time for homework after dinner.

Deciding About Self-Care

When deciding whether your child is ready for self-care, consider the questions listed in the accompanying evaluation. Because each child and situation is different, weigh all the answers to make an appropriate decision for your family.

Self-Care Evaluation

		Yes	No
1.	Do you consider your child old enough to assume self-care re-sponsibilities?	☐	☐
2.	Do you believe your child is mature enough to care for himself or herself?	☐	☐
3.	Has your child indicated she or he would be willing to try self-care?	☐	☐
4.	Is your child able to complete daily tasks?	☐	☐
5.	Can your child unlock and lock the doors to your home?	☐	☐
6.	Is there an adult living or working nearby that your child knows and can rely on in case of an emergency?	☐	☐
7.	Is your house safe?	☐	☐
8.	Is your neighborhood safe?	☐	☐
9.	Does your child:		
	Handle responsibility well?	☐	☐
	Consistently complete his or her homework?	☐	☐
	Get along with his or her brothers and sisters?	☐	☐
	Get frightened easily?	☐	☐
	Ask you to solve most problems?	☐	☐
	Get chores done without a lot of supervision?	☐	☐
	Communicate his or her feelings to you easily?	☐	☐
	Understand why she or he is being left alone?	☐	☐
	Handle being alone for short periods of time?	☐	☐
	Know emergency and safety procedures?	☐	☐
	Know how to reach you by phone?	☐	☐
10.	Are you comfortable with the idea of self-care?	☐	☐

If you answered no to any of the questions, it is highly rec-ommended that you delay or abandon plans to leave your child in self-care until positive responses can be given for all the questions.

Communication with Self-Care Children

Effective communication with children who are home alone after school will help you relax and be productive at work. It also pro-motes the confidence the child needs to handle situations alone.

Prepare your child.

- Work with your child to prepare her or him for success-fully taking care of himself or herself. Safety is the number one issue that causes parents to worry.
- Use good communication skills by not only telling your child what to do in an emergency by also *showing* him or her.
- Role-play situations by simulating a fire, accidents, or break-ins.
- Have the child practice giving emergency information quickly.
- Write a script together of what to say. Put the script near the telephone.
- Work with the child to set and establish a routine and clear rules. Teach your child how to prepare simple snacks, clean up after themselves, and set a schedule for home-work and chores.
- Work with your child to develop a variety of activities that will prevent boredom and loneliness. Consider community services as a source of support. Some communities sponsor telephone volunteers who call latchkey children.
- Be clear about when your child should call you at work.
- Find creative ways to welcome the child home after school. It can be very lonely to walk into an empty home day after day. Write little notes, leave messages on an audiocassette, or leave surprise snacks. If it doesn't interfere with your work, call and chat for a moment. If you don't have a pet, think about one that won't require a lot of work, like a cat, bird, hamster, or fish. Children often find companionship with animals. For older children, consider a dog.
- Use good probing and clarifying skills to find out some of your child's fears about being alone. For example: When was the last time you were scared at home while being alone? What made you feel that way? What did you do to help yourself? Or you can begin a problem-solving activity by opening a dialogue. Start with something like, "Some-times there are sounds that make us feel scared. Let's talk about them so you won't be frightened when you hear them." Explore all the sounds inside and outside of your

house—the wind blowing, a shutter flapping, water dripping, the water pump going off and on. Help the child to identify what is just an ordinary sound versus a sound that merits concern.

- Clarify with your child the rules about having other friends over or going to their houses, watching TV, going outside, answering the door or the phone, or using the stove. Be clear with the child about the consequences of not following the rules. This will avoid misunderstandings and conflict.

- Define what constitutes an emergency clearly. Many children frequently call their parents at work for things that aren't an emergency. If that situation occurs, use good open-ended questions to find out what is really going on— is the child lonely, bored, upset, and so on. Learn to diffuse the potentially volatile situation. Ask questions and extract the information you need to determine whether you have a true emergency.

- Be sure you have checked the safety of your house thoroughly before your child is home alone. Make sure there are smoke alarms and windows are secure to avoid a break-in. Investigate neighbors or community resources available in emergency situations.

- Have a regular family meeting so you can discuss what is working and not working. Use good observation skills to detect any situation that is uncomfortable for the child but the child is embarrassed to admit. Help your child voice concerns and discuss alternate arrangements.

- There are some excellent workbooks for you and your child as well as reading books for you on the topic of latchkey children. See the list at the end of this chapter.

RESOURCES

Books

Apter, Terri. *Why Women Don't Have Wives: Professional Success and Motherhood.* New York: Schocken Books, 1985.

Auerback, Stevanne. *Choosing Child Care: A Guide for Parents.* New York: E. P. Dutton, 1981.

Banks, Ann. *Alone At Home: A Kid's Guide to Being in Charge.* New York: Puffin Books, 1989.

Bauer, Caroline Feeler. *My Mom Travels a Lot.* New York: Viking Press/ Penguin Books, 1981.

Beardsley, Lyda. *Good Day/Bad Day: The Child's Experience of Child Care.* Homewood, Ill.: Richard D. Irwin, Inc., 1990.

Berg, Barbara J. *The Crisis of the Working Mother: Resolving the Conflict between Family and Work.* New York: Summit Books, 1986.

Bergstrom, Joan, *School's Out.* Berkeley, Calif.: Ten Speed Press, 1984.

Boston Children's Hospital. *New Child Health Encyclopedia: The Complete Guide for Parents.* New York: Delacorte Press/Merloyd Lawrence, 1987.

Brack, Pat and Ben. *Moms Don't Get Sick.* Aberdeen, S.D.: Melius Publishing, 1991.

Brazelton, T. Berry. *The Earliest Relationship: Parents, Infants and the Drama of Early Attachment.* Reading, Mass.: Addison-Wesley Publishing, 1985.

Brazelton, T. Berry. *On Becoming a Family: Growth of Attachment.* New York: Delacorte Press/Merloyd Lawrence, 1981.

Brazelton, T. Berry. *Toddlers and Parents: Declaration of Independence.* New York: Delacorte Press/Merloyd Lawrence, 1974.

Brazelton, T. Berry. *To Listen to a Child: Understanding the Normal Problems of Growing Up.* Reading, Mass.: Addison-Wesley Publishing, 1984.

Brazelton, T. Berry. *Working and Caring.* Reading, Mass.: Addison-Wesley Publishing, 1985.

Brazelton, T. Berry, and Victor C. Vaughan. *The Family: Setting Priorities.* New York: Science and Medicine Publishing Co., 1979.

Bredekamp, Sue, ed. *Developmentally Appropriate Practice in Early Childhood Programs Serving Children from Birth through Age 8 (Expanded Edition).* Washington, D.C.: National Association for the Education of Young Children, 1987.

Brenner, Barbara. *Preschool Handbook: Making the Most of Your Child's Education.* New York: Pantheon Press, 1990.

Brooks, Andree Aelion, *Children of Fast Track Parents: Raising Self-Sufficient and Confident Children in an Achievement Oriented World.* New York: Viking Press, 1989.

Clarke-Stewart, Alison. *Daycare.* Cambridge, Mass.: Harvard University Press, 1982.

Crary, Elizabeth. *Mommy, Don't Go: A Children's Problem Solving Book*. Seattle, Wash.: Parenting Press, 1989.

Dana, Nancy, and Anne Price. *Successful Breastfeeding*. Deep Haven, Minn.: Meadowbrook Press, 1985.

Elliot, Ruth S. *Minding the Kids: A Practical Guide to Employing Nannies, Caregivers, Baby-sitters and Au Pairs*. New York: Prentice Hall Press, 1990.

Ferber, Richard. *Solve Your Child's Sleep Problems*. New York: Fireside Books/Simon & Schuster, 1985.

Galinsky, Ellen, and William Hooks. *The New Extended Family: Day Care That Works*. Boston: Houghton Mifflin, 1977.

Galinsky, Ellen, and Judy David. *The Preschool Years: Family Strategies That Work—From Experts and Parents*. New York: New York Times Books, 1988.

Genevie, Lois, Ph.D. *The Motherhood Report: How Women Feel about Being Mothers*. New York: Macmillan, 1987.

Gillis, Jack, and Mary Ellen R. Rise. *The Childwise Catalogue: A Consumer Guide to Buying the Safest and Best Products for Your Children*. New York: Pocket Books, 1986.

Gilman, Lois. *Adoption Resource Book: The Comprehensive Guide to All the Things You Need to Know and Ought to Know*. New York: Harper & Row, 1984.

Helmering, Doris Wild. *Husbands, Wives and Sex*. Holbrook, Mass.: Bob Adams, Inc., 1990.

Hirsch, Roseann. *Superworking Mom's Handbook*. New York: Warner Books, 1986.

Hochschild, Arlie Russel, with Anne Machung. *The Second Shift: Working Parents and the Revolution at Home*. New York: Viking Press, 1989.

Kimball, Gayle, Ph.D. *The 50/50 Marriage*. Boston: Beacon Press, 1983.

Kimball, Gayle, Ph.D. *50/50 Parenting: Sharing Family Rewards and Responsibilities*. Lexington, Mass.: Lexington Books, 1988.

Klinman, Debra G., and Thinan Kohl. *Fatherhood U.S.A.* New York: Garland Publications, 1984.

La Leche League International. *The Womanly Art of Breastfeeding*, 4th rev. ed. Franklin Park, Ill.: La Leche League International, 1987.

Lansky, Vicki. *Best Practical Parenting Tips*. Minnetonka, Minn.: Meadowbrook Press, 1980.

Lansky, Vicki. *Practical Parenting Tips for the School-age Years*. Toronto and New York: Bantam Books, 1985.

Levine, Karen, and Conalee Levine-Shneidman. *Too Smart for Her Own Good? The Impact of Success on the Intimate Lives of Women*. Garden City, N.Y.: Doubleday Publishing, 1985.

Long, Lynette, and Thomas Long. *Handbook for Latchkey Children and Their Parents*. New York: Arbor House, 1983.

Magid, Renee Y., with Nancy E. Fleming. *When Mothers & Fathers Work: Creative Strategies for Balancing Career and Family*. New York: AMACOM, 1987.

Mayer, Anne. *How to Stay Lovers While Raising Your Children: A Burned-Out Parent's Guide to Sex*. Los Angeles: Price Stern Sloan, Inc., 1990.

Miller, Jo Ann, and Susan Weissman. *The Parent's Guide to Day Care: Everything You Need to Know to Find the Best Care for Your Child—And to Make It Happy, Safe and Problem-Free from Day to Day*. Toronto and New York: Bantam Books, 1986.

Phillips, Deborah A. *Quality in Child Care: What Does Research Tell Us?* Washington, D.C.: National Association for the Education of Young Children, 1987.

Rice, Robin D. *The American Nanny: A Comprehensive Guide to Finding Highly Qualified Childcare Providers*. Washington, D.C.: TAN Press, 1985.

Rust, Frances O'Connell, and Leslie R. Williams, ed. *The Care and Education of Young Children*. Homewood, Ill.: Richard D. Irwin, Inc., 1989.

Scarr, Sandra. *Mother Care/Other Care: The First Authoritative Guide to Child Care Decisions That Takes into Account the Child's Needs and the Working Mother's Dilemma*. New York: Basic Books, 1984.

Schaefer, Charles E. *How to Talk to Children About Really Important Things*. New York: Harper & Row, 1984.

Shell, Adeline G., and Kay Reynolds. *Working Parent Food Book*. New York: Cornerstone Library, 1979.

Smith, Dayle M. *Kincare*. Homewood, Ill.: Richard D. Irwin, Inc., 1991.

Spaide, Deborah, *Day Care Kit: A Parent's Guide to Quality Child Care*. New York: Carol Publishing, 1990.

Swan, Helen L. *Alone after School: A Self-Care Guide for Latchkey Children & Their Parents*. Englewood Cliffs, N.J.: Prentice Hall, 1985.

Woolover, Elizabeth, ed. *Better Homes and Gardens: Your Child . . . The Latchkey Years*. Des Moines, Ia.: Meredith Corporation, 1990.

Yeiser, Lin. *Nannies, Au Pairs, Mothers' Helpers—Caregivers: The Complete Guide to Home Child Care*. New York: Vintage Books, 1987.

Zigler, Edward F., and Meryl Frank. *The Parental Leave Crisis: Toward a National Policy*. New Haven: Yale University Press, 1988.

Publications

Working Mother magazine.

Organizations

American Academy of Pediatrics
141 Northeast Point Road
Elk Grove Village, IL 60001
(708) 228-5005
Free booklets on parenting, child care, and other family issues.

The Capable Kid Counseling Centers
1615 Orrington Avenue
Evanston, IL 60201
(708) 866-7335

Catalyst
2500 Park Avenue South
New York, New York 10003
(212) 777-8900

Publications on child care.

The Child Care Action Campaign (CCAC)
99 Hudson Street, Room 1233
New York, NY 10013
(212) 334-9595

Children's Defense Fund
122 C Street, N.W.
Washington, DC 20001
(202) 628-8787

Compassionate Friends
P. O. Box 1347
Oak Brook, IL 60521
(708) 323-5010
Assists parents coping with the death of a child.

Family Resource Coalition
200 S. Michigan Ave., Suite 520
Chicago, IL 60604
(312) 341-0900

National Association for the Education of Young Children
1834 Connecticut Avenue, NW
Washington, DC 20009
(202) 232-8777; (800) 424-2460

Send for the publications list and standards for accreditation of child-care providers.

National Association of Family Day Care
725 15th Street, N.W., Suite 505
Washington, DC 20005
(202) 347-3356

National Black Child Development Institute, Inc.
1463 Rhode Island Avenue, NW
Washington, DC 20005
(202) 987-1281

National Coalition of Hispanic Mental Health and Human Services Organizations
1030 15th Street, N.W., Suite 1053
Washington, DC 20005
(202) 371-2100

Parent Action
230 N. Michigan Ave., Suite 1625
Chicago, IL 60601
(312) 726-4750

Parents Without Partners
8807 Colesville Road
Silver Spring, MD 20910

The Partnership Group
840 West Main Street
Lansdale, PA 19446
(215) 362-5070

School-Age NOTES
(National Resource Organization on School-Age Care)
P. O. Box 40205
Nashville, TN 37204-0205
(615) 242-8464

Resources and information on school-age care, programming, conflict management administration. professional news.

Au pairs.

The American Institute for Foreign Study
Greenwich, CT
(203) 869-9090
Provides au pairs for a fee.

Au Pair in America
(203) 869-9090

Au Pair Homestay Program
(202) 371-1000

Hotlines.

Early Childhood Center
8730 Alden Drive
Los Angeles, CA 90048
(219) 855-3639
A "warm line" offering parenting tips.

National Parenting Center
(900) 246-MOMS
Advice on 1000 topics.

Parents Anonymous
606 South Federal, Suite 204
Chicago, IL 60605
(312) 427-0161

Toughlove
(800) 333-1069
Information and referrals to parents who are troubled about their teenager.

Social Service and Public Agencies

Social Security Administration
(800) 234-5772
To obtain an application for a social security number for your child and to find
out what your obligations are for in-home providers.

Tax Information

Internal Revenue Service
Kansas City, MO
(800) 424-3676
Information about taxes for parents who employ caregivers in their homes.

Chapter Eight

Caring for Elders

OUR POPULATION IS AGING

Our nation is aging. According to the American Association of Retired Persons (AARP), 15 percent of Americans will be older than 65 by the year 2000. We refer to people over age 65 as "elders." Elders over the age of 75 are the fastest-growing (in terms of percentages) group of the population. In *Talking with Your Aging Parents,* author Mark Edinberg says it is now likely that at least one of our parents will be alive when we reach age 65.[1] Four-generation families are no longer uncommon.

So what does this mean to our work and family puzzle? Most of us will at some time need to fit the role of elder caregiver into our lives. Twenty percent of the work force is caring for elders now, according to a recent study by the Families and Work Institute. The average elder requires 18 years of some form of special care. It is important to note that over 80 percent of elders do *not* experience senility, dementia, or other forms of serious mental deterioration. Many remain competent to manage their own affairs. Commonly, however, elders need assistance with physical activities, and their need for assistance with daily living increases over time.

Family members provide 80 percent of the needed care, spending an average of 12 to 16 hours a week in the role of elder caregiver. In the majority of cases, there is one primary caregiver, most frequently a spouse (50 percent) or adult daughter (46 percent) (half of whom find they must quit work or reduce their work hours to meet elder-care demands). Because individuals are marrying and having children later, many people will find themselves in the "sandwich" generation, caring for children and elders at the same time. One study from the House Select Committee on Aging predicts that when baby boomers reach 40, more than half will care for both older and younger family members.

As the need for elder care grows, social service agencies, communities, and employers are developing supportive services for elders and the relatives who care for them. It is a slow process, however, and affordable elder care remains hard to find in many parts of the country. It is therefore all the more important to plan for caring for your elders—and to plan for your own future.

BECOMING AN ELDER CAREGIVER

Caring for an elder, especially a parent, can be a disturbing experience. These are the people we have depended on all of our lives. Eventually, the nature of the caring relationship changes, and the person you depended on depends on you. This new role, like any transition, requires adjustments as you take on new responsibilities. The same skills we discussed earlier can help you handle it with flying colors—communication, organization, and managing guilt.

When Does It Start?

When do you begin to be an elder caregiver? When do you know you should become more involved in your elder's life? Age is not usually the determining factor. Rather, it is a question of the ability of the elder to function safely and competently on his or her own. The accompanying questionnaire will help you evaluate your elder's level of independence. Some of the questions may require a little snooping or active questioning of the elder.

What Do I Know About My Elder(s)?

Circle either true or false for each of the following statements. Examples or explanations of the statements are in parentheses.

1. My elder had no interests or hobbies when I was growing up.   True False
2. My elder has not pursued these or is not engaged in new activities.   True False

3. My elder does not attend social functions or visit with
    friends.   True   False
4. I have noticed a significant personality change in my el-
    der (withdrawal, fits of anger or other emotional out-
    bursts, verbal abusiveness, crying bouts, etc.).   True   False
5. My elder is physically impaired.   True   False
    Definition of impaired:
    My elder can feed him/herself unassisted.   Yes No
    My elder can walk unassisted.   Yes No
    My elder can bathe unassisted.   Yes No
    My elder can use the toilet unassisted.   Yes No
    If you answered any of these questions no, your elder
    may be considered impaired.
6. My elder is taking multiple medications.   True   False
    My elder's medications:

Medication	Ailment
1.	
2.	
3.	
4.	
5.	

    Note: Have your elder's medications all been
    prescribed by the same doctor or is one doctor aware
    of all medications (to guard against medications that
    interact with adverse effects)? If not, choose a primary
    physician and make sure she or he knows about all
    treatments and medications. Also, use the same phar-
    macist as an additional safeguard against unintentional
    drug interactions. If your elder experiences mental or
    physical side effects from medication, consult the physician.
7. My elder has difficulty medicating himself or herself
    (due to confusion, forgetfulness, etc.) (check pill counts
    versus the date of prescription and prescribed dose).   True   False
8. I have noticed a change in my elder's memory.   True   False
9. My elder seems confused and/or becomes disoriented.   True   False
10. My elder cannot pass a mini-mental status examination.   True   False
    Mini-mental status examination
    A preliminary test of a lessening of cognitive ability,
    perhaps indicating the beginning of dementia or senil-
    ity, consists of the following questions. If you or your
    elder are uncomfortable having you administer the
    exam, ask another family member, social worker, or
    your physician to do it.
    1. Can you tell me the month and date?
    2. What year is it?
    3. Who is president of the United States?

4. Repeat this phrase: "The dog ate the cat's food as well as his own."
5. Say the names of the 12 months backwards.
6. Can you count backwards from 20?
7. What is the phrase I told you before?

If your elder is unable to pass this test, seek medical attention. Dementia is an illness caused by many factors, some of which may be effectively treated with medication.

Did your elder become hostile, defensive, or evasive during or following the exam? If yes, there may be a problem your elder is unwilling to admit.

11. My elder has fallen or shown signs of bruises due to frequent accidents or mishaps.   True   False

12. My elder has been having frequent accidents with appliances (e.g., iron, stove, or oven left on, burn marks on counters or pots).   True   False

13. My elder has spells of dizziness or weakness (like when getting up from a chair or climbing stairs).   True   False

14. My elder's nutritional needs are not being met (she or he no longer shops or cooks meals).   True   False

15. I have noticed a significant loss of energy or chronic fatigue in my elder.   True   False

Malnutrition:

Malnutrition can be a problem for elders. Fatigue, weight loss, hair loss, dizziness, falling, mouth sores, and brittle nails can be signs of malnutrition. Taking over the grocery shopping, providing precooked meals and a microwave, or calling "Meals on Wheels" can provide the answer.

16. My elder's driving is unsafe and/or she or he has had accidents.   True   False

17. My elder's home is not as clean as it was.   True   False

18. My elder frequently can't find or loses common things (purse, keys, glasses).   True   False

19. Things are misplaced in my elder's home (soup cans in the oven, ice cream in the refrigerator, bills in the trash, etc.).   True   False

20. My elder's hearing has deteriorated (complaints of mumbling by others, frequent requests to repeat, TV or music turned up very loud, misunderstood communications).   True   False

21. My elder refuses to wear a hearing aid.   True   False

22. My elder is having trouble with his or her vision (cataracts, glaucoma, deteriorating sight).   True   False

23. My elder refuses to visit an ophthalmologist or optometrist.   True   False

24. My elder's neighbors or friends have hinted at or com-
    mented on potential problems in my elder's daily activi-
    ties.   True   False
25. My elder does not remember appointments and is not
    ready or is ready several hours early.   True   False
26. My elder's personal appearance and hygiene have dete-
    riorated.   True   False
27. My elder's bills are not paid or not paid on time. (Does
    your elder get nervous when finances are discussed? Do
    you see past due notices or piles of bills in the kitchen
    or a desk drawer?)   True   False
28. My elder is particularly aggravated and/or confused at
    tax time and can't find records (or records are in com-
    plete disarray).   True   False
29. My elder handles money inappropriately (six checks to
    one charity in six months, subscriptions to many maga-
    zines, overpayment of bills, failure to cash checks).   True   False
30. My elder behaves inappropriately in public (threatens
    others, shouts or yells, exposes self).   True   False
31. My elder exhibits fears about routine activities.   True   False
32. My elder has lost a significant amount of weight.   True   False
33. My elder has insomnia or has trouble sleeping.   True   False
34. My elder drinks to excess.   True   False
35. My elder is depressed and expresses a desire to die.   True   False
    Depression:
       Sleeplessness, alcohol/drug abuse, and weight loss/
       gain are sometimes signs of depression. Depression is
       treatable and a psychiatrist or psychologist should be
       consulted. Also, investigate side effects or possible
       drug interaction from medications as the potential
       cause of depression and mood swings.
36. My elder refuses to use a walker or other device that is
    clearly needed.   True   False
37. My elder exhibits a noticeable change in his or her abil-
    ity to walk.   True   False
38. My elder complains of pain.   True   False

If you answer "true" to any of the questions on the questionnaire, your elder may have a problem that requires assistance. At
the least, answers marked "true" are a warning you need to plan
to provide assistance in the future. If more than a few items were
marked "true," you may need to take immediate action.

Be aware of the possibility of a "hidden" patient. If the primary caregiver is also an elder, usually a spouse, the caregiving role may be taking a toll on his or her emotional and/or physical health. He or she may be unaware of his or her own decline, or the caregiver may be hiding it from you. He or she may need assistance just as much as the obviously disabled elder.

Where to Begin

Once you determine that you need to take some action, start by talking to your elder. Your elder is an adult and should be allowed and encouraged to make decisions about his or her own life to the greatest extent possible. Too often, the elder's preferences are ignored. Arguments and intense resistance to proposed changes often result when someone else tries to take over. Have an open and honest conversation about your concerns and possible solutions. Find out what concerns and ideas your elder may have as well as his or her preferences about what steps to take.

The issues involved (death, funerals, housing care preferences in the event of illness) can be very sensitive and emotional. You'll often find yourselves focused on different concerns. The elder tends to focus on control and independence, while the caregiver centers on safety and health. If necessary, get help from a third party (a member of the clergy, a social worker, a counselor, or another family member) to promote a cooperative and productive atmosphere. Get information on health, finances, insurance, and so on so that you are all making informed decisions. Put together a file of all important papers and information such as wills, insurance policies, social security records, doctors' telephone numbers, and emergency information and keep it somewhere safe. Make sure all members of the family know where the file is kept.

It is important to acknowledge and talk about the issues of death, finances, living arrangements, or loss of mental or physical capabilities, even though they may cause discomfort. Good communication is important but does not guarantee that your elder will do what *you* want. Your elder may make decisions you don't agree with or that you worry about. It is hard to accept the fact that your elder makes choices you would not make. Try to discover and understand your elder's reasons. Is it simply his or her preference, or does the choice reflect another concern (finances, loss of control)? If so you may be able to then address that underlying problem. If you think the elder's choice is unsafe, or that the elder is incapable of making the decision, you'll have to try again. Enlist other family members in a group problem-solving process.

Get Help

From your evaluation and the checklist you have completed, make a list of your elder's care needs.

For example:

1. Can't drive or use public transportation.
2. Doesn't eat regularly or nutritiously.
3. Can't remember to take medication.

Once you know the needs, you can fulfill them by taking on the task yourself, finding assisting products, or finding services to assist your elder.

Education and Information

The aging process and the consequences of getting old in our society are complicated. Read all you can about the effects of aging on your elder:

- Physically.
- Mentally.
- Emotionally.
- Socially.
- Financially.

Many community groups and organizations offer classes and workshops on growing older and caregiving for the elderly.

Professional Help

Get help from professionals. You may need to seek out:

- Doctors
    - For medical advice and geriatric assessments.
    - To investigate significant physical/mental changes.
    - To get prescribed help from home health professionals (which may then be covered by insurance).
    - To ask questions about medical conditions and medications.
- Lawyers for
    - A will—provides for property distribution in the event of death.
    - Estate planning—other ways to pass assets to designated persons after (or before) death.
    - Durable power of attorney for health care—allows the agent to make health-care decisions if the principal is not able.
    - Living will—specifies the principal's wishes regarding death-delaying treatment; only applies in the event of terminal illness.
    - Power of attorney—legal document that permits the elder to give another person (usually the primary caregiver) the authority to act on his or her behalf in specified ways (for banking, financial and real estate transactions, etc.).
    - Durable power of attorney—remains valid even if the principal becomes incompetent (avoids the need to get a court-orderd guardianship).
    - Irrevocable trusts (which can make the elder eligible for financial assistance) and other legal planning for potential lifetime disability.
    - Medicare/Medicaid problems.
- Financial consultants for advice on financial alternatives such as
    - Investments and investment strategies.
    - Tax-free gifts.
    - Loans (rather that cash gifts), which can be repaid tax-free from the estate.
    - Reverse mortgages (converts home equity to cash—See Appendix A at the end of this chapter).

- Trusts.
- Cashing in or borrowing against insurance policies.
- Financial management in the event of disability.
- Pension plan benefits and options.
- Insurance brokers who can help your elder with options like
  - Medigap coverage, which picks up the difference between the cost of Medicare-covered services and the actual cost of the service. (See Appendix B for an explanation of what Medicare covers.)
  - Medicare supplement and/or long-term care insurance (see Appendix C at the end of this chapter). Investigate Medicare/Medicaid coverage carefuly before buying additional insurance.
  - Health insurance.
  - Life insurance.
- Social workers.
  - Can identify resources and benefits for which your elder may qualify.
  - Clinical social workers offer counseling services.
- Home health professionals.
  - Nurse (medication needs, bandage changing, medical supervision).
  - Physical therapist (evaluates, designs, and implements treatment programs to relieve pain and restore or improve movement).
  - Speech pathologist (works with patient to relearn or improve speech or hearing).
  - Respiratory therapist (works with patient to improve breathing).
  - Occupational therapist (can make or suggest adjustments in home, appliances, etc. to allow elder to manage daily activities).

There is overlap between what professionals can do for you (a lawyer may be able to give financial advice, a doctor or hospital can help figure out what treatments are covered by Medicare). The issues are specialized, however. In choosing professionals, make sure they have experience in dealing with elders.

Be realistic. You can't handle the situation alone or without pursuing the interests in your own life. Remember you aren't only an elder caregiver; you're a worker, spouse, parent, brother/sister, and friend too. Get help when you need it.

ELDER-CARE OPTIONS

Moral Support

Usually, caregiving for an elder starts with providing moral support. Often being old means a loss of friends and companionship. Simple contact can mean a lot.

Making contact is a way of strengthening your relationship with others. Making contact can be harder than it sounds. So often we listen with only half an ear, particularly if our elder seems to be rambling. We lead busy lives and sometimes it's hard to slow down long enough to see or hear what is happening to another individual. We miss the real message. We hear the words but not the underlying message.

Making contact can also mean physical contact. Touching can be very meaningful for older individuals. Some are without partners or daily contact. A hug or warm embrace can make their day.

In Virginia Satir's book, *Making Contact*, she emphasizes the importance of making true contact through the ability to see, hear, understand, and to touch someone else.[2] It is important to put forth the effort to really make contact with our elders.

Making contact can mean making a special effort to:

- Stay in touch by phone or letters.
- Encourage regular medical and dental checkups.
- Share special events (graduations, baptisms, parties).
- Visit (or have them visit you) on holidays or just for fun.
- Ask them for help, favors.
- Provide encouragement to continue activities and social engagements.
- Do social things together.
- Empathize with their losses (of friends, mobility, work, etc.).

- Send lots of pictures.
- Give lots of hugs.
- Help them find an outlet for their experience and energy. Ask your elders to consider volunteering for the
  - Gray Panthers—an elder advocacy group.
  - Service Corps for Retired Executives (SCORE)—offers experience and services to for-profit and not-for-profit businesses.
  - Foster Grandparents—makes telephone contact with latchkey children or takes kids on outings.
  - Older Women's League (OWL)—political and social organization.
  - Area hospitals, child day-care centers, homeless shelters, museums, schools, churches, or synagogues.
  - Retired Senior Volunteer Program (RSVP)—organizes volunteer opportunities for elders.
  - Senior Companion Program (SCP)—federal program for low-income people over 60 who provide assistance to other elders who are homebound. Tax-free stipend and transportation allowances are provided.
  - Peace Corps.
- Take classes/pursue education.
- Exercise regularly.
- Travel (maybe with senior groups that will handle day-to-day arrangements and special accommodations).
- Take a part-time job.
- Start a hobby (painting, music, quilting, biking).
- Go to senior centers that provide social, recreational, and educational services for older adults. Often they offer financial, legal, and psychological services as well. They may also offer meals.

Many of these organizations provide transportation.

Elder-Care Services

Many types of elder care are available. We have grouped the options into four main categories.

1. Assistance in elder's home.

2. Adult day-care center.
3. Special-care community or facility.
4. Elder care in your home.

Your choices may be limited by money (though money can be stretched with professional advice) and by the physical and/or mental condition of your elder. Also, as the condition of your elder changes, you may need to revisit the type and extent of care.

Helen's Story

Helen and Al were vital people who lived in the East in an apartment. (They had sold their home when Al retired.) Their two children were grown and lived with their families in the Midwest. Helen and Al had friends and an active social life and did well on their own for about 10 years after Al's early retirement. When Al became sick, it was hard for Helen to cope alone. Helen and Al's daughter flew out to help when she could. She still had children at home, so she couldn't come often. Together with their children, Helen and Al decided to move to the Midwest. It was hard for them to leave their friends, but they were excited about being closer to their children and grandchildren.

They moved into an apartment complex about 20 minutes away from their daughter. All went well for several years. Eventually, however, Al was no longer able to drive safely. Helen had never learned, so their daughter arranged to take them shopping, to doctor's appointments, and so on. After several years of illness, during which daily visits from a home health nurse were necessary, Al died. Helen was his principal caregiver, assisted by their daughter and the visiting nurses.

Helen now faced the prospect of what to do now that she was alone. She was determined not to be a burden to her family and to remain as independent as possible. Helen and her daughter investigated the alternatives, and they visited them together. A continuous-care facility run by a religious order seemed the best answer. Although the financial commitment represented a substantial percentage of her resources, creating real financial concerns, Helen decided to buy in. She moved into an apartment in the complex. While she had her own apartment, lunch and dinner were served in a common dining room. Transportation was available to shopping centers, grocery stores, and movies. Special events like the opera and theater were available for a fee. Various entertainments and interest groups were available on-site. Helen made friends and prospered. Over the years, as her health declined, Helen's daughter (now the primary caregiver) arranged special services as Helen needed them: daily visits by staff members to check on Helen and give her medication, a companion who visited in the afternoons and helped Helen with bathing, dressing, and so on. Helen's daughter took over financial matters (with a durable power of attorney) when Helen agreed she could no longer handle them, and did laundry, grocery shopping, and so on.

The time required for elder-care responsibilites grew to 15 to 25 hours per week as Helen's daughter assumed more and more duties as well as the responsibility to locate and arrange for special services. Social workers and staff members at the facility were of tremendous help during this time.

After several falls and lengthy bouts of confusion and disorientation, Helen moved into the nursing-home wing of the facility. While the decision to give up the apartment was a wrenching one for her and her family, the issue was not compounded by having to find and pay for nursing-home care. Helen's friends can still see her and she them. She is well cared for in a bright, cheerful environment. Helen's daughter continues to provide additional support, often spending up to 15 hours a week on care of her mother. Now 87, Helen has several illnesses and requires 24-hour supervision and assistance. She is pleased that she provided for her own care financially and that her daughter can travel with her husband and live her own life despite her significant elder-care responsibilities. Helen maintains her dignity, her lively sense of humor, and the twinkle in her eyes.

Many companies acknowledge the need to support their employees with elder-care responsibilities. Some companies offer a resource and referral service through a toll-free telephone number or outside consultant. Others help you locate care and resources through their Employee Assistance Program (EAP), which generally also can provide counseling and support. Through a Dependent Care Assistance Program, your employer may be able to help you pay for elder care with pretax dollars (see your benefits department for details). A few companies have begun intergenerational day-care facilities. Some companies also extend health-care coverage to dependent elders and/or make long-term care an optional benefit. Talk to your human resources department to find out what support your employer offers.

Assistance in the Elder's Home

If your elder is still physically and mentally able to take care of his or her basic needs, most elders and their families prefer to have the elder remain in his or her own home as long as possible. They will appreciate your support and encouragement to retain their independence.

Many families find themselves needed to help with certain aspects of daily life. You can help:

- Make your elder's home safe (install grab rails or other safety devices in the bathroom, nonslip mats in the bathroom, lower hot water temperature, remove rugs that slip or carpet with holes, put in smoke detectors and night lights, ensure adequate light and heat).
- Encourage good health practices (medical or dental attention).
- Medicate properly (count out pills, put them in a pill counter with a beeper).
- Make sure the elder has a nutritious diet (help with grocery shopping, food preparation).
- Do chores (housework, yard work, errands, keeping walkways clear of leaves or snow).
- Manage finances (budgeting assistance, paying bills, doing taxes).
- Assist memory (post a list of important phone numbers near the phone or install a telephone programmed with emergency and family numbers).
- Provide or provide for transportation.
- Make ends meet (direct financial assistance or help getting the financial assistance to which your elders may be entitled).

- Check in regularly or set up a buddy system with a nearby friend or neighbor.

You can also locate a wide variety of services to assist your elder, like:

- Phone check-in/companion services.
- Senior centers for meals, social activities, or services.
- Social Security Office for Medicare/Medicaid advice.
- Meals on Wheels programs (one to two hot meals a day, five days a week for $2 to $4 a meal).
- Medical/emergency alert beepers or call button systems.
- Elder transportation services (call your public transportation agency to see if special services are offered for elders).
- Visiting nurses/home health professionals (generally $28 an hour or $50 a visit).
- Volunteer programs through school, churches, synagogues, community groups (for companionship and helpful services like home repair, shopping, transportation, meals).
- Homemaker aide to help with grooming, dressing, taking medications (approximately $9 an hour).
- Home alterations (a chair lift, ramps, grab bars, elevated toilet, bath bench, a downstairs bathroom, a tubless shower).

The services can be located in a variety of ways. Does your employer offer an elder-care resource and referral system? If so, use it! A common source of free information is your local Area Agency for Aging (AAA) funded by the federal government as part of the Older Americans Act. The AAA will be able to tell you about a wide range of services available in your community. Other sources of information include senior centers, the local Social Security Office, family service agencies, AARP, and similar groups, as well as any resource listed under "Seniors" in the Yellow Pages. A list is also included at the end of this chapter. Case management services are also available where a social worker or other trained professional works with you and/or your elder to develop a long-term plan.

Using such services, the solution to our earlier example might be:

1. I'll drive Mom to doctor's appointments, the grocery store, and our house for dinner once a week. A bus from the Senior Center will take her there for bridge and a movie.

2. I'll help Mom shop and choose easy-to-prepare frozen meals for weekends and breakfast. We'll give her a microwave for Christmas. Meals on Wheels will provide hot, fresh lunches and dinners during the week (except after bridge when she can eat at the center).

3. I'll get Mom a pill counter with a beeper. After our weekly outing, I'll count out medication and fill the counter for the week. I'll also check to make sure the medicines were taken the previous week.

In-home care may also mean a daily visit by a nurse or caregiver is necessary to make sure medicine is taken, nutritional meals are eaten, and basic housekeeping and hygiene needs are met. As time goes on, you may find yourself taking on increasing responsibilities for paying the elder's bills, home repair, doing or arranging for laundry and/or housekeeping, and so on. Full-time care may become necessary if your elder's physical and/or mental condition requires constant assistance or supervision.

The questions you need to ask a caregiver who will come into your home to care for your elder are very similar to those you would ask someone who would provide child care. (See Chapter Seven.) You would, of course, modify the questions to find out about their experience with and ability to relate to older people.

Unless the elder is homebound and requires nursing care, and the treatment plan is set up and supervised by a doctor, Medicare will not cover in-home services. Medicaid might be available. Consult your local Social Security Office.

House sharing. Some elders choose to take in or move in with other elders and share the cost of a home and various in-home services. This option can make home-based care more affordable and provide companionship. The problems faced by any roommates (lack of privacy, different lifestyles and preferences) may present problems.

Adult Day-Care Center

If your elder requires constant supervision during the day, you may find that an adult day-care center (or family-care home) is more affordable than in-home care and more enjoyable for the elder since it provides social opportunities. Adult day-care centers care for an elder during the workday. There are half- and full-day programs. They usually provide medical, social, and recreational programs. Transportation to and from home may be included. Physical, occupational, and speech therapy and social workers may also be available. Adult day-care centers can be facilities devoted to elder care (run by a community group or a not-for-profit or for-profit corporation) or be part of a nursing home or hospital, or be part of a combined elder/child-care facility (an intergenerational-care facility). Costs range from $30 to $150 per week.

Day-care questions are also similar to those you would ask about a child-care center (see Chapter Seven), modified to require elder-care qualifications for the caregiver. You might want to add additional questions about the available medical services and emergency procedures.

Special-Care Community or Facility

Residential homes and communities for the elderly are being built at an increasing rate. There are many types of such facilities. Consider your elder's need for care, lifestyle, and budget when examining your options. Also consider getting professional help from a social worker or geriatric care specialist.

Continuing-care community. Continuing-care communities allow an elder to buy lifetime care. Generally, entrants must be in good mental and physical health. They live in separate apartments and receive as much care as necessary from nurses, companions, therapists, social workers, and so on. Two meals are served in a common dining room, and housekeeping and laundry services are provided. Social and recreational activities are provided as well as transportation to shopping, theater, movies, and other activities. When it is no longer possible for the individual to live on his or her own, nursing-home facilities in the same complex are provided. Generally, there is a substantial upfront fee and monthly charges. Additional services may also entail extra fees.

Congregate-care facility. A congregate-care facility is similar to a continuing-care community but without the long-term care component.

Retirement home. Retirement homes are usually privately operated and provide a room, meals, and some personal services. They may also organize social events and outings. Costs vary dramatically with the number of rooms and the standard of living provided.

Nursing home. For some elders (only 5 percent), loss of health (mental and physical) eventually requires care in a nursing home. It can be an extremely difficult decision for the family. Nursing-home care is for people who are chronically ill or recovering from acute illness or who need full-time extended care but do not need to be hospitalized. There are various types of care, from skilled nursing care to intermediate care to custodial care. Good nursing homes often have long waiting lists, so crisis planning should be avoided if at all possible.

If your elder requires care in a nursing home, you can make the transition easier. Bring pictures and furniture (a bureau, a favorite chair) from your elder's home to make the environment a little more familiar and less sterile. Visit often (but not so frequently that your elder has no time to adjust). If they are able, take them home with you for holidays or out for an occasional movie or dinner.

Choosing the right nursing home for another family member or close friend is usually time consuming and emotionally draining. When visiting a nursing home, use the accompanying checklist to compare the facilities. Give yourself enough time to visit and evaluate several facilities thoroughly. The best time to visit a nursing home is around mealtime. This gives you a chance to observe how the staff members interact with the residents, how the meals are prepared and served, and the overall efficiency of the facility. Do not hesitate to visit a facility more than once if you need to ask further questions before making a decision. Remember, placing a family member or close friend in a nursing home is difficult at best, so make sure it is a place where the goal is to provide a quality of life for all its residents.

Selecting the Right Nursing Home[3]

General	Yes	No
1. Do the services offered by the nursing home meet the needs of the individual? Consider not only the medical care services offered, but also whether the facility/staff can support the emotional and social needs of the individual.	☐	☐
2. Is the facility Medicare and/or Medicaid certified? If the individual entering the nursing home is there for a short time (rehabilitating after a hospitalization) and meets Medicare eligibility, some of the expenses will be reimbursed by Medicare, up to the first 100 days. However, if the individual is planning to stay at the nursing home facility for a long time, but has limited financial resources, it is important to know if the nursing home accepts Medicaid recipients.	☐	☐
3. Are payment schedules available? Describe:	☐	☐
4. Will the nursing home take a Medicare assignment?	☐	☐
5. Does the nursing home offer skilled, intermediate, and/or custodial services? This is important because as an individual physically improves or declines, so do the type of services she or he may require.	☐	☐
6. Does the nursing home have an ombudsman program/grievance procedure? If yes, talk with the ombudsman representative to assess the type of problems that have arisen in the past.	☐	☐
7. Is the nursing-home staff adequate? Depending on the needs of the individual, the following areas need to be assessed: • Registered nurse (RN) to patient ratio. • Number of RN's on each shift. • Type of training all staff members have completed. • Staff turnover rates (e.g., average length of employment).	☐ ☐ ☐ ☐	☐ ☐ ☐ ☐
8. Is the nursing home religiously affiliated?	☐	☐
9. Does the facility provide for different religious services?	☐	☐
10. Does the nursing home provide physical therapy, occupational therapy, or other supportive services?	☐	☐
11. Are these therapeutic departments Medicare certified?	☐	☐
12. On behalf of a resident, does the facility bill Medicare for all eligible services?	☐	☐
13. Is there warmth and/or affection between residents and staff members (e.g., touching between individuals)?	☐	☐
14. Is the overall feeling you get when entering the nursing home positive?	☐	☐

Environment	Yes	No
15. Does the nursing home smell of urine or fecal matter?	☐	☐
16. Is there an outdoor and/or indoor area(s) where residents can socialize with other residents or visitors?	☐	☐
17. Are the outside areas clean and well maintained?	☐	☐
18. Does the nursing home provide for outside activities (e.g., field trips)?	☐	☐
19. Are the visiting hours reasonable?	☐	☐
20. Is there a "drop ins welcome" policy?	☐	☐
21. Does the nursing home have a sprinkler system?	☐	☐
22. Is there an emergency evacuation plan?	☐	☐

Patient Rooms	Yes	No
23. Are the patient rooms bright and well ventilated?	☐	☐
24. Are the residents allowed to furnish their own rooms with personal touches or furniture?	☐	☐
25. Do the rooms have windows?	☐	☐
26. Is there privacy, even in a semiprivate room?	☐	☐
27. Does each room have its own bathroom with a tub and/or shower?	☐	☐
28. Are there nonsmoking rooms?	☐	☐
29. Is there an emergency and/or call button next to each resident's bed?	☐	☐

Food	Yes	No
30. Is the food well prepared and pleasant to look at?	☐	☐
31. Is there a dietitian or nutritionist on staff?	☐	☐
32. Do all residents eat in a centralized area (e.g., dining room)?	☐	☐
33. Are meals served at regular times?	☐	☐
34. Does the staff provide assistance with eating if necessary?	☐	☐

Medical Services	Yes	No
35. Is there a physician on staff?	☐	☐
36. If not, does the nursing home have a contractual relationship with a physician and/or medical group?	☐	☐
37. Can personal physicians have nursing-home staff privileges (e.g., write physician orders)?	☐	☐
38. Is there a pharmacy in the nursing home?	☐	☐
39. If not, does the nursing home have a contractual relationship with an outside vendor or pharmacy?	☐	☐
40. Can the resident supply his or her own medication?	☐	☐
41. Does the nursing home offer dental services? If no, how does a resident receive dental care?	☐	☐

Len's Story

Len works in a corporation and often travels. He has been looking after his 95-year-old aunt since she was 70 years old. His aunt, Dora, had been in good health and lived alone in an apartment complex in a large city. Dora had many friends in her building who also checked in on her occasionally. However, her condition deteriorated after she fell. There were signs of confusion, lack of appetite, and general apathy. She was unable to do some simple tasks such as bathe, go out for a walk, or fix meals. Because of Len's job, he was unable to see her daily.

After many conversations, Len convinced her that she needed some help. Finding a solution to keep her in her own home was important. Based on a friend's recommendation, Len called an organization that offered case assessments for a reasonable fee. The social worker determined Dora needed help with simple tasks such as bathing, preparing meals, dressing, and walking outside. Part-time help was arranged for several hours in the morning and several in the late afternoon.

This arrangement worked well until Dora fell during the night. The fall injured her arm severely. She needed hospitalization and long-term therapy (8 to 12 weeks). The doctor recommended a full-time care arrangement after hospitalization. The situation was explained to Dora, who agreed. The long, painful task of looking for a nursing home began. The hospital gave a list of names. Len inquired among friends, and the search began. There were many considerations—cost, location (near friends or Len), types of services, staffing, and so on.

Len's mother and dad (Dora's brother), who are in their 80s and still live in their home, made a recommendation that hadn't been considered. They live five hours from the city in a small town. The town has several good nursing homes at a reasonable cost, and, most importantly, they would be available to visit Dora daily. After many discussions of the pros and cons and asking Dora what she wanted to do, Len and his wife arranged to take her to a nursing home in the country.

Dora made a rapid adjustment to the nursing home. She is well taken care of, made new friends, and had family who could visit regularly. She gained weight, went out for lunch occasionally, participated in activities, and is happy again.

In 1991, she celebrated her 97th birthday. She went out to lunch with friends and family.

Hospice care. Hospices provide special care for the terminally ill and their families, supplying medical, psychological, and emotional support. In a hospice facility, cost can run up to $200 a day. Hospice care is available at home for $50 to 80 a day.

Adult Care in Your Home

Thirty-seven percent of elders choose to move in with a child's family, or their families choose it for them. This arrangement will stir up a lot of emotions on the part of both the elder and the family, including baggage from the past. The dynamics of the new living arrangement can create tension between spouses and parents and children, as well as loss of privacy. *Don't* make the decision out of guilt or against your elder's wishes. If possible, try an extended visit before making the arrangement permanent. Investigate other options, including an apartment or shared home nearby.

The accompanying questionnaire may help you decide if your elder should be cared for in your home or if care in your home is best for all concerned.

Should My Elder Live With Me?[4]

	Health and Safety	Yes	No
1.	Would your home require major modifications to provide an adequate environment for your elder (heating, plumbing, laundry facilities, accessible bathrooms, etc.)?	☐	☐
2.	Would it be necessary to modify your home to increase safety (add railings, etc.) or allow mobility?	☐	☐
3.	Does your elder require nursing services that are too physically difficult or demanding for you (turning, transfer to toilet, etc.)?	☐	☐
4.	Is your elder likely to regularly disturb the sleep of others by calling out, needing care, or wandering?	☐	☐
5.	Is your elder likely to wander away from you or the house if left unsupervised?	☐	☐
6.	Is your elder likely to create safety hazards for other family members because of forgetfulness or carelessness (falling asleep while smoking, misuse of appliances, etc.)?	☐	☐

Time and Energy	Yes	No
7. Does your elder require someone available at all times to provide personal care?	☐	☐
If yes, do you have backup and support?	☐	☐
8. Must clothing and bed linens be changed and laundered so frequently that this becomes an excessive physical demand (on you, children, spouse)?	☐	☐
9. Do you have other family responsibilities that could result in split loyalties and/or emotional overload?	☐	☐

Personal Communications	Yes	No
10. Does your elder interfere with the running of your household?	☐	☐
11. Would loss of privacy become a problem for the adult members of the household (a strain on marriage)?	☐	☐
12. Is there conflict between younger adults and adolescent family members and your elder?	☐	☐

Emotional Considerations	Yes	No
13. Has your elder become emotionally explosive or verbally abusive?	☐	☐
14. Has your elder accused you or others of trying to kill him or her (poisoning food, etc.) or of stealing money?	☐	☐
15. Would you become cut off from friends and other family members because of the demands of caring for your elder?	☐	☐
16. Would you have to give up activities and interests that are important to you because of the demands of caring for your elder?	☐	☐

Situational Considerations	Yes	No
17. Is it necessary for the family to change homes or move to another community to make continued care realistic?	☐	☐
18. Would the financial demands make continued employment or longer work hours necessary?	☐	☐
If yes, are the financial consequences acceptable?	☐	☐
19. Would the care demands make continued employment impossible or require reduced work hours?	☐	☐
20. Has an additional family emergency created conflict or competition for time and energy?	☐	☐

If you have answered yes to many of the questions, you will probably want to reconsider caring for your elder in your own home and begin to explore a change in living arrangements for your elder.

LONG-DISTANCE CAREGIVING

Those of you caring for elders who live at a distance have the extra burden of not being able to be physically in touch with your elder. There is also the added stress of trying to make personal arrangements only by phone. Effective communication skills can help you find out how your elder is doing and what you can do to help.

Here are some guidelines for getting started:

- Identify another adult who lives near your elder who can give you feedback regularly (a minister, priest, or rabbi, a neighbor, another relative, or friend).
- Stay in regular phone contact.
- Assess your elder's needs or get the assistance of a professional geriatric-care manager who knows the area.
- Determine the person and/or services that can help your elder in your absence.
- Make the most of your infrequent visits by observing, asking good questions, and checking health and finance records, health and safety procedures.
- Set up a formal or informal network of support.

Be prepared to make alternative arrangements. Many elders' physical and mental conditions change periodically. More or less assistance may be needed over time. Most importantly, know you are doing the best you can as a long-distance caregiver.

When the situation becomes impossible to manage from a distance, begin the process to bring your elder closer to you. This step deserves special attention as you will need to discuss honestly many considerations for both of you—your elder's social contacts, support systems, the amount of time you have to spend on elder care, the resources available in your area, the cost of moving, the cost of living where you live, the relationship between the two of you, and so on.

THE CAREGIVER: TAKING CARE OF YOURSELF

One of the most important issues related to caregiving for elders is taking care of yourself, the caregiver. You can get so wrapped up in the caregiving role that there is little thought to getting what *you* need. Getting support for yourself not only will help your stress and energy levels but also will help you keep a healthy perspective on your elder's situation. Most caregivers are involved in some aspect of elder care for 18 years. You need to get support now so that you will be able to go the distance. Moreover, unlike children who grow progressively more independent, the trend in care for elders is the reverse. Most elders will become more dependent and need more and more assistance.

Taking care of an elder can be physically demanding. It takes strength to get someone in and out of bed and a bath, take them to the toilet, bathe, or feed them. It can also be an emotional drain as you watch a once vigorous and alert loved one become frail, fearful, forgetful, confused, or disoriented.

To truly help your elder, you must take care of yourself. For most of us, that means asking for help. Taking advantage of community or other services will increase the quality of life for both you and your elder. Consider the following:

- Take a break with respite care.
  - Short-term respite care—hire someone to come in for short periods so that you can go out to lunch, go shopping, see a movie.
  - Longer-term respite care—get help so that you can take a vacation, deal with an emergency, or just take an extended break. Maybe another family member or friend can take over for a week or your elder can go to a nursing home.
- Get backup and assistance. Go though the list of options presented earlier carefully and find resources near you. Contact the Area Agency on Aging to find out more about elder-care services to support you.
- Read books and newsletters that will keep you up to date on available resources, health insurance, and financial planning for elders. Take action.
- Get enough rest, exercise, and nutritious food.
- Maintain a positive attitude.
  - Part of keeping your own spirits up requires acceptance of the fact that there are many things you can't control and can't make better no matter what you do. You must be realistic. Most illnesses or mental problems will not

get significantly better. Many elder caregivers recommend a "one day at a time" perspective that can temper the emotional highs and lows that can occur.

- Don't get caught up in feelings of guilt. You did not cause your elder to grow old, did you? Neither did you cause the person's mental or physical changes or the loss of friends or the death of a mate. Nor can you be blamed for wishing the burden would be lifted from your shoulders. You are doing the best you can.

- Avoid isolation.
  - Get support. Don't try to go it alone. It will be very difficult to get help if you hide your elder's condition or the burden on you from others. Ask other family members to share the responsibilities.
  - Consider joining an elder-care support group where you can share your experiences with others.
  - Attend workshops and lectures to learn more about aging, resources, and solutions to difficult situations.

If your elder suffers from Alzheimer's disease (which 20 percent of elders over 80 will), you are particularly vulnerable to stress and burnout. Studies have shown that over 50 percent of caregivers in this situation suffer mental and physical deterioration themselves from the stress of the situation. A support system and frequent breaks are vital.

Fill out the accompanying questionnaire to help determine your need for support.

Caregiver Assessment

	Never	Rarely	Sometimes	Frequently	Always
1. I support my elder(s) daily.	1	2	3	4	5
2. I ask others for help with routine chores for my elder(s) like:					
Shopping	1	2	3	4	5
Errands	1	2	3	4	5
Finances	1	2	3	4	5
Laundry	1	2	3	4	5
Housekeeping	1	2	3	4	5
Transportation	1	2	3	4	5

3. I discuss my feelings and concerns about my elder(s) with friends, family, counselors, or others.	1	2	3	4	5
4. My caregiving responsibilities do not affect my work.	1	2	3	4	5
5. I have enough or get the information about aging I need to make effective decisions with my elder(s).	1	2	3	4	5
6. I feel a balance between my caregiving and personal life.	1	2	3	4	5
7. I get enough rest and eat properly.	1	2	3	4	5
8. I exercise regularly.	1	2	3	4	5
9. I take regular breaks from my caregiving responsibilities.	1	2	3	4	5
10. My spirits/attitude are generally positive.	1	2	3	4	5

Total up your score.

41–50 Great job! Keep up the good work.

31–40 You are on the right track. Continue to strive for balance and get help when you need it.

21–30 You could use more help. Delegate some of your responsibilities to family, volunteers, or support services.

10–20 You don't have adequate support. Check out some of the resources we have described.

CONCLUSION

Elder care is a difficult issue, but it can be very rewarding. It can be a chance to really get to know your elders as people and to give back some of the love and support they have shown you over the years. Like every other aspect of our lives, it can only be one piece of the puzzle. Take what steps you need to make sure the piece fits and does not overwhelm the other parts of your life.

Appendix A
HOME EQUITY CONVERSION: MORTGAGE INSURANCE DEMONSTRATION PROGRAM (U.S. Department of Housing and Urban Development)[5]

Under the Home Equity Conversion Mortgage Insurance Demonstration Program, the U.S. Department of Housing and Urban Development (HUD) will insure reverse mortgages on the homes of elder homeowners, enabling them to convert their equity into monthly payments or line-of-credit draws. Those eligible are homeowners 62 years of age or older who live in homes that they own free and clear, or nearly so. Between 1988 and 1991, HUD was authorized to insure 2,500 reverse mortgages. Through the Fannie Mae program (low-cost housing loans for low- and middle-income consumers), HUD was authorized in 1991 to insure another 25,000 loans.

HUD will insure a reverse mortgage that allows homeowners to choose from three basic payment options: tenure, term, and line of credit.

- The tenure option provides monthly payments to a homeowner as long as the homeowner occupies the home as a principal residence.
- The term option provides monthly payments for a fixed period selected by the homeowner.
- The line-of-credit option permits homeowners to draw money at times and in amounts of their own choosing up to a maximum amount.

The homeowner may receive lump-sum draws, combine a line of credit with monthly payments, and change the payment plan if needed.

Regardless of the payment option selected, homeowners may continue to live in the house until they move, sell, or die. They may sell their property at any time, retaining any proceeds that exceed the amount needed to pay off the mortgage. They cannot be forced to sell their home to pay off the mortgage. HUD will insure lenders against the risk that the mortgage balance may grow to exceed the value of the property.

Payments to borrowers will be based on the age of the youngest borrower, the mortgage interest rate, and the property value up to a maximum claim amount. A reverse mortgage may bear interest at either a fixed or adjustable rate. HUD also proposes to insure reverse mortgages that provide for shared appreciation between borrower and lender.

Appendix B
MEDICARE BENEFITS 1992[6]
Elder Link, Inc., Chicago, IL (312–929–4514)

Part A Benefits: Hospital Insurance (per benefit period)

Services	Benefit	Medicare Pays	You Pay
Hospital inpatient	First 60 days	All but $652	$652
• Semiprivate room	61st to 90th day	All but $163/day	$163/day
• General nursing care			
• Hospital services and supplies	91st to 150th day*	All but $326/day	$326/day
	Over 150 days	Nothing	All costs
Psychiatric hospital (Psychiatric care in a general hospital)	190 lifetime days	All costs for 190 days	All costs after 190 days
Skilled nursing			
Qualifications for Medicare payment:	First 20 days	100% of approved cost	Nothing (if approved)
• Hospitalized for at least 3 days	20–100 days	All but $81.50/day	$81.50/day
• Admitted within 30 days of hospitalization	Over 100 days	Nothing	All costs
• Facility and bed is Medicare approved			
• Services are medically necessary (not custodial) and related to condition treated in the hospital			
• Physician certifies that you need services on a daily basis			
• Medicare intermediary or facility's utilization review committee does not disapprove the stay			

Part A Benefits: Hospital Insurance (per benefit period)

Services	Benefit	Medicare Pays	You Pay
Hospice			
Qualifications for Medicare payment: • Doctor certifies that a patient is terminally ill • Patient chooses to receive care from a hospice instead of standard Medicare benefits for the terminal illness • Care is provided by a Medicare participating hospice program	Maximum 210 days (Two 90 day periods and one 30 day period) If Medicare hospice benefits are exhausted and patient still wants and needs hospice services, hospice must continue. Hospice may bill patient for continued care.	All costs except for some outpatient drugs and inpatient respite care	Limited cost-sharing for outpatient drugs and inpatient respite care
Blood	Blood	All but first 3 pints/year	First 3 pints/year
Home health[†]			
Qualifications for Medicare payment: • Care includes intermittent skilled nursing care, physical therapy, or speech therapy • You are confined to home • Under the care of a physician who determines that home health care is needed and develops a home health plan • Home health care agency is Medicare approved	Medicare approved part-time or intermittent nursing care and health care services	100% of approved amounts 80% of approved amounts for durable medical equipment	Nothing 20% of approved amount for durable medical equipment

*60 reserve days may be used only once during a lifetime.
[†]Part A pays for home health care benefits only when Medicare recipient does not have Part B.

Part B Benefits: Medical Insurance (per benefit period)

Services	Benefit	Medicare Pays	You Pay
Medical expenses • Physician services (hospital, clinics, office, or home) • Inpatient/outpatient medical and surgical services and supplies • Diagnostic tests (e.g., mammography) • Ambulance • Durable medical equipment • Physical and speech therapy	Medicare pays for eligible medical expenses* in or out of the hospital	After $100 deductible, Medicare will pay for 80% of eligible expenses	$100 deductible plus 20% of Medicare eligible expenses and all costs above eligible expenses
Clinical laboratory services	Blood tests, urinalysis, biopsies, etc.	100% of eligible expenses	Nothing for eligible expenses
Home health care Covers eligible home health care visits for those who are not covered under Part A.	Part-time or intermittent medically necessary skilled care, home health aide services, etc.	100% of eligible expenses; 80% of approved amount for durable medical equipment	20% of approved amount for durable medical equipment and all costs above eligible expenses
Outpatient hospital treatment Reasonable and necessary services for the diagnosis or treatment of an illness/injury.	Unlimited if medically necessary	After $100 deductible, 80% of eligible expenses	Subject to deductible, 20% of eligible expenses, and all costs above eligible expenses

*Medicare determines what services are eligible for payment and then pays 80% of those expenses. Medicare recipient pays the 20% difference and any charges higher than the amount approved by Medicare, unless physician accepts assignment (accepting Medicare approved amount as payment in full). Physicians who do not accept assignment are limited as to the amount they can charge: 1992 – 120% of the fee schedule amount for non-participating physicians, and 115% thereafter.

Part B Benefits: Medical Insurance (per benefit period)

Services	Benefit	Medicare Pays	You Pay
Blood (If blood deductible is met under one part of Medicare during calendar year, it does not have to be met under the other part)	Blood	After $100 deductible and starting with 4th pint, 80% of approved amount	Subject to deductible, first 3 pints and 20% of approved amount

Source: U.S. Department of Health and Human Services, Washington, D.C., 1992.

Appendix C
MEDICARE SUPPLEMENT INSURANCE POLICIES[7]

Questions to Ask Yourself and Your Insurance Agent

1. Does this policy cover the following benefits per benefit period?
   - Part A hospital deductible and copayments.
   - Skilled nursing copayments and expenses that are not eligible under Medicare.
   - Home health-care benefits not eligible under Medicare.
   - Part B annual deductible and copayments.
   - Physician charges not approved by Medicare.
2. Are all benefits based on Medicare eligibility?
3. Is the annual premium for this policy affordable?
4. Does this policy have any added features and/or benefits that make this plan better than other Medicare Supplement policies?
5. Is this policy guaranteed renewable?
6. Does this policy exclude coverage for any preexisting condition(s)?
7. What are the waiting periods?
8. Does this policy offer a Stop-Lease provision? Example: pays 100 percent of Medicare eligible expenses after you have paid the first $5,000 during a calendar year.

9. Does this policy offer any foreign travel benefits?
10. Does this policy require that all applicants be medically evaluated by the insurance company to determine insurability? What percentage of applicants are accepted?
11. How quickly does the insurance company pay claims? What percent of claims are denied?
12. What is the insurance company's Best rating?
13. What does the policy cost per year?

Appendix D
LONG-TERM CARE INSURANCE POLICIES[8]

Before selecting a long-term care insurance policy, the elder must make two decisions:

- You must evaluate your present health status and determine realistically which types of health-care services you require now and may in the future.
- You must decide what type of housing (i.e., retirement community, nursing home, etc.) and/or services (i.e., home health care, homemaking, etc.) you will want in the future if your health deteriorates to the point where you can no longer take care of yourself.

Once you make these decisions, you will be able to select a long-term care insurance policy that meets your needs.

Checklist for Selecting an Insurance Policy

1. What services does this policy cover?
   _____ Skilled nursing
   _____ Intermediate care
   _____ Home health care
   _____ Custodial care
   _____ Homemaking
   _____ Respite care
   _____ Adult day care
   _____ Other _____

2. What are the daily benefits for each service outlined in the policy?
3. Are daily benefits for home health care a percentage of the nursing home benefit?
   _____ Yes
   _____ No
   If so, what percentage?
4. Is there a waiting period before you are eligible for benefits?
   _____ Yes
   _____ No
5. What are the deductibles associated with the daily benefits?
   _____ No deductible
   _____ 20-day deductible
   _____ 100-day deductible
   _____ Other _____
6. Does the policy offer the option of increasing the daily benefit amount (inflation option rider)?
   _____ Yes
   _____ No
7. How does a policyholder qualify for benefits?
   _____ Physician certification of need
   _____ Functional assessment
   _____ Prior hospitalization for nursing-home and home health-care benefits
   _____ Prior nursing-home stay for home health-care benefits
   _____ Other _____
8. What are the limits on all policy benefits?
   _____ 1 year
   _____ 2 years
   _____ 3 years
   _____ 4 years
   _____ 5 years
   _____ Lifetime
   _____ Other
9. Does this policy have a maximum length of coverage for each "period of illness"?
   _____ Yes
   _____ No
   If yes, what are the limits? _____
10. Does this policy cover preexisting conditions?
    _____ Yes
    _____ No
    If yes, are there restrictions? _____

11. Does this policy cover Alzheimer's disease?

_____ Yes

_____ No

If yes, are there restrictions? _____

12. Is the policy "guaranteed renewable" for life?

_____ Yes

_____ No

If no, can the policy be canceled?

_____ Yes

_____ No

13. What are the age requirements for enrollment?

14. Will the policy cover you if you move to another area? If you live outside the United States?

15. Does the policy require that applicants be medically evaluated by the insurance company to determine insurability?

16. Is a physician statement required for medical underwriting purposes?

17. How quickly does the insurance company pay claims? What percentage of claims are denied?

18. How long has the insurance company been selling long-term care policies?

19. What is the insurance company's Best rating (A or A+)?

20. What does the policy cost per year? Do premiums increase with age?

RESOURCES

Bumagin, Victoria, and Kathryn F. Hirn. *Aging Is a Family Affair*. New York: Thomas Y. Crowell, 1979.

Crichton, Jean. *The Age Care Sourcebook: A Resource Guide for Aging and Their Families*. New York: Simon & Schuster, 1987.

Daniels, Norman. *Am I My Parents' Keeper?* New York: Oxford University Press, 1988.

Edinberg, Mark A. *Talking with Your Aging Parents*. Boston: Shambhala, 1987.

Elder Services: The Greater Chicago Area Guide to Eldercare. Phoenix, Ariz.: The Oryx Press, 1991.

Family Home Caring Guides. Eight brochures published by the National Council on Aging. Write NCOA, Dept. 5087, 600 Maryland Ave. S.W., West Wing 100, Washington, D.C. 20061.

For Those Who Care. Metro-Dade County Elderly Services Division, nine-hour video series or five audiocassettes. (305) 375-5335.

Jarvik, Lissy, M.D., Ph.D., and Gary Small, M.D. *Parentcare: A Common Sense Guide to Helping Our Parents Cope with the Problems of Aging.* New York: Crown Publishers/Bantam Paperback, 1988.

Kubler-Ross, Elisabeth. *On Death and Dying.* London: Macmillan, 1969.

Kubler-Ross, Elisabeth, and David A. Tomb. *Growing Old: A Handbook for You and Your Aging Parent.* New York: Viking Press, 1984.

Lester, Andrew and Judith L. *Understanding Aging Parents.* Philadelphia: The Westminister Press, 1980.

Levin, Nora Jean. *How to Care for Your Parents: A Handbook for Adult Children.* Washington, D.C.: Storm King Press, 1987.

Mall, E. Jane. *Caregiving: How to Care for Your Elderly Mother and Stay Sane.* New York: Ballantine Books, 1990.

Parent Care. Geronotology Center, 316 Strong Hall, University of Kansas, Lawrence, KS 66045; 913-864-4130. Six-times-a-year newsletter for the caregiver—tips, book reviews, health advice, and hot-line numbers.

Porcino, Jane. *Growing Older, Getting Better: A Handbook for Women in the Second Half of Life.* Reading, Mass.: Addison-Wesley Publishing, 1983.

Portnow, Jay, M.D., with Martha Houtmann, R.N. *Home Care for the Elderly.* New York: McGraw-Hill, 1987.

Shulman, Bernard, and Raeann Berman. *How to Survive Your Aging Parents.* Chicago: Surrey Books, 1988.

Springer, Dianne, and Timothy Brubaker. *Family Caregiving and Dependent Elderly.* Beverly Hills, Calif.: Sage Publications, 1984.

Stong, Maggie. *Mainstay: For the Well Spouse of the Chronically Ill.* Boston: Little, Brown, 1988.

Support Groups/Taking Care of the Caregiver

Benjamin, Ben. *Are You Tense?* New York: Pantheon Books, 1978.

Benson, Herbert. *The Relaxation Response.* New York: Morrow, 1975.

Lieberman, Morton. *Self-Help Groups for Coping with Crisis: Origins, Members, Processes and Impact.* San Francisco: Jossey-Baas, 1979.

Roberts, Jeanne D., M.A. *Taking Care of Caregivers.* Palo Alto, Calif.: Bull Publishing, 1991.

Children of Aging Parents
2761 Trenton Road,
Levittown, PA 19056.
(215) 945–6900

National Association of Private Geriatric Care Managers
1315 Talbott Tower
Dayton, OH 45402
(513) 222-2621
Association that can provide lists of geriatric care managers.

National Council on Aging Publications
Idea Book on Caregiver Support Groups.

Adult Day-Care

National Council on Aging, *Adult Day Care Annotated Bibliography.* Washington, D.C., 1982.

National Association for Home Care, Washington, D.C. (202) 547-7424

Housing

Shared Housing Resource Center
6344 Green Street
Philadelphia, PA 19144
(215) 848-1220
National clearinghouse for groups that provide housing for people who need part-time assistance; referral service but doesn't evaluate groups.

The Continuing Care Retirement Community: A Guidebook for Consumers
American Association of Homes for the Aging
1129 20th St., N.W., Suite 400
Washington, DC 20036

**The National Center for State Long Term
Care Ombudsman Resources**
2033 K St. N.W., Suite 304
Washington, DC 20006
Organization that will put you in touch with an ombudsman.

American Health Care Association
How to Select a Nursing Home
1200 15th St., N.W.
Washington, DC 20005.

U.S. Department of Health and Human Services, *How to Select a Nursing Home.* Baltimore, MD: Health Care Financing Administration, 1980.

Hospice Care

National Hospice Foundation and Home Care
519 C Street, N.E.
Washington, DC 20002
(202) 547-6586

Handicapped Services

Sargent, Jean Vieth. *An Easier Way: Handbook for the Elderly and Handicapped.* New York: Walker, 1981.

Health or Personal-Care Aid

National Homecaring Council. *Directory of Homemaker/Home Health-Aide Services in the United States, Puerto Rico and Virgin Islands.* New York: National Homecaring Council, 1982.

Nutrition

Watkin, Donald M. *Handbook of Nutrition, Health and Aging.* Park Ridge, N.J.: Noyes Publications, 1983

Zaccarelli, Herman E. *The Cookbook That Tells You How: The Retirement Food and Nutrition Manual.* Boston: Cahners Publishing Company, 1972.

Mental Health

Butler, Robert N., and Myrna I. Lewis. *Aging and Mental Health: Positive Psychosocial Approaches.* St. Louis: The C.V. Mosby Company, 1977.

Glasscote, Raymond M., Jon E. Gudeman, and Donald G. Miles. *Creative Mental Health Services for the Elderly.* Washington, D.C.: The Joint Information Service of the American Psychiatric Association and the Mental Health Association, 1977.

Mace, Nancy. *The 36-Hour Day: A Family Guide to Caring for Persons with Alzheimer's Disease, Related Dementia Illness and Memory Loss at Later Life.* Baltimore, Md.: Johns Hopkins University Press, 1991.

Insurance

Your Medicare Handbook. Available from your local Social Security Office.

Inlander, Charles B., and Charles K. MacKay. *Medicare Made Easy.* Reading, Mass.: Addison-Wesley Publishing, 1989.

Polniaszek, Susan. *Long-Term Care: A Dollar and Sense Guide*. Washington, D.C.: United Seniors Health Cooperative.

Law and Finance

Shane, Dorlene V., and The United Seniors Health Cooperative. *Finances after 50: Financial Planning for the Rest of Your Life*. New York: Harper & Row/Perennial, 1989.

The National Academy of Elder Law Attorneys
665 N. Alvernon, Suite 108
Tucson, AZ 85711
(602) 881–4005
Send a stamped, self-addressed envelope to this group to receive a list of nearby lawyers familiar with seniors' legal problems.

Associations

Alzheimer's Association
70 E. Lake Street, Suite 600
Chicago, IL 60601
(312) 253–3060

American Association of Retired Persons (AARP)
1909 K Street, N.W.
Washington, DC 20049
(202) 872–4700
An association that offers many services and publications.

American Psychiatric Association
400 K Street, N.W.
Washington, DC 20005

American Psychological Association
1200 17th Street, N.W.
Washington, DC 20036

American Society on Aging
833 Market Street, Suite 516
San Francisco, CA 94103
(415) 543–2617

Arthritis Foundation
1314 Spring Street
Atlanta, GA 30309
(404) 872–7100

Center for the Study of Aging
706 Madison Avenue
Albany, NY 12208
(518) 465–6927

Family Service America
11700 West Lake Park Drive
Milwaukee, WI 53224
(414) 359–2111

Can refer you to your local Family Service Agency for suggestions on home care, services, day care, and long-term care facilities.

The Gray Panthers
3635 Chestnut Street
Philadelphia, PA 19104

The National Association of Social Workers
7981 Eastern Avenue
Silver Springs, MD 20910

National Caucus and Center on Black Aged, Inc.
1424 K Street, N.W., Suite 500
Washington, DC 20005
(202) 637–8400

National Council on the Aging (NCOA)
600 Maryland Avenue, S.W.
West Wing 100, Suite 208
Washington, DC 20024
(202) 479–1200

National Council for Homemaker/Health and Services
67 Irving Place
New York, NY 10003

Older American Volunteer Programs/ACTION
806 Connecticut Avenue, N.W.
Room M-1006
Washington, DC 20525
(202) 643–9355

Older Women's League
730 11th Street, N.W.
Washington, DC 20001
(202) 783–6686

U.S. Administration on Aging
Department of Health and Human Services
Office of Management and Policy
330 Independence Avenue, S.W.
Washington, DC 20201
(202) 245–0641

NOTES

1. Mark A. Edinberg, *Talking with Your Aging Parents* (Boston: Shambhala Publications, 1987), p. 2.
2. Virginia Satir, *Making Contact* (Berkeley, Calif.: Celestial Arts, 1976).
3. Adapted from *Choosing the Right Nursing Home* by Elder Link, Inc., Chicago, Illinois. Reprinted with permission. References: American Association of Retired Persons, *Nursing Home Life: A Guide for Residents and Families* (Washington, D.C., AARP, 1991) and Susan Polniaszek, *Long Term Living: How to Live Independently as Long as You Can and Plan for the Time When You Can't* (Washington, D.C., Acropolis Books, 1990).
4. Adapted and reprinted from *Elder Services 1990–1991: The Greater Chicago Area Guide to Elder Care.* Copyright 1990 by The Oryx Press, 4041 N. Central at Indian School Rd., Phoenix, AZ 85012. Used by permission of The Oryx Press.
5. By Elder Link, Inc., Chicago, Illinois (312) 929–4514. Reprinted with permission. Reference: U.S. Department of Urban Development, "Home Equity Conversion Mortgage Program," Washington, D.C. (P.L. 100–242, 2/5/88 and P.L. 101–508, 11/5/90).
6. By Elder Link, Inc., Chicago, Illinois. Reprinted with permission.
7. By Elder Link, Inc., Chicago, Illinois. Reprinted with permission.
8. By Elder Link, Inc., Chicago, Illinois. Reprinted with permission.

Chapter Nine

Managing Special Family Situations

If a child is to keep alive his inborn sense of wonder without any such gift from the fairies, he needs the companionship of at least one adult who can share it, rediscovering with him the joy, excitement, and mystery of the world we live in.

Rachel Carson[1]

SINGLE PARENTING

Six out of 10 children in this country will at some time live in a single-parent household. About 25 percent of American children (including about half of black children) live in single-parent households today. The majority of single parents are women.[2] Every single parent's situation is different. Many have no help paying for and raising their child(ren), some have occasional help, and fewer still have substantial support and cooperation from the other parent. Nevertheless, most single parents find their role as parent to be the most rewarding part of their life.

Bonnie's Story

Having survived single parenthood, I can now reflect on the positive contributions it made to my life. It was clearly the most difficult challenge I will ever face. Single parenting taught me to focus my energy on a few things rather than on many. It promoted skills I never knew I had, such as financial planning, on-the-spot decision making, resourcefulness, goal setting, and discovering innovative family programs. I found strength, energy, and spiritual belief that has been the basis of my life ever since.

Becoming a Single Parent

Going back to work. If you suddenly find yourself a single parent without a job, you will probably need to get into the job market. Here are some things to consider when reentering the work force.

1. Skills review/career counseling.
2. Identify your ideal job, and variations of it.
3. Full- or part-time work.
4. Salary requirements.
5. Training (additional or refresher courses) needed.
6. Child-care arrangements and costs.
7. Transportation costs and considerations.
8. Clothes investment.

After reviewing them, begin your job search in a systematic way and use all the resources you have available. Often the best leads come from former co-workers, friends, and family members. Consider all your options, even work at home that might cut down on commute time and child-care costs. Those of you who did not finish your education or training for a career may have to find ways to pay for your training and create a network of support to help you raise your child while you go to school. If your child is of school age, try doing "homework" together.

Depression. Getting hit with the reality of single parenting can cause depression, which is sometimes severe. Seeing couples together can be frustrating and emotionally hard to cope with. Being at home alone with a child and without spousal support can be exhausting. That fatigue combined with omnipresent feelings of being trapped, lonely, or overwhelmed can lead to depression.

One of the best ways to cope with possible depression and even prevent it is to keep a clear focus on what is (reality) and not to get caught up in worrying about what could be or should be. One method is visualization.

Visualization for single parents[3]

To begin the visualization process, take any quiet moments you have and stop thinking. Take some long, deep breaths and calm yourself. Once you have calmed your thoughts, start to develop a clear mental focus. Begin to visualize your responsibilities for the day. If you start to overwhelm yourself with a monthly projection, depression and burnout is inevitable. In your mind, picture what you need to do today—just today. Then calmly plan how you will get it done.

Don't forget to give yourself a chance to enjoy your time with your child. Make sure there are fun times even if it means the house is dirty. Keep your priorities clear. The love shared between parent and child can erase any self-doubt and fatigue.

If depression persists, seek professional help. Remember the influence you have as a role model for your child and get help to be happy and balanced.

Life as a Single Parent

A support network. No matter what your single-parenting situation is, the day-to-day responsibilities can be overwhelming. While all parents need support, a good outside support network is essential for single parents. Take stock of your current support systems by completing the accompanying worksheet.

My Support Network

	Name	*Phone Number*	*Availability (Days)*
Sick-child care			

Emergency child care			
Overnight child care			
Budget			
Financial planning			
Housecleaning/ Upkeep			
Electrician			
Plumber			
Handyman			
Painter			
Running errands			
Car repair			
Doctors Yours			
Child(ren)'s			
Emotional support Friends			
Family			
Counselors			
Other single parents			

Support works. Even "impossible" situations can work with grace and joy.

Amy's Story

Amy is the mother of quadruplets. She has raised the four children alone since soon after they were born. She is a professional who works full time. She believes in good organization and communication, as well as taking advantage of support. Amy has a strong family support system, and she relied on it heavily when the children were young. She lived with her parents while the children were little. But her positive attitude and creative problem solving have been the main elements that have supported her through some difficult times.

All four children have had responsibilities since they were young. Their duties increased as they got older. Amy uses a chore chart and rotates tasks weekly. She has learned to manage her family with flexibility. The family has rules, but not too many. The family system runs on trust, traditions, and having fun.

She has been innovative in keeping close communication with her children even when working late or traveling. She leaves notes on their pillows when she travels. "Tea time" together every Sunday is family time, a tradition the children enjoy even now that they are teenagers. It is a constant in their lives. They also take annual camping trips and enjoy biking and other outdoor activities as a family. Amy also believes listening is important. When they were younger, she often talked to each child separately at night, in the dark when they were in bed. Each child also went on outings alone with Mom.

Now that her children are teenagers, she has gotten a beeper that allows them to reach her at any time, without restricting her own social life. Amy continues to fill her life with good friends, a supportive family, and interesting work. She attributes those things to helping her keep her morale and energy up.

To reach out and ask for help or support is the healthiest choice you can make for yourself. Try some of the following ideas to find people for your network:

1. Parents Without Partners, an organization to support single parents. Look in the phone book for your local chapter.

2. Look for single-parent group meetings in the Sunday paper or on the bulletin board at your grocery store, church or synagogue, health club, or doctor's office.

3. Your child-care provider might organize support groups. If not, ask if the provider will help you start a group.

4. Contact agencies listed in the phone directory and family service associations.

5. Big Brothers/Big Sisters can provide volunteers to be role models and companions for children when the other parent is not available regularly. In addition, they may give you some time off.

Check out books that relate to stress, parenting, and child development. Information and education is always helpful.

Getting organized.   In Chapter Five, we discussed the importance of life management skills—organizing, eliminating time, delegating, and so on. For the single parent, staying organized is one of the most crucial steps for survival. Setting priorities to conserve your time will also relieve stress in the long run. Bartering with other single parents can be very helpful. Explore equally creative options to take some of the burden off your shoulders.

Mary's Story

Mary is a 35-year-old single parent with limited financial resources. She has a 13-year-old daughter, and her parents live two hours away. Most of her friends are married. Getting to the grocery store was difficult because of her work schedule. She worked out an arrangement with a neighbor who had the time to shop regularly. The neighbor did the shopping. Mary, in turn, did the neighbor's laundry. Mary also needed some financial advice and called on a friend who is a financial consultant. To pay for the service, she offered to baby-sit her friend's children until the debt was paid. She and her daughter took turns baby-sitting.

Take care of yourself.   Take a close look at the weekly planner you created in Chapter Five. Is there time for you? It is

especially important to make time for yourself, to rest and reju-
venate, when you are the primary caregiver. If you have an ex-
spouse who takes the children periodically, use that time for
yourself and your social life. Plan to do chores during the week
whenever possible so you can have fun on weekends.

The single part-time parent.   Being a noncustodial parent has its share of ups and downs, rewards and frustrations.
Part-time parents often have difficulty finding a balance in their
time with their children, walking a tightrope between overindul-
gence and discipline.

Ralph's Story

Ralph believes the "unnatural intensity" associated with short visits with his children, versus a normal flow of everyday visits, made
it difficult for him to be a single parent. The parenting role seemed
unnatural; too much attention had to be always on the children
when they were with him. Ralph believed he had lost touch with
the daily happenings—his children's friends, homework assignments, little accomplishments.

His solution was to plan more time, frequently at his home, doing normal things. He worked out an arrangement at work to
leave early once a week to pick up his children directly after
school. They had dinner at his house, did their homework, and
then went home. This allowed Ralph to be more a part of his children's "regular" lives. (It also gave his ex-wife an evening to herself.) Many times his children invited friends to come along, so
Ralph could meet them too. He felt more quality and continuity
from these visits than from every-other weekend.

The more you can work together with your former spouse to
negotiate and accommodate everyone's needs (including the
children's), the easier it will be for everyone involved. Communicating with an ex-spouse and working out the details of visitation may be very difficult. Try to keep your personal feelings
about your ex-spouse to yourself. Complain to your friends, not
your children. When dealing with your ex, keep your focus on

the children's best interests. It is important to his or her development that your child have a relationship with both parents. It is generally better for your child to know the other parent personally than to go through life with unanswered questions and frustrations.

Communication with your children is equally important. Mommy may let them do things Daddy doesn't. The rules at Daddy's house may be different than at Mommy's. Try not to turn the differences into a competition or a battleground. Just explain why you have your rules and that's that. If one parent has only "fun" times, try to get him or her to take on more "regular" time so that you're not the only disciplinarian. When communication is impossible, try to find a third-party intermediary or get professional help.

Finances. For many single parents, financial concerns are one of the hardest issues to manage, particularly if you receive no (or erratic) child-support payments. Whether you have help or not, this is an area to take charge of immediately. Get the advice you need, and plan accordingly. Take stock of your current financial state now. Fill in the budget you have set for yourself and then track your expenses for a month to see where you are on target and where you may need to make some adjustments.

Monthly Budget

	Budget	Actual
Food		
Mortgage/rent		
Child care		
Household help		
Phone		
Electricity		
Gas		
Doctors Yours		

Child(ren)'s		
Dentist Yours		
Child(ren)'s		

Insurance
  Medical
  Home		

Car		
Emergency fund		
Car upkeep/transportation		
Educational training		
Entertainment		
Grooming (hair, nails)		
Clothes Child(ren)'s		
Yours		
Loans		
Vacation fund		
Savings		
Total expenses		
Income after taxes		
Child support		
Other assistance		
Total income		
Difference		

When your expenses exceed your income, it is time to find ways to cut back. Answer the following questions:

What can I live without?

How can I save money on food or clothing?

Should I get a loan? Could I pay it back?

What could I do to increase my income?

Short term?

Long term?

Working and paying for child care is one of the biggest obstacles. Can you barter services with another parent who either doesn't work or has a different schedule? Or can you get the necessary training to have your own home child-care program so that you can take care of your child and make money, too? Or can you find a job with an employer that provides assistance with child-care expenses?

Child support.   As a single custodial parent, you must realize you *deserve* child support. If you are not receiving support, seek legal counsel, either from a private attorney or from a government agency. Many states have set up ombudsman offices to help women collect support. Consult your Department of Child and Family Services.

You need certain information about your child's other parent to start collection proceedings. Find out his or her:

- Social security number.
- Past and/or present employer.
- Names and addresses of relatives and friends.
- Present or past address and phone number.
- Past legal history (overdue bills, arrests, etc.) (if you know it).

Keep in mind that if you must resort to legal proceedings, it will take time to get the support you deserve. Even then you may not receive the payments as ordered. "About half the mothers who have been awarded child support by the courts do not get full payments regularly."[4] You should build this possibility into your financial plan.

Sleep—how little you get/how much you need. Studies show that women today who work and raise a family have lost one-and-a-half hours of sleep nightly. As we listen to comments from seminar participants and focus groups, we hear that lack of sleep is a major problem, particularly for single parents.

With young children, your sleep is often erratic because of the child's erratic sleep habits. As children grow, there are more opportunities to get sound sleep. Whatever your situation, try some of the following techniques to help you feel more rested and relaxed.

1. Take cat naps. Find a quiet place at lunch time and close your eyes for 5 to 10 minutes. Take a five-minute rest before dinner. Get extra sleep on the weekends—sleep when your young child naps.
2. Take deep breaths often during the day.
3. Learn to meditate and visualize.
4. Use friends and support groups to let off steam.
5. Exercise daily—if you cannot get out because of a lack of a baby-sitter, walk after dinner with your child(ren) or do a video exercise program with them or while they do homework.
6. Let your child sleep over at someone else's house and sleep in the next morning. (You can swap once in a while with the parents of your child's friend.)

Final Thoughts

Single parenting can be an extremely rewarding experience for you and your child. You'll probably need a strong support network though to keep balance so that you can enjoy it and find time for fun.

- Try to keep a perspective on your life by surrounding yourself with support from others.
- Learn from others who have gone through it.
- Ask for help from others, including your child(ren). Don't try to do everything yourself.
- Remember to stay organized and plan for the long term.

- Be sure to keep your personal and career aspirations alive. They may be on "hold" today, but tomorrow is a new day.
- Have hope. It will help you get through the bad times.
- Try the following meditation exercise.

You're not alone meditation[5]

In the darkness of night when you cannot sleep and you worry about the bills and your job and your parenting, take four deep breaths and begin to visualize the millions of single parents in this country, your friends and family holding hands and surrounding you with understanding and support. Feel their strength, hope, and perseverance. As they draw closer to you, feel the energy and acknowledgment that you are doing a good job. Keep the image alive and slowly close your eyes. Feel the stress and worry leaving your body. Know that you are not alone. Say it out loud, "I am not alone."

BLENDED FAMILIES

Because 45 to 50 percent of marriages end in divorce and 80 percent of those divorced remarry (and more than half divorce again), you may be part of a blended family at some time, if you are not already. At least 7 million children become part of a blended family each year. By the end of this decade, more than 60 percent of all families in this country will be blended families.

The term *blended families* has replaced what was once referred to as stepfamilies. The word *blended* is a more harmonious word, but it is deceiving. Blending a family is quite often not a harmonious process. In 40 percent of blended homes, the conflict between the new parent and children is so strong that it destroys the new family.

Deciding to Remarry and Become Part of a Blended Family

In Carolyn Johnson's book, *How to Blend a Family*, she writes about the need to reestablish a family unit after divorce. There is such a strong desire to feel "whole" again after divorce that re-marriage and blending a family can take on a fantasy quality.[6] Re-marriage is not necessarily the solution to single parenting, however. The decision to remarry has grave consequences for you and your children. Do your best to stay grounded in reality.

Complete the accompanying questionnaire honestly to help you establish your readiness for remarriage.

If you answer many of the questions no, you may not be ready to blend your two families. Discuss the answers with your intended spouse and decide whether the two families are ready to be blended. Ask whether you need time as individuals and as parents to heal the wounds sustained by previous divorce. Ask whether your children need time and/or counseling.

To successfully blend, there must be:

- Common values and goals.
- A commitment to the marriage.
- Understanding.
- Patience.
- Good communication among all family members.

Discuss with your proposed spouse, how you would handle the following scenarios.

Scenario 1. You and your new spouse have one child each, 15 and 17. Your husband's daughter leaves her clothes all over the house. When you arrive home before your husband and you ask her to pick up her things, she replies, "You are not my mother! And anyway my dad doesn't care if I leave them."

What would you reply? How would the other parent react? What would you need to work out?

Scenario 2. You and your spouse have two children, 12 and 16 years old. Your wife has partial custody of the 12-year-old (weekends) and you have full custody of the 16-year-old. You and your spouse have agreed it is important to have some time alone out of the house. You travel frequently during the week. You are looking forward to a nice quiet evening on Saturday. On Saturday morning, your stepdaughter informs you she is joining you that evening.

Are We Ready To Blend?

		Yes	No
1.	Have you reestablished yourself as a whole person? We define a "whole" person as one who has dealt honestly with the past (divorce, etc.) and is able to take care of oneself emotionally, physically, financially, and intellectually without a relationship or marriage.	☐	☐
2.	Have you given yourself a sufficient period of time to deal with your grief and anger from your previous marriage?	☐	☐
3.	Are your children recovered from the divorce and emotionally stable?	☐	☐
4.	Have you dated your proposed spouse for at least six months?	☐	☐
5.	Have you discussed the possibility of remarriage with your children?	☐	☐
6.	Do your children like and get along with your intended spouse?	☐	☐
7.	Do your children like and get along with your intended spouse's children?	☐	☐
8.	What will your living arrangements be like?	☐	☐
9.	Will your family have to move?	☐	☐
10.	Will your potential partner's family have to move?	☐	☐
11.	Will any of the children have to change schools?	☐	☐
12.	Will there be children from both parents in the house?	☐	☐
13.	Do you have a compatible system of values?	☐	☐
14.	Are your family norms compatible?	☐	☐
15.	Do you believe you should parent your intended spouse's children?	☐	☐
16.	Does your spouse believe she or he should parent your children?	☐	☐
17.	Do you and your intended spouse have similar parenting styles?	☐	☐
18.	Will your children resist parenting by another person?	☐	☐
19.	Do you agree on what the house rules will be?	☐	☐
20.	Do you agree on how rules should be enforced (discipline)?	☐	☐
21.	Are there noncustodial children to consider?	☐	☐
22.	Have you and your intended spouse both completed the Values Clarification Exercise in Chapter Two?	☐	☐
23.	Have you discussed your differences and potential solutions to conflicts?	☐	☐
24.	Have you discussed the reasons for previous divorce(s)?	☐	☐
25.	Have you discussed adjustments/changes that may be required of or from ex-spouses (visitation rights, etc.)?	☐	☐

Scenario 3.   You have joint custody of a 10-year-old (alternate weekends, some days during the week). Your husband has partial custody of two children (9 and 11) on weekends. Your husband works five days, two nights a week and all day Saturday. On Sunday, he invites his mother for the day. You have agreed that time together without other family is important to your relationship.

Strategies for Blended Families

Once you have dealt with these issues, you are ready to commit to a new relationship and a blended family.

Experts agree that the relationship between you and your new spouse should be primary, and the relationship between parents and children secondary.

> The first ingredient for a happy family is a well put-together mother and father. They will not be perfect, but they are working at evicting the dragons from their souls and have established a loving relationship together that gives their children a sense of security. Within the circle of home there is safety, safety because there is genuine love, open communication and a way of handling conflict that is well defined and acceptable.[7]

Recognize that the transition between you and your new family members will be more successful if children are well informed of what will happen to them, they are given their own personal space, and you respect the relationship between the child and the other biological parent. Here are some other ideas to keep your new family healthy and on track.

- Be yourself.
- Be a spouse first, and stepparent second.[8]
- Be honest about your feelings and needs.
- Communicate your feelings and needs and encourage others to do so as well.
- With your spouse, define your limits for dealing with each other's children.
- Keep a sense of humor.
- Be flexible.
- Join a blended family support group.

- Make sure children have personal space and room for their belongings.
- Get counseling when you can't work things out.
- Risk asserting authority.
- Learn and respect the history that exists among children and their parents.
- Commit to working out problems.
- Be prepared for trade-offs and compromises.

Use communication and organizational skills to redefine your balance and make your new family life work.

BUSINESS TRAVEL WHILE CARING FOR OTHERS

Many of us have jobs that require travel. Travel adds another dimension to your work and family life. To manage your travel and home responsibilities, you have to use some of the skills we have already discussed such as planning, delegating, arranging for overnight care, and communicating effectively.

Leaving home with a sense of confidence and comfort is no easy task. To manage travel, it takes strong organizational skills and an ability to clearly communicate your plans and ideas. Complete the accompanying questionnaire to see how you are doing combining business travel and family.

Traveler: Do You Need Aid?

Rate yourself on a scale of 1 to 5, with 1 being strongly agree and 5 strongly disagree. The higher your total score, the more you need to pay attention to this section.

I leave for a trip feeling secure and organized about the arrangements I have made for my family.   _____

I am confident about my child's well-being while I am away.   _____

I am comfortable that others monitor my child's daily activities when I am away.   _____

It is easy to reconnect with my partner after a business trip.   _____

Business travel is a positive experience for myself and my family.   _____

    Total score   _____

In addition to the energy work normally requires, travel adds stress and exhaustion due to commuting from airports, jet lag, interrupted and insufficient sleep, and a general worry over making connections, hotel reservations, and the like. To be able to handle that extra stress, you need to leave knowing everything is all right at home.

Each trip can be divided into three stages:

- Planning the trip.
- The trip itself.
- Reentry.

Before You Leave

It takes serious planning and well-informed support systems to be able to leave for a trip with peace of mind.

For you. Make reasonable travel and hotel arrangements. Be realistic; don't schedule in exhaustion or increase the chances of missed flights and lost luggage. If you can do it in a day, even if it's a long day, do it. You'll be surprised what's possible. If you travel frequently, make it easy for yourself. Keep a prepacked toiletry bag so all you have to add is clothes. Take a sweat suit or casual clothes for after work and cold hotel rooms. Pack clothes that don't wrinkle. Take one carryon bag.

For your caregiver. Discuss any information and special instructions on medications, visitation rights, child's preferred foods, household rules, bedtime routines, night fears, and so on. Leave suggested menus or preprepared foods. Leave a notebook or "While I'm Away" report sheet for your caregiver to track the child's activities, development, foods eaten, and emotions while you're gone. If you have multiple care arrangements with special pickups, make sure each caregiver has information on each other (phone number, address). Discuss ways to make each day a bit special—a new book, a trip to the ice cream shop.

For your child. Communicate when you are leaving, what you will be doing, and especially when you will return. Set a time when you will call home. Tell them you will miss them.

For the younger child, reassure any fears. Listen to their concerns and acknowledge that they are real. For young children, the concept of time is difficult. Help them realize what it means to be away for a day, or three days, or a week. Compare it to things they understand in their own world, such as how long it takes to visit a distant relative or the time they sleep at night. Relate it to something they might have experienced. For a young child, make a special calendar showing the days you will be away. Show the child on a map where you are going. For an older child, discuss ways she or he can help while you are gone. Make sure limits are set and consequences are clear. Let them know how they can reach you. Children can gain confidence and independence when they pitch in for a parent.

For your elder. Communicate the same information you did with your children. Listen to any concerns about your absence. Recognize they too may have fears about your absence. Reassure them by letting them know you will keep in contact. Make sure neighbors, friends, or other relatives are notified of your absence and are asked to check on them or take over what you normally do. Arrange for temporary support services if necessary. Leave detailed written information on medication, doctors, and where you can be reached.

For your spouse/partner. Go over lists of responsibilities, caregivers for children/elders, and any concerns. Probe for clarification and listen for any signs of discomfort. For the spouse/partner left behind, it is often difficult to assume more responsibilities. Expect some feelings of resentment. Figure out together how the things you normally do will get done. Plan a special time together or something special you can do for your spouse/partner when you return.

For co-workers. Leave all flight and hotel information. Let them know when and how often you will check in. Leave a list of urgent matters and who else can handle them in your absence.

Use the accompanying checklist to help you be organized.

Traveler's Checklist

Work

- [ ] Notify supervisor and secretary of the dates of your trip and when you will return
- [ ] Make travel and hotel reservations; leave your itinerary
- [ ] Where you can be reached
- [ ] How often you will call for messages
- [ ] Who can cover your calls, duties, and/or emergencies in your absence

Home

Child(ren)
- [ ] Talk to child(ren) about your trip, the rules while you're gone, when you'll call, when you'll return
- [ ] Child-care arrangements
  - _____ Meals
  - _____ Transportation
  - _____ Appointments
  - _____ Overnight/extended hour care, if necessary
  - _____ Tape a favorite bedtime story
  - _____ Mark a calendar
  - _____ Mark a map
  - _____ Leave a note on their pillow

Caregiver
- [ ] Notify caregiver of your travel plans
- [ ] Make any special arrangements (like if you need to give the caregiver permission to let your child go home with a neighbor for a few days)
- [ ] Notify the caregiver of any changes in backup procedures
- [ ] Special instructions

Elders
- [ ] Notify elders of your travel plans and reassure them you will take care of everything you normally do
- [ ] Arrange for backup care or supervision
- [ ] Let them know how they can reach you

Spouse/Partner
- [ ] Notify them of travel plans
- [ ] Let them know what extra things will need to get done while you are gone (child pickup, transportation, deliveries, chores). Figure out together how it will be handled.

You
- [ ] Pack
- [ ] Travel arrangements

Miscellaneous
- [ ] Pet care
- [ ] Plant care
- [ ] Yard work
- [ ] Stop newspaper/mail for long trips

Taking Care of Yourself While Traveling

Business travel is hard work. It is not as glamorous as those who stay home imagine. Even with all the work and stress, however, travel time is an opportunity to take some time for yourself. Make sure you take care of yourself. Eat healthy, regular meals. Get enough sleep (some of us need mild sleep aids in hotels). Exercise.

Travel can be a relief from all your responsibilities at home and at work. It gives you an opportunity to focus on one task. But try to utilize the time away for you as well as work—relax in your hotel room, read a good book, get a massage, enjoy the peace and quiet, use the hotel's exercise facility, go to a museum, see the sights, and/or enjoy a good restaurant.

Travel can give you time to yourself, time to think. It gives you an opportunity to assess what you need and want and to go back directed and refocused on work and family responsibilities. Give yourself permission to rest or read for fun on the way home rather than working. If at all possible, don't push your schedule so hard that you are exhausted when you get home. One traveling mom we know sometimes plans to get home from hectic trips after her children are asleep so that she can respond to their enthusiastic greetings with equal enthusiasm the next morning.

Stay in touch with your family. Call home at the designated time and share your day. Send a postcard to each child and elder. Even if it gets home after you do, your family will know you were thinking of them. Bring little souvenirs home—t-shirts, models of a famous landmark, convention toys, and gizmos. Your kids will love it. Maybe they'll even take the gifts to school for show-and-tell.

Reentry

There is no place like home! Practically everyone looks forward to getting back into his or her own surroundings. Plus, there is the initial excitement of being greeted by those you left behind. Once the initial fanfare has subsided, it may take time to find the rhythm again. Everyone adjusts in his or her own time. Check in with everyone.

With children, ask the high and low points of their days while you were gone. Acknowledge and support their changes and new independence.

With the caregiver, find out about any physical or emotional concerns or any developmental changes. Ask what she or he would change next time you travel.

With elders, call or visit. Find out how things went in your absence and if they'd like something done differently next time.

With spouse/partner, ask what worked and what did not. Decide what you will change the next time you travel. Allow the spouse/partner to vent some feelings. Show appreciation for the extra effort she or he put out in your absence.

For yourself, assess what made the trip easy or difficult. Try not to have too high expectations on how home responsibilities will get done in your absence. Others will do things differently. Don't come home and complain that chores were done incorrectly. Be glad you had the help you needed while you were away. Praise those that did the caregiving while you were away. They will appreciate your acknowledgment of their efforts. Remember, your traveling can be hard on those left behind. Identify what you need to get back into your rhythm and end the trip, unpacking, playing with the children, or finishing your travel expense report, for example.

A Learning Experience for All

Travel experiences can be shared in many ways with your family. Make the most of your time away by sharing what you have seen and heard. Even if you have seen only the inside of hotels, airports, and restaurants, you can share differences and similarities in local accents, customs, geographical information, and history of the areas. The more you can communicate your experiences while traveling, the more you will stay connected to your family.

Bonnie's Story

When I traveled, I would bring postcards or representative items of the city to share with my family. I would tell stories of anything I had learned, even if it was from a cabdriver. My daughter still remembers anecdotal stories of the trips, and occasionally she brings it up as a topic of conversation. We reminisce, laugh, and find that it had bonded us in a way other experiences have not.

Traveling can be hard, but it can also be rewarding to all. By sharing what you have seen and done, you will have the chance to put some closure on what you have experienced. Instead of just another business trip, it can be a trip that enhances your life experience.

Take the Children with You

You may want to consider taking your child with you, always or on special trips.

Beverly's Story

Beverly was married and had a 9-year-old daughter and a 3-month-old son when she got a promotion. She works for a large corporation, and her new job required her to travel frequently. Her husband often travels, too. Beverly looked at her options of hiring a full-time, in-house caregiver when she traveled (her son was in family day care), but she wanted to continue breast-feeding.

She discovered she was able to get her travel schedule in advance. Knowing she was going to travel in the summer, she researched the cost of taking both children with her. She discovered the baby could fly for free and her daughter's fare cost from $1 to $94. Then she called the hotels in the destination city and requested sitters. Her first trip was very successful, and she was glad to be able to be with her children in the evening. The cost of the flights and sitters was still cheaper than a full-time in-home caregiver. But most importantly, Beverly could stay close to her children while working and continue to breast-feed.

Beverly is very creative. She traveled to many different cities, and often she had relatives or friends who could also help out. She continued these creative arrangements until her son became a toddler. He wasn't quite as portable then and was ready for a child-care center experience.

Beverly's story is unusual but not unique. Like Beverly, others have traveled with their children as a way to fulfill parenting and working goals simultaneously. Traveling and parenting is not for everyone, but it really works for some. Other parents have told us they take children occasionally, particularly if they are going to a historic city or somewhere relatives live who can watch the child while the parent works.

RESOURCES

Averick, Leah Shifrin. *How In-Laws Relate: It's All Relative.* New York: Shapolsky Publishers, 1989.

Bauer, Caroline Feeler. *My Mom Travels A Lot.* New York: Puffin Books, 1981.

Bingham, Mindy, and Sandy Stryker. *More Choices: A Strategic Planning Guide for Mixing Career and Family.* Santa Barbara, Calif.: Advocacy Press, 1987.

Chusmir, Leonard H. *Thank God It's Monday: The Guide to a Happier Job.* New York: New America Library, 1990.

Dietz, Susan. *Single File: How To Live Happily Forever after with or without Prince Charming.* New York: St. Martin's Press, 1990.

Einstein, Elizabeth. *The Stepfamily: Living, Loving and Learning.* New York: Macmillan, 1982.

Einstein, Elizabeth, and Linda Albert. *Strengthening Your Stepfamily.* New York: Random House, 1986.

Gilbert, Sara D. *By Yourself.* New York: Lothrop, Lee and Shepard Books, 1983.

Hirsch, Roseann. *Super Working Mom's Handbook*. New York: Warner Books, 1986.

Hunt, M. Gladys. "Guidelines to Happy Families." *Raising a Joyful Family*. New York: Harper & Row, 1983.

Johnson, Carolyn. *How To Blend a Family*. Grand Rapids, Mich.: Zondervan Publishing House, 1989.

Lansky, Vicki. *Traveling with Your Baby*. Toronto and New York: Bantam Books, 1985.

Lansky, Vicki. *Vicki Lansky's Divorce Book for Parents*. New York: New America Library, 1989.

Portnoy, Sanford, and Joan Flynn Portnoy. *How to Take Great Trips with Your Kids*. Harvard, Mass.: Harvard Common Press, 1983.

Step Family Association of America
215 Centennial Mall South, Suite 212
Lincoln, NE 68508-1834

The Capable Kid Counseling Centers
1615 Orrington Avenue
Evanston, IL 60201
(708) 866-7335

NOTES

1. Anne Wilson Schaef, *Meditations for Women Who Do Too Much* (San Francisco, Calif.: Harper & Row, 1990), quoting Rachel Carson.
2. Kenneth Labich, "Can Your Career Hurt Your Kids?" *Fortune*, May 20, 1991, p. 48.
3. Anna Michaels, *Single Parent's Survival Guide* (unpublished, 1991)
4. Labich, p. 48
5. Michaels.
6. Carolyn Johnson, *How to Blend a Family* (Grand Rapids, Mich: Zondervan Publishing House, 1989), p. 15.
7. M. Gladys Hunt, "Guidelines for Happy Families," in *Raising a Joyful Family* (New York: Harper & Row, 1983), p. 10.
8. Paul Rand, "No Easy Mix for Blended Families," Pioneer Press, April 4, 1991, p. 5.

Chapter Ten

Getting the Organization to Work with You

. . . improving the quality of work life and considering the human consequences of organizational arrangements are as important a measure of a system's "effectiveness" as economic indicators.[1]

Rosabeth Moss Kanter, *Men and Women of the Corporation*

Throughout this book, we have referred to the support that might be available from your employer. National demographics and work force trends have made it clear that all employers eventually must address the work/family conflict to continue to recruit and retain talented workers. While all employees need supportive policies and benefits, the needs of working parents have emerged at the forefront of the work/family agenda.

The corporation's efforts not only help its employees manage their work and family conflicts, but they also relate directly to corporate profitability. Studies by Catalyst, The Conference Board, Families and Work Institute, and others have demonstrated the value of policies such as parental leave, flexible work options, and sick days for children on bottom-line issues such as productivity, absenteeism, tardiness, recruitment, and retention.

CORPORATE CULTURE

A corporate culture that is truly supportive of work/family initiatives shows it not only with benefits and services. It supports the concept from top to bottom, inside and out. It does not just pay lip service to being "family-friendly." It embraces and respects family. Its top-level executives are examples of its philosophy and role models for others.

Within a corporate culture supportive of balanced employee lives, top management articulates that belief and then clearly defines the guidelines for managers to follow in supervising employees with families. Openness between managers and employees is encouraged so that they may work together to find solutions to work/family conflicts. Employees and managers are given the resources they need to do their jobs well while also managing a healthy personal and family life.

How Does Your Company Rate?

Answer each of the following questions by circling either yes or no. Circle no if you don't know the answer. Even if an investigation would reveal that the answer was yes, the corporate failure to publicize the policy or program counts as a no. While not a comprehensive guide to a work/family initiative, your answers will help you assess the corporate culture.

1. Has the company done a complete work/family organizational needs assessment? Yes No
2. Have the results been communicated to all employees? Yes No
3. Are there women who hold senior-level jobs? Yes No
4. Are flexible benefits such as DCAP in place? Yes No
5. Has upper management articulated its philosophy on work and family issues? Yes No
6. Is that philosophy in writing? Yes No
7. Has upper management set guidelines for middle management on how to handle work/family conflicts? Yes No
8. Is parental or family leave available? Yes No
9. Has anyone taken a parental or family leave? Yes No
10. Are flexible work options available? Yes No
11. Are flexible work options in use? Yes No
12. Has upper management set guidelines or a policy for flexible work options? Yes No
13. Have managers been trained to implement the policy? Yes No
14. Have employees been trained in strategies to combine work and family (through workshops, seminars, training programs)? Yes No
15. Has an individual in upper management taken a leave of absence for family reasons? Yes No
16. Was that person male? Yes No

17. Has the company held a Family Day event?   Yes   No
18. Did senior management attend the Family Day event?   Yes   No
19. Do you have a work/family coordinator?   Yes   No
20. Does the work/family coordinator or individual responsible
     for work/family programs report to a senior executive? Yes   No

Ratings: 16–20 points   Excellent: Family-friendly company
          11–15 points   Good: Good company to work for; on the right track
          6–10 points   Fair: Fair company
          0–5 points   Poor: This company needs help

WHAT CAN BE DONE?

A company, large or small, can take a number of steps that do not require major changes to help employees balance work and family. Encourage your company to provide resources. If your company already does, take advantage of them.

Education and Information

The company can provide a forum for education and a source for information for working parents to get ideas and strategies for balancing their work and family demands. A resource library can include books, pamphlets, videos, and audiocassettes. Educational programs presented by local consultants or representatives of community groups (generally held on-site for those who are interested) can offer insight into particular areas for "quick hits" of useful information. Topics can include:

- Parenting skills.
- Communicating with children.
- Talking with your elders.
- Discipline.
- Planning your maternity leave.
- Fathering and partnering in the 90s.
- Raising adolescents.
- Financial planning.
- Latchkey children.

- Traveling and parenting.
- Career and life planning.
- The ins and outs of summer care.
- Talking with your supervisor about work/family conflicts.
- Stepparenting.
- Single parenting.
- Taking care of yourself.
- How to talk to your children about difficult subjects (like drugs, sex, AIDS).

Support groups of working parents can also be of enormous benefit. Lunchtime meetings of parents with children of similar ages or similar concerns (latchkey, preschool, single parenting, stepparenting, divorce) allow employees to share their solutions, frustrations, and guilt in a constructive way. Some companies have brought in leaders from outside the company. Others asked human resources personnel to coordinate and facilitate these groups, or involved members of their work and family task force. Sometimes these groups can also generate an informal database of information on child-care providers, before/after-school and summer-care programs and other community resources available to working parents.

Policies and Benefits

There are a wide range of benefits and policies employers can offer to assist working parents. Many options can be planned and put into action in a consortium approach with other nearby employers to alleviate the financial and other concerns of any one employer. Benefits and policies most often requested by employees in our assessments include:

- Flexibility in management style and practices.
- Flexible work options (flextime, telecommuting, part-time work, job sharing, compressed workweek, summer hours).
- Reserved slots or corporate discounts in child-care centers near the work site or employees' homes.
- Pretax payment of child-care expenses (DCAP).

- Cafeteria benefits.
- Reimbursement for child-care expenses incurred due to overtime or business travel.
- On-site/near-site child-care center.
- A sick-child-care center, program or policy; subsidies for sick-child-care expenses.
- Child-care programs (summer and holiday care, before/after-school care).
- Revised sick day policies that allow an employee to take time off to care for a sick child (without lying about the reason for the absence).
- Resource and referral (a hot line or other assistance in finding child and/or elder care).
- Compensation time for personal time spent on business travel.
- The ability to take personal or vacation days in hours or half days.
- A family leave, generally unpaid but with benefits and job guarantee.
- A "Family Day at Work" where employees can introduce their families to their workplace and co-workers and teach their children more about what they do and why they do it.

Which policies or services will work best for your organization depends on an accurate assessment of the employee population's needs and upper management's commitment to changes that will address those needs.

HOW CAN YOU HELP START A WORK/FAMILY INITIATIVE AT YOUR COMPANY?

If your company has done very little to initiate a work/family program, you can help it begin by taking the following steps.

1. Contact your human resources director and ask what benefits and policies are in place. You might be surprised what is available but hasn't been well communicated. Find out the future direction of the company.

2. Gather articles and data on companies known for their work/family support, particularly companies which compete with your company for talented employees. (*Working Mother* provides a yearly list of the "Best Companies for Working Mothers.") Also read about companies actively addressing work/family issues in *Companies That Care* and *Kincare*, listed in Resources.

3. Suggest an employee task force be formed to identify the issues and potential solutions.

4. Suggest the company do an organizational needs assessment to find out more about employee needs and how they affect productivity.

5. Find a champion at a high level who is willing to support and promote the work/family initiative.

6. Don't give up! Sometimes companies take a long time to get started.

To learn more about what employers can do, contact us at Managing Work & Family, Inc., 912 Crain Street, Evanston, IL 60202, or call 1-800-472-4698. Managing Work and Family, Inc., is a work/family consulting and training firm. We conduct organizational needs assessments, train managers and employees, assist in the development of flexible working options and benefits, consult on a wide range of work/family benefits and provide supportive products such as work/family Kopy Kits, training videos, child/elder care pamphlets, and Family Days at Work events.

RESOURCES

Fernandez, John P. *Child Care and Corporate Productivity: Resolving Family/Work Conflicts.* Lexington, Mass.: Lexington Books/D. C. Heath, 1986.

Jamieson, David, and Julie O'Mara. *Managing Workforce 2000: Gaining the Diversity Advantage.* San Francisco: Jossey-Bass, 1991.

Kanter, Rosabeth Moss. *Men and Women of the Corporation.* New York: Basic Books, 1977.

Morgan, Hal, and Kerry Tucker. *Companies That Care.* New York: Simon & Schuster, 1991.

Olmstead, Barney, and Suzanne Smith. *Creating a Flexible Workplace: How to Select and Manage Alternative Work Options.* New York: AMACOM, 1989.

Smith, Dayle M. *Kincare and the American Corporation.* Homewood, Ill.: Richard D. Irwin, Inc., 1991.

Sweeney, John J., and Karen Nussbaum. *Solutions for the New Workforce: Policies for a New Social Contract.* Washington, D.C.: Seven Locks Press, 1989.
Work and Health: Strategies for Maintaining a Vital Workforce. Greenvale, N.Y.: Panel Publishers, Inc., 1989.

Newsletters

Buraff Publications, Washington, D.C.: *The National Report on Work & Family*
Work and Family Connection, Inc., Minnetonka, Minn.: *Work & Family Newsbrief*

Organizations

Bureau of National Affairs, Inc.
1231 25th Street, N.W.
Washington, DC 20037
(202) 452-4895

New Ways to Work
149 Ninth Street
San Francisco, CA 94103
(415) 552-1000
Specialists in flexible management and flexible work options.

The Partnership Group, Inc.
840 West Main Street
Lansdale, PA 19446
(215) 362-5070
A Family Resource Service for employers, employees and their families.

Women's Bureau
U.S. Department of Labor
Office of the Secretary
Washington, DC 02010
(202) 523-8916

NOTES

1. Rosabeth Moss Kanter, *Men and Women of the Corporation* (New York: Basic Books, 1977), p. 265.

Chapter Eleven

Taking Care of Yourself

Yesterday is a canceled check. Tomorrow is a promissory note. Today is cash in hand; spend it wisely.

Anonymous

"I never have time for myself."
"I couldn't possibly find an hour to exercise."
"I don't have any time left in the day for me."

We have heard these comments from many individuals who work and care for others. Somehow time for ourselves always sinks to the bottom of our list. While we would never break an appointment with a client or a co-worker and try hard to meet our agreements with family members, most of us will cancel an appointment with or for ourselves at the drop of a hat.

Taking care of yourself should be as high on your priority list as getting to work on time and spending time with children and elders. If it's not high on your priority list, you need to reevaluate. What are the risks if you don't?

- Poor health.
- Poor judgment/fatigue.
- Poor energy.
- Poor attitude.
- Poor caregiver.
- Poor partner.

Here is an exercise to see how you treat yourself.

	Never	Rarely	Sometimes	Frequently	Always
1. I exercise at least three times a week.	1	2	3	4	5
2. I take a midmorning break that is relaxing or fun such as breathing deeply, closing my eyes, reading something light or eating a healthy snack.	1	2	3	4	5
3. I often have lunch away from my desk in a relaxing environment.	1	2	3	4	5
4. I walk outside during the day.	1	2	3	4	5
5. On my commute home from work, I focus on relaxing (not thinking about work, chores, etc.).	1	2	3	4	5
6. I plan time alone during the week for at least one hour.	1	2	3	4	5
7. If a family member asks me to do something for them and I have planned an evening out for relaxation, I say no.	1	2	3	4	5
8. I get yearly physical checkups.	1	2	3	4	5
9. I enjoy my life on the whole.	1	2	3	4	5
10. I laugh at least once a day.	1	2	3	4	5

Rating scale:

41–50 Doing great! Keep up the good work.

31–40 Good job. Look at the questions where you had a low score and see if you can find a way to incorporate those items into your life.

21–30 Not bad, but you probably treat others better than you treat yourself. Plan some activities just for you.

10–20 Reevaluate your priorities—you need to take better care of yourself.

If you rated on the low end, take time now to mark some days on the calendar just for you. Remember, if someone asks you to do something for them on those days, give yourself permission to say no. At first, tell a white lie if you have to to protect that time. With practice, you'll be able to acknowledge that time for you is as good a reason as any for not changing your plans.

What can you do at work?

- Stretch at break time.
- Take a walk.
- Climb stairs.
- Meditate.
- Read a novel or book for information you need on your lunch hour.
- Listen to relaxing music.
- Do breathing exercises.
- Avoid caffeine and sugar.

What can you do at home?

- Listen to music.
- Develop an exercise program.
- Meditate.
- Take a walk after dinner.
- Take a warm bath or shower.
- Do yoga.
- Lie down alone and do relaxation exercises.
- Visit with a friend.
- Take up a hobby that emphasizes different skills than those you use at work.
- Get a back rub or massage.
- Buy yourself a flower.

Don't wait for other people to take care of you (e.g., buy you a nice dinner, invite you out for a relaxing evening). Take charge and plan it for yourself. It is important for everyone to have something to look forward to, and not just your vacation. You deserve to have something to look forward to every day. But speaking of vacations—take them. And not just an occasional day here and there but a full week (better yet, two or three) to give yourself a real break from routine and replenish your energy. When you come home, keep being good to yourself.

Inspiration. Here is a way to get started. Make a list of simple pleasures, things that would enhance the quality of your everyday life. Develop a way of integrating those pleasures into your everyday life. Look for things that can fit into your busy work and family life. Taking care of yourself doesn't always require a quantity of time. It is the quality that will refresh you and keep you energized.

Things that Bring Joy to My Life

Activity	When I Could Do It
1.	
2.	
3.	
4.	
5.	

When you are happy and content, it will be that much easier to love and care for the people in your life who matter. We hope that some of the ideas presented in or sparked by this book will help you find a more satisfying balance between work and family life.

Bibliography

Abraham, Danielson, Eberle, Green, Rosenberg, and Stone. *Reinventing Home: Six Working Women Look at Their Home Lives*. New York: Plume, 1991.

American Health Care Association. *How to Select a Nursing Home*. 1200 15th St. N.W., Washington, D.C. 20005.

Apter, Terri. *Why Women Don't Have Wives: Professional Success and Motherhood*. New York: Schocken Books, 1985.

Ashery, Rebecca Sager, and Michelle Margolin Basen. *Guide for Parents with Careers: Ideas on How to Cope*. Washington, D.C.: Acropolis Books, Ltd., 1991.

Auerbach, Stevanne. *Choosing Child Care: A Guide for Parents*. New York: Dutton, 1981.

Averick, Leah Shifrin. *How In-Laws Relate: It's All Relative*. New York: Shapolsky Publishers, 1989.

Banks, Ann. *Alone at Home: A Kid's Guide to Being in Charge*. New York: Puffin Books, 1989.

Barret, Patti. *Too Busy to Clean: Over 500 Tips and Techniques to Make Housecleaning Easier*. Pownal, Vt.: Storey Communications, 1990.

Barrett, Nina. *I Wish Someone Had Told Me: Comfort, Support & Advice for New Moms from More Than 60 Real-Life Mothers*. New York: Simon & Schuster, 1990.

Bartholomew. *I Come as A Brother*. Taos, N.M.: High Mesa Press, 1986.

Bauer, Caroline Feeler. *My Mom Travels a Lot*. New York: Puffin Books, 1981.

Beardsley, Lyda. *Good Day/Bad Day: The Child's Experience of Child Care*. New York: Columbia University Teachers College Press, 1990.

Benjamin, Ben. *Are You Tense?* New York: Pantheon Books, 1978.

Benson, Herbert. *The Relaxation Response*. New York: Morrow, 1975.

Berg, Barbara J. *The Crisis of the Working Mother: Resolving the Conflict between Family and Work*. New York: Summit Books, 1986.

Bergstrom, Joan. *School's Out*. Berkeley, Calif.: Ten Speed Press, 1984.

Bingham, Mindy, and Sandy Stryker. *More Choices: A Strategic Planning Guide for Mixing Career and Family.* Santa Barbara, Calif.: Advocacy Press, 1987.

Bliss, Edwin. *Getting Things Done: The ABC's of Time Management.* New York: Scribner, 1976.

Block, Joyce. *Motherhood as Metamorphosis.* New York: Penguin Books, 1990.

Blotnick, Srully, Ph.D. *Otherwise Engaged.* New York: Penguin Books, 1985.

Bolles, Richard Nelson. *What Color Is My Parachute?* Berkeley, Calif: Ten Speed Press, 1991.

Borysenko, Joan. *Guilt Is the Teacher, Love Is the Lesson.* New York: Warner Books, 1990.

Boston Children's Hospital. *New Child Health Encyclopedia: A Complete Guide for Parents.* New York: Delacorte Press/Merloyd Lawrence, 1987.

Brack, Pat and Ben. *Mom's Don't Get Sick.* Aberdeen, S.D.: Melius Publishing, 1991.

Bradshaw, John. *Healing the Shame that Binds You.* Deerfield Beach, Fla.: Health Communications, 1988.

Brazelton, T. Berry, M.D. *The Earliest Relationship: Parents, Infants and the Drama of Early Attachment.* Reading, Mass.: Addison-Wesley Publishing, 1985.

Brazelton, T. Berry, M.D. *On Becoming a Family: Growth of Attachment.* New York: Delacorte Press/Merloyd Lawrence, 1981.

Brazelton, T. Berry, M.D. *Toddlers and Parents: Declaration of Independence.* New York: Delacorte Press/Merloyd Lawrence, 1974.

Brazelton, T. Berry, M.D. *Working and Caring.* Reading, Mass.: Addison-Wesley Publishing, 1985.

Brazelton, T. Berry, M.D. *To Listen to a Child: Understanding the Normal Problems of Growing Up.* Reading, Mass.: Addison-Wesley Publishing, 1984.

Brazelton, T. Berry, M.D., and Victor C. Vaughan. *The Family: Setting Priorities.* New York: Science and Medicine Publishing Co., 1979.

Bredekamp, Sue, ed. *Developmentally Appropriate Practice in Early Childhood Programs Serving Children from Birth through Age 8 (Expanded Edition).* Washington, D.C.: National Association for the Education of Young Children, 1987.

Brenner, Barbara. *Preschool Handbook: Making the Most of Your Child's Education.* New York: Pantheon Press, 1990.

Briles, Judith. *Confidence Factor: How Self-Esteem Can Change Your Life.* New York: Mastermedia, 1990.

Brooks, Andree Aelion.*Children of Fast Track Parents: Raising Self-Sufficient and Confident Children in an Achievement Oriented World.* New York: Viking Press, 1989.

Bumagin, Victoria, and Kathryn F. Hirn. *Aging Is a Family Affair.* New York: Thomas Y. Crowell, 1979.

Burke, Jane B., and Lenora M. Yuen. *Procrastination: Why You Do It, What To Do.* Reading, Mass.: Addison-Wesley Publishing, 1983.

Butler, Robert N., and Myrna I. Lewis. *Aging and Mental Health: Positive Psychosocial Approaches.* St. Louis: The C.V. Mosby Company, 1977.

Caine, Lynn. *What Did I Do Wrong? Mothers, Children, Guilt.* New York: Arbor House, 1985.

Campbell, Jeff. *Speedcleaning.* New York: Dell Publishing, 1985.

Canape, Charlene. *Part-Time Solution: The New Strategy for Managing Your Career While Managing Motherhood.* New York: Harper & Row, 1990.

Cardozo, Arlene Rossen. *Sequencing: Having It All But Not All at Once.* New York: Atheneum Publishers, 1986.

Chusmir, Leonard H. *Thank God It's Monday: The Guide to a Happier Job.* New York: New America Library, 1990.

Clarke-Stewart, Alison. *Daycare.* Cambridge, Mass.: Harvard University Press, 1982.

Conrad, Pam. *Balancing Home and Career: Skills for Successful Life Management.* Los Altos, Calif.: Crisp Publications, 1986.

Covey, Stephen R. *Seven Habits of Highly Effective People.* New York: Simon & Schuster, 1989.

Crary, Elizabeth. *Mommy, Don't Go: A Children's Problem Solving Book.* Seattle, Wash.: Parenting Press, 1989.

Crichton, Jean. *The Age Care Sourcebook: A Resource Guide for the Aging and Their Families.* New York: Simon & Schuster, 1987.

Cuozzo, Jane Hershey. *Power Partners: How Two-Career Couples Can Play to Win.* New York: Master Media Ltd., 1990.

Dana, Nancy, and Anne Price. *Successful Breastfeeding.* Deep Haven, Minn.: Meadowbrook Press, 1985.

Daniels, Norman. *Am I My Parents' Keeper?* New York: Oxford University Press, 1988.

Dietz, Susan. *Single File: How To Live Happily Forever after with or without Prince Charming.* New York: St. Martin's Press, 1990.

Dinkmeyer, Don, and Gary D. McKay. *The Parent's Guide: Systematic Training for Effective Parenting.* Circle Pines, Minn.: American Guidance Services Inc., 1976.

Dinkmeyer, Don, and Gary D. McKay. *The Parent's Handbook: Systematic Training for Effective Parenting of Teens.* Circle Pines, Minn.: American Guidance Services, Inc., 1982.

Dinkmeyer, Don, Gary D. McKay, and James S. Dinkmeyer. *Parenting Young Children.* New York: Avon, 1969.

Donkin, Scott W. *Sitting on the Job: How to Survive the Stresses of Sitting Down to Work: A Practical Handbook.* Boston: Houghton Mifflin, 1989.

Edinberg, Mark A. *Talking with Your Aging Parents.* Boston: Shambhala Publications, Inc., 1987.

Edwards, Paul and Sarah. *Working from Home: Everything You Need to Know About Living and Working under the Same Roof.* Los Angeles: Jeremy P. Tarcher, Inc., 1990.

Einstein, Elizabeth. *The Stepfamily: Living, Loving and Learning.* New York: Macmillan, 1982.

Einstein, Elizabeth, and Linda Albert. *Strengthening Your Stepfamily.* New York: Random House, 1986.

Elder Services: The Greater Chicago Area Guide to Eldercare. Phoenix, Ariz.: The Oryx Press, 1991.

Elliot, Ruth S. *Minding the Kids: A Practical Guide to Employing Nannies, Caregivers, Babysitters and Au Pairs.* New York: Prentice Hall Press, 1990.

Eyre, Linda and Richard. *Lifebalance: Priority Balance, Attitude Balance, Goal Balance in All Areas of Your Life.* New York: Ballantine Books, 1987.

Faber, Adele, and Elaine Mazlish. *How to Talk So Kids Will Listen and Listen So Kids Will Talk.* New York: Avon Books, 1980.

Feinstein, Karen Wolk, ed. *Working Women and Families,* vol. 4. Beverly Hills, Calif.: Sage Publications, 1979.

Ferber, Richard. *Solve Your Child's Sleep Problems.* New York: Fireside Books/Simon & Schuster, 1985.

Fernandez, John P. *Child Care and Corporate Productivity: Resolving Family/Work Conflicts.* Lexington, Mass.: Lexington Books/D. C. Heath, 1986.

Fulghum, Robert. *All I Really Needed to Know I Learned in Kindergarten.* New York: Ivy Books, 1986.

Gabany, Steve G., Ph.D. *The Working Person's Survival Guide.* Terre Haute, Ind.: Hunt & Peck Publishing, 1990.

Galinsky, Ellen, and Judy David. *The Preschool Years: Family Strategies That Work—From Experts and Parents.* New York: New York Times Books, 1988.

Galinsky, Ellen, and William Hooks. *The New Extended Family: Day Care That Works.* Boston: Houghton Mifflin, 1977.

Genevie, Lois, Ph.D. *The Motherhood Report: How Women Feel about Being Mothers.* New York: Macmillan, 1987.

Germer, Jim G. *How To Make Your Boss Work for You: More than 200 Hard-Hitting Strategies, Tips, and Tactics to Keep Your Career on the Fast-Track.* Homewood, Ill.: Richard D. Irwin, Inc., 1991.

Gerson, Kathleen. *Hard Choices: How Women Decide About Work, Career and Motherhood.* Berkeley and Los Angeles: University of California Press, 1985.

Gilbert, Sara D. *By Yourself.* New York: Lothrop, Lee and Shepard Books, 1983.

Gillis, Jack, and Mary Ellen R. Rise. *The Childwise Catalogue: A Consumer Guide to Buying the Safest and Best Products for Your Children.* New York: Pocket Books, 1986.

Gillespie, Clark. *Prime Life Pregnancy: All You Need To Know About Pregnancy After 35.* New York: Perennial Library, 1987.

Gilman, Lois. *Adoption Resource Book: The Comprehensive Guide to All the Things You Need to Know and Ought to Know.* New York: Harper & Row, 1984.

Ginott, Haim G. *Between Parent and Child: New Solutions to Old Problems.* New York: Macmillan, 1969.

Ginott, Haim. *Between Parent and Teenager.* New York: Macmillan, 1969.

Glasscote, Raymond M.; Jon E. Gudeman; and Donald G. Miles. *Creative Mental Health Services for the Elderly.* Washington, D.C.: The Joint Information Service of the American Psychiatric Association and the Mental Health Association, 1977.

Grollman, Earl A., and Gerri L. Sweder. *The Working Parent Dilemma: How to Balance the Responsibilities of Children and Careers.* Boston: Beacon Press, 1986.

Gusdor, Georges. *Speaking (La Parole).* Evanston, Ill.: Northwestern University Press, 1966.

Hallett, Jeffrey J. *Worklife Visions.* Alexandria, Va.: American Society for Personnel Administration, 1987.

Harris, Amy Bjork, and Thomas A. Harris, M.D. *Staying OK.* New York: Avon Books, 1985.

Harris, Thomas A., M.D. *I'm OK, You're OK.* New York: Avon Books, 1969.

Helmering, Doris Wild. *Husbands, Wives and Sex.* Holbrook, Mass.: Bob Adams, Inc., 1990.

Hewlett, Sylvia Anne. *When the Bough Breaks.* New York: Basic Books, 1991.

Hirsch, Roseann. *Superworking Mom's Handbook*. New York: Warner Books, 1986.

Hochschild, Arlie Russel, with Anne Machung. *The Second Shift: Working Parents and the Revolution at Home*. New York: Viking Press, 1989.

Hunt, M. Gladys. "Guidelines to Happy Families," *Raising a Joyful Family*. New York: Harper & Row, 1983.

Inlander, Charles B., and Charles K. MacKay. *Medicare Made Easy*. Reading, Mass.: Addison-Wesley Publishing, 1989.

Jamieson, David, and Julie O'Mara. *Managing Workforce 2000: Gaining the Diversity Advantage*. San Francisco: Jossey-Bass, 1991.

Jarvik, Lissy, M.D., Ph.D., and Gary Small, M.D. *Parentcare: A Common Sense Guide to Helping Our Parents Cope with the Problems of Aging*. New York: Crown Publishers/Bantam Paperback, 1988.

Jeffers, Susan, Ph.D. *Feel the Fear and Do It Anyway*. New York: Ballatine Books, 1987.

Johnson, Carolyn. *How To Blend a Family*. Grand Rapids, Mich.: Zondervan Publishing House, 1989.

Josefowitz, Natasha. *Natasha's Words for Families*. New York: Warner Books, 1986.

Judson, Sylvia Shaw. *The Quiet Eye*. Chicago: Regnery/Gateway, Inc., 1982.

Kahn-Hut, Rachel; Arlene Kaplan Daniels; and Richard Colvard, ed. *Women and Work: Problems and Perspectives*. New York: Oxford University Press, 1982.

Kanter, Rosabeth Moss. *Men and Women of the Corporation*. New York: Basic Books, 1977.

Kaufman, Gershen. *Shame: The Power of Caring*. Cambridge, Mass.: Schenkman Publishing Company, 1985.

Kaye, Beverly. *Up is Not the Only Way: A Guide for Career Development Practitioners*. San Diego, Calif.: University Associates, 1985.

Kiley, Dan. *Dr. Dan's Prescriptions*. New York: Coward, McCann and Geoghegan Publishers, 1982.

Kimball, Gayle, Ph.D. *The 50/50 Marriage*. Boston: Beacon Press, 1983.

Kimball, Gayle, Ph.D. *50/50 Parenting: Sharing Family Rewards and Responsibilities*. Lexington, Mass.: Lexington Books, 1988.

Klinman, Debra G., and Rhiana Kohl. *Fatherhood U.S.A.* New York: Garland Publications, 1984.

Kottler, Jeffrey A. *Private Moments, Secret Selves: Enriching Our Time Alone*. Los Angeles: Jeremy P. Tarcher, Inc., 1990.

Kubler-Ross, Elisabeth. *On Death and Dying*. London: MacMillan, 1969.

Kubler-Ross, Elisabeth, and David A. Tomb. *Growing Old: A Handbook for You and Your Aging Parent*. New York: Viking Press, 1984.

La Leche League International. *The Womanly Art of Breastfeeding*, 4th rev. ed. Franklin Park, Ill.: La Leche League International, 1987.

Labich, Kenneth. "Can Your Career Hurt Your Kids?"*Fortune*, May 20, 1991.

Lakein, Alan. *How to Get Control of Your Time and Life*. New York: N.A.L.-Dutton, 1973.

Lansky, Vicki. *Best Practical Parenting Tips*. Minnetonka, Minn.: Meadowbrook Press, 1980.

Lansky, Vicki. *Practical Parenting Tips for the School-age Years*. Toronto and New York: Bantam Books, 1985.

Lansky, Vicki. *Traveling with Your Baby*. Toronto and New York: Bantam Books, 1985.

Lansky, Vicki. *Vicki Lansky's Divorce Book for Parents*. New York: New America Library, 1989.

Leinberger, Paul, and Bruce Tucker. *The New Individualists*. New York: Harper Collins Publishers, 1991.

Lester, Andrew and Judith L. *Understanding Aging Parents*. Philadelphia: The Westminister Press, 1980.

Levin, Nora Jean. *How to Care for Your Parents: A Handbook for Adult Children*. Washington, D.C.: Storm King Press, 1987.

Levine, Karen, and Conalee Levine-Shneidman. *Too Smart for Her Own Good? The Impact of Success on the Intimate Lives of Women*. Garden City, N.Y.: Doubleday Publishing, 1985.

Lewan, Lloyd S. *Women in the Workplace: A Man's Perspective*. Denver, Colo.: Remington Press, 1988.

Lewin, Elizabeth. *Financial Fitness for New Families: A Guide for Newlyweds and Parents of Young Children*. New York: Facts on File, Inc., 1989.

Lewis, Hunter. *A Question of Values: Six Ways We Make the Personal Choices that Shape Our Lives*. San Francisco: Harper Collins Publishers, 1990.

Lieberman, Morton. *Self-Help Groups for Coping with Crisis: Origins, Members, Processes and Impact*. San Francisco: Jossey-Bass, 1979.

Lindbergh, Anne Morrow. *Gifts from the Sea*. New York: Pantheon Books, 1955.

Long, Lynette, and Thomas Long. *Handbook for Latchkey Children and Their Parents*. New York: Arbor House, 1983.

Mace, Nancy. *The 36-Hour Day: A Family Guide to Caring for Persons with Alzheimer's Disease, Related Dementia Illness and Memory Loss at Later Life*. Baltimore: Johns Hopkins University Press, 1991.

Magid, Renee. *The Work and Family Challenge*. New York: American Management Association Publications, 1990.

Magid, Renee Y., with Nancy E. Fleming. *When Mothers & Fathers Work: Creative Strategies for Balancing Career and Family*. New York: AMACOM, 1987.

Mall, E. Jane. *Caregiving: How to Care for Your Elderly Mother and Stay Sane*. New York: Ballantine Books, 1990.

Marzollo, Jean. *Your Maternity Leave: How to Leave Work, Have a Baby, and Go Back to Work Without Getting Lost, Trapped or Sandbagged Along the Way*. New York: Poseidon Press/Simon & Schuster, 1989.

Mayer, Anne. *How to Stay Lovers While Raising Your Children: A Burned-Out Parent's Guide to Sex*. Los Angeles: Price Stern Sloan, Inc., 1990.

McCullough, Bonnie Runyan. *Bonnie's Household Organizer*. New York: St. Martin's Press, 1980.

McCullough, Bonnie Runyan. *401 Ways to Get Your Kids to Work at Home*. New York: St. Martin's Press, 1981.

McKaughan, Molly. *Biological Clock: Balancing Marriage, Motherhood and Career*. New York: Penguin Books, 1987.

Miller, Jo Ann, and Susan Weissman. *The Parent's Guide to Day Care: Everything You Need to Know to Find the Best Care for Your Child—And to Make It Happy, Safe and Problem-Free from Day to Day*. Toronto and New York: Bantam Books, 1986.

Mitchell, Susan E., and Jill Fox. *30-Minute Meals*. San Francisco: California Culinary Academy, 1986.

Morgan, Hal, and Kerry Tucker. *Companies That Care*. New York: Simon & Schuster, 1991.

National Council on Aging, *Idea Book on Caregiver Support Groups*. Washington, D.C.: National Association for Home Care.

National Council on Aging, *Adult Day Care Annotated Bibliography*. Washington, D.C.: National Association for Home Care, 1982.

National Homecaring Council. *Directory of Homemaker/Home Health-Aide Services in the United States, Puerto Rico and Virgin Islands*. New York: National Homecaring Council, 1982.

Olds, Sally Wendkos. *The Working Parent's Survival Guide*. Toronto and New York: Bantam Books, 1983.

Olmstead, Barney, and Suzanne Smith. *Creating a Flexible Workplace: How to Select and Manage Alternative Work Options*. New York: AMACOM, 1989.

Parke, Ross. *Fathers*. Cambridge, Mass.: Harvard University Press, 1981.

Paulson, Pat A.; Sharon C. Brown; and Jo Ann Wolf. *Living On Purpose*. New York: Simon & Schuster, 1988.

Phillips, Deborah A. *Quality in Child Care: What Does Research Tell Us?* Washington, D.C.: National Association for the Education of Young Children, 1987.

Polniaszek, Susan. *Long-Term Care: A Dollar and Sense Guide*. Washington, D.C.: United Seniors Health Cooperative.

Porcino, Jane. *Growing Older, Getting Better: A Handbook for Women in the Second Half of Life*. Reading, Mass.: Addison-Wesley Publishing, 1983.

Portnow, Jay, M.D., with Martha Houtmann, R.N. *Home Care for the Elderly*. New York: McGraw-Hill, 1987.

Portnoy, Sanford, and Joan Flynn Portnoy. *How to Take Great Trips with Your Kids*. Harvard, Mass.: Harvard Common Press, 1983.

Rice, Robin D. *The American Nanny: A Comprehensive Guide to Finding Highly Qualified Childcare Providers*. Washington, D.C.: TAN Press, 1985.

Roberts, Jeanne D., M.A. *Taking Care of Caregivers*. Palo Alto, Calif.: Bull Publishing, 1991.

Rohrlich, Jay B. *Work and Love: The Crucial Balance*. New York: Harmony Books, 1980.

Rust, Frances O'Connell, and Leslie R. Williams, ed. *The Care and Education of Young Children*. Homewood, Ill.: Richard D. Irwin, Inc., 1989.

Sangar, Sirgay, M.D., and John Kelly. *The Woman Who Works, the Parent Who Cares*. New York: Harper & Row, 1987.

Sargent, Jean Vieth. *An Easier Way: Handbook for the Elderly and Handicapped*. New York: Walker, 1981.

Satir, Virginia. *Helping Families to Change*. New York: J. Aronson, 1975.

Satir, Virginia. *Making Contact*. Berkeley, Calif.: Celestial Arts, 1976.

Satir, Virginia. *Meditations and Inspirations*. Berkeley, Calif.: Celestial Arts, 1985.

Satir, Virginia. *The New Peoplemaking*. Mountain View, Calif.: Science and Behavior Books, Inc., 1972.

Scarr, Sandra. *Mother Care/Other Care: The First Authoritative Guide to Child Care Decisions That Takes into Account the Child's Needs and the Working Mother's Dilemma*. New York: Basic Books, 1984.

Schaef, Anne Wilson. *Meditations for Women Who Do Too Much*. San Francisco: Harper & Row, 1990.

Schaefer, Charles E. *How to Talk to Children About Really Important Things*. New York: Harper & Row, 1984.

Shaevitz, Margorie. *The Superwoman Syndrome*. New York: Warner Books, 1984.

Shane, Dorlene V., and the United Seniors Health Cooperative. *Finances after 50: Financial Planning for the Rest of Your Life*. New York: Harper & Row/Perennial, 1989.

Shapiro, Jerold Lee. *When Men Are Pregnant: Needs and Concerns of Expectant Fathers*. San Luis Obispo, Calif.: Impact, 1987.

Shell, Adeline G., and Kay Reynolds. *Working Parent Food Book*. New York: Cornerstone Library, 1979.

Shulman, Bernard H., M.D., and Raenann Berman. *How to Survive Your Aging Parents*. Chicago: Surrey Books, 1988.

Shwebel, Andrew. *Guide to a Happier Family: Overcoming the Anger, Frustration and Boredom that Destroy Family Life*. Los Angeles: Jeremy P. Tarcher, Inc., 1989.

Smedes, Lewis B. *Choices: Making Right Decisions in a Complex World*. San Francisco: Harper & Row, 1986.

Smith, Dayle M. *Kincare and the American Corporation*. Homewood, Ill.: Richard D. Irwin, Inc., 1991.

Spaide, Deborah. *Day Care Kit: A Parent's Guide to Quality Child Care*. New York: Carol Publishing, 1990.

Springer, Dianne, and Timothy Brubaker. *Family Caregiving and Dependent Elderly*. Beverly Hills, Calif.: Sage Publications, Inc., 1984.

Stong, Maggie. *Mainstay: For the Well Spouse of the Chronically Ill*. Boston: Little, Brown, 1988.

Swan, Helen L. *Alone after School: A Self-Care Guide for Latchkey Children & Their Parents*. Englewood Cliffs, N.J.: Prentice Hall, 1985.

Sweeney, John J., and Karen Nussbaum. *Solutions for the New Workforce: Policies for a New Social Contract*. Washington, D.C.: Seven Locks Press, 1989.

Swigart, Jane. *The Myth of the Bad Mother: The Emotional Realities of Mothering*. Garden City, N.Y.: Doubleday Publishing, 1991.

Tannen, Deborah. *That's Not What I Meant: How Conversational Style Makes or Breaks Relationships*. New York: Morrow, 1986.

Tannen, Deborah. *You Just Don't Understand: Men and Women in Conversation*. New York: Ballantine Books, 1990.

Tilly, Louise, and Joan W. Scott. *Women, Work, and Family*. New York: Holt, Rinehart & Winston, 1978.

U.S. Department of Health and Human Services. *How to Select a Nursing Home*. Baltimore: Health Care Financing Administration, 1980.

Watkin, Donald M. *Handbook of Nutrition, Health and Aging.* Park Ridge, N.J.: Noyes Publications, 1983.

Weschler, Rabbi Harlin J., Ph.D. *What's So Bad About Guilt?* New York: Simon & Schuster, 1990.

Wheatley, Meg, and Marcie Schorr Hirsch. *Managing Your Maternity Leave.* Boston: Houghton Mifflin, 1983.

Woolover, Elizabeth, ed. *Better Homes and Gardens: Your Child . . . The Latchkey Years.* Des Moines, Iowa: Meredith Corporation, 1990.

Work and Health: Strategies for Maintaining a Vital Workforce. Greenvale, N.Y.: Panel Publishers, Inc., 1989.

Yeiser, Lin. *Nannies, Au Pairs, Mothers' Helpers—Caregivers: The Complete Guide to Home Child Care.* New York: Vintage Books, 1987.

Zaccarelli, Herman E. *The Cookbook That Tells You How: The Retirement Food and Nutrition Manual.* Boston: Cahners Publishing Company, 1972.

Zigler, Edward F., and Meryl Frank. *The Parental Leave Crisis: Toward a National Policy.* New Haven: Yale University Press, 1988.

Index

A

Accreditation, child-care programs, 157
Action plan, goals and, 15–17
Active listening, 59–63
Adolescents, communicating with, 73–76
Adult day-care center, 210
Alternate career paths, 20–33
  options for, 29–33
Antiguilt strategies, 40–45
Appropriate language, and communication, 53
Area Agency for Aging (AAA), 208
Attitude/tone, communication and, 56–57
Au pairs, 151–52

B

Baby-sitters, 152
Backup child care, 181–82
Bartering services, 115–16
Big Brothers/Big Sisters, 240
Blended families, 246–50
Body language, 54–56, 73
Borysenko, Joan, 36, 37
Business travel while caring for others, 250–57

C

Cardozo, Arlene Rossen, 17
Career and beginning family
  career and family life values assessment, 131–35

Career and beginning family—*Cont.*
  child-care arrangements, 146
  leave of absence planning, 135–40
  maternity leave, 140–41
  paternity leave, 141–46
  planning return to work, 146–47
Career path decisions, 28–29
Caregiver's home, and elder caregiving, 215–16
Carson, Rachel, 235
Checklists
  child-care, 171–75
  traveler's, 253–54
Child abuse, 179–80
Child care
  checklists for, 171–75
  child abuse question, 179–80
  criteria for, 156–61
  day-care centers and preschools, 154
  family day-care homes, 153
  in home, 150–53
  need for flexibility and patience, 155
  needs for determination, 161–63
  preparing for, 175–79
  provider selection, 163–71
  for school-aged, 183–87
  special needs for, 180–83
  at work, 153
Child-care arrangements, 146
Child development stages, 93
Children, communicating with, 67–73
Children concerns, guilt and, 41–43
Children with special needs, care for, 182–83
Child support, and single parenting, 244

Communication
active listening, 58–63
with adolescents, 73–76
and attitude/tone, 56–57
body language, 54–56
with children, 67–73
communication skills assessment,
50, 51
effective confrontation, 63–67
with elders, 76–81
elements of effective, 50, 52–58
open-ended questions, 60–63
and play with children, 72–73
with spouse/significant other, 81–85
with supervisor, 85–89
and timing and setting, 58
and voice quality, empathy, and
trust, 57–58
words, and messsge accuracy, 50,
52–54
Communication review, 89–90
Compressed workweek, 31
Congregate-care facility, 211
Continuing-care community, 210
Cost, child-care programs, 159–60

D

Day-care centers, 154
Delegating responsibilities, 106–13
Dependent Care Assistance Program,
206
Depression, and single parenting,
236–37
Different company or different shift,
and career plan options, 29–30
Doctors, and elder caregiving, 201
Durable power of attorney, 201

E

Edinberg, Mark, 194
Effective communication, elements
of, 50, 52–58
Effective confrontation, 63–67

Elder caregiving
adult day-care center, 210
in caregiver's home, 215–16
caregiver self-care, 217–20
concerns of elderly, 199–200
demographics on elderly, 194–95
in elder's home, 207–9
guilt concerning, 43–44
level of independence, elderly,
195–99
by long distance, 217
and moral support for elderly,
203–4
sources of aid for, 200–203
special-care community or facility,
210–15
Elder's home, caregiving in, 207–9
Elders, communicating with, 76–81
Emergencies, child care and, 181
Empathy and trust, and communication, 57–58
Employee Assistance Program
(EAP), 206
Employers and work/family conflict,
259–64
Employment agreement, in-home
child-care provider, 169–70
Estate planning, 201
Expectations barrier, and alternate
career paths, 23–27

F

Family day-care homes, 153
Fantasy plan creation, 13
Fear barrier, and alternate career
paths, 21–23
Feedback, 54
Field of experience, communication
and, 53
50-50 Marriage, The (Kimball), 82
Finances, single parenting and,
242–44
Financial consultants, and elder care-
giving, 201–2

Flexibility, and child-care programs, 154–57
Flextime, 30
Foster Grandparents, 204
Friends concerns, and guilt, 45
Fulghum, Robert, 49, 95
Full-time and less than full-time work options, 30–33

G

Goals identification, and whole-life planning, 7, 9–20
Goals prioritization, 18–20
Gray Panthers, 204
Guilt Is the Teacher, Love Is the Lesson (Borysenko), 36, 37
Guilt management
    antiguilt strategies, 40–45
    and child care, 41–43
    delegating responsibilities and, 106
    and elder caregiving, 43–44
    extent of problem, 36–37
    getting rid of guilt, 45–46
    healthy and unhealthy guilt, 37–40

H

Healthy and unhealthy guilt, 37–40
Healthy relationship communication assessment, 82–83
Hiring help, 116–17
Historical context, family/work issue, 1–3
Holidays, and child care, 181
Home Equity Conversion: Mortgage Insurance Demonstration Program, 221–22
Home health, and Medicare, 224
Home health professionals, and elder caregiving, 202
Hospice care, 215
    under Medicare, 224, 225
Housekeepers, 152
House sharing, 209

How to Blend a Family (Johnson), 246
How to Survive Your Aging Parents (Shulman and Berman), 80

I

"I" message confrontation, 63–67, 76
"I'm guilt-free" exercise, 46
Insurance brokers, and elder caregiving, 202
Interviews and observation, child-care providers, 167–68
Irrevocable trusts, 201

J

Job-sharing, 32
Johnson, Carolyn, 246

K

Kantner, Rosabeth Moss, 259
Kimball, Gayle, 82, 149
Knowlton, Judith M., 130

L

Language skills development, 94
Lawyers, and elder caregiving, 201
Leave of absence planning, 135–40
Level of independence, elder's, 195–99
Licensing, child-care programs, 157
Lifeline, 18
Life management organization
    bartering services, 115–16
    choosing not to perform, 104–5
    delegation of duties, 106–13
    hiring help, 116–17
    making time, 100–117
    new and reaffirmed priorities, 120
    priorities and organization in action, 117–22
    priorities identification, 96–100

Life management organization—*Cont.*
  responsibilities postponement,
    105–6
  task processes improvement,
    113–15
  weekly routines, 118–20
Life satisfaction index, 10
Living will, 201
Location change, and career plan
  options, 30
Long-distance caregiving for
  elderly, 217
Long-term care insurance policies,
  226–28

M

Making Contact (Satir), 82
Making time, 100–117
Maternity leave, 140–41
Meals on Wheels, 208
Medical eligible expenses, Medicare
  and, 224
Medicare coverage, 222–25
Medicare supplement insurance
  policies, 225–26
Montaigne, 49
Monthly planner, 124
Moral support, and elder caregiving,
  203–4

N

Nannies, 150–51
New and reaffirmed priorities, 120
Nonperformance choice, 104–5
Nurse, 202
Nursing home, 211
  selection of, 212–13

O

Occupational therapist, 202
Older Americans Act, 208

Older Women's League (OWL), 204
Open-ended questions, 60–63
Outpatient drugs, Medicare and, 225
Overload, and communication, 54
Overnight, child care and, 181

P

Parenting Young Children (Dinkmeyer
  et al.), 41
Parents Without Partners, 239
Part-time work option, 31–33
Paternity leave, 142–46
Payment for child care, assistance in,
  160–61
Phase-in after leave of absence, 32
Physical therapist, 202
Planning return to work after leave,
  146–47
Plateau, and career plan options, 29
Play, and communication, 72–73
Power of attorney, 201
Preparation, child care, 175–79
Preschools, 154
Priorities and organization in action,
  117–22
Priorities identification, 96–100
Professional help, elder caregiving,
  201–203
Professional relationship with child-
  care providers, 168–71
Provider selection, child care, 163–71

R

References check, child-care provid-
  ers, 166–67
Reisman, Barbara, 42
Relatives and friends, and child care,
  152–53
Reliability, and child-care pro-
  grams, 157
Repetition, and communication, 54
Respiratory therapist, 202
Responsibilities postponement, 105–6

Retirement home, 211
Returning to work, and single
    parenting, 236
Roles, and whole-life planning, 8–9

S

Sanger, Sirgay, 41, 141
Satir, Virginia, 82
School-aged children, care for, 183–87
Self-care, 266-70
    children and, 183–87
    and elder caregiving, 217–20
    single parents, 240
    while traveling, 254
Self-employment, and career plan
    options, 30
Sequencing, and whole-life planning,
    17–18
Service Corps for Retired Executives
    (SCORE), 204
Setting, and communication, 58
Shared child care, 152
Sick children, care of, 180–81
Single parenting
    child support and, 244
    depression and, 236–37
    finances and, 242–44
    as part-time parent, 240–42
    returning to work, 236
    self-care and, 240
    sleep and, 245
    and support network, 237–40
    visualization, 237
Single part-time parent, 240–42
Skilled nursing, and Medicare,
    223–24
Sleep, and single parenting, 245
Smaller company, and career plan
    options, 30
Social workers, and elder care-
    giving, 202
Sources of aid, elder caregiving,
    200–203
Sources of information, child-care
    providers, 164

Special-care community or facility,
    elderly and, 210–15
Special child-care needs, 180–83
Special family situations
    blended families, 246–49
    business travel and caring for
        others, 249–57
    single parenting, 235–45
Speech pathologist, 202
Spouse/partner concerns, guilt and,
    44–45
Spouse/significant other, communi-
    cating with, 81–85
Stability, and child-care pro-
    grams, 159
Staff/child ratio, child-care programs,
    157–58
Staff qualifications, child-care pro-
    grams, 158–59
Supervisor, communicating with,
    85–89
Support network and single parent-
    ing, 237–40
Szanton, Eleanor, 41

T

Talking with Your Aging Parents (Edin-
    berg), 194
Tannen, Deborah, 85, 113
Task processes improvement, 113–15
Telecommuting/work at home, 31
Telephone calls at work, 88–89
Telephone screening, child-care pro-
    viders, 165–66
Temporary work, 32
Timing, and communication, 58
Tomlin, Lily, 7
Traveler's checklist, 253–54

U

Unhealthy guilt, 37–40
Unplanned events, flexibility and, 33

V

Values clarification index, 11–13
Visit with child, child-care providers, 168
Visualization, 237
Voice quality, communication and, 57
Voluntary reduced work time, 32

W

Weekly planner, 126–29
Weekly routines, 118–20
Weschler, Harlan J., 36
Whole life plan creation
    action plan, 15–17
    alternate career paths, 20–33
    career path decisions, 27–29
    expectations barrier, 22–27
    fantasy plan creation, 13
    fear barrier, 21–22
    full-time work options, 30–31
    goal prioritization, 18–20
    goals identification, 7, 9–20

Whole life plan creation—*Cont.*
    less than full-time alternatives, 31–33
    lifeline, 18
    life satisfaction index, 10
    options, alternative career paths, 29–33
    roles, 8–9
    sequencing, 17–18
    unplanned events, flexibility and, 33
    values clarification index, 11–13
Will, 201
Woman Who Works, Parent Who Cares, The (Sanger), 142
Words, and message accuracy, 50, 52–54
Work facilities for child care, 153
Working Mother magazine, 36

Y

You Just Don't Understand (Tannen), 113

Also Available from Business One Irwin . . .

SECOND TO NONE
How Our Smartest Companies Put People First
Charles Garfield

Discover how you can create a workplace where both people and profits flourish! *Second to None* by Charles Garfield, the best-selling author of *Peak Performers*, gives you an inside look at today's leading businesses and how they became masters at expanding the teamwork and creativity of their work force. Using this unique mix of practical strategies gleaned from our smartest companies, you can respond to the challenges of today's global marketplace, provide superior service to your customers—and your own employees, maintain a competitive edge during times of rapid transition and restructuring, and much more!
ISBN: 1–55623–360–4

WORKFORCE MANAGEMENT
How Today's Companies Are Meeting Business and Employee Needs
Barbara Pope

Provides practical advice for organizations struggling to respond to ongoing change. Pope shows how to integrate business and employee needs in order to recruit and retain the best employees. She shows how you can manage work force problems before they become critical, work collaboratively to develop human resource programs and policies that match business plans, jobs, and people, and much more!
ISBN: 1–55623–537–2

TEAM-BASED ORGANIZATIONS
Developing a Successful Team Environment
James H. Shonk

Shonk shows you how to structure and manage an organization that is built around teams versus forcing a team approach into an existing structure. He identifies the advantages and challenges associated with team-based organizations so that you'll be prepared to deal with and resolve any issues that arise. You'll find valuable planning tools to assist you in implementation and help you avoid wasted time.
ISBN: 1–55623–703–0

SURVIVE INFORMATION OVERLOAD
The 7 Best Ways to Manage Your Workload by Seeing the Big Picture
Kathryn Alesandrini

Gives you a step-by-step action plan to survive the information onslaught and still have time to effectively manage people, increase productivity, and best serve customers. You'll find innovative techniques, such as Priority Mapping, Context Analysis, Visual Organization, and the use of a Master Control System to manage details by seeing the big picture.
ISBN: 1–55623–721–9

CONTINUOUS IMPROVEMENT AND MEASUREMENT FOR TOTAL QUALITY
A Team-Based Approach
Dennis C. Kinlaw
Copublished by Pfeiffer & Company/Business One Irwin

You'll find the tools, processes, and models for success that assist you in measuring team performance, improving customer satisfaction, and solving unique challenges your company faces. No matter if you're a team member, manager, or consultant, Kinlaw gives you valuable insight so your organization can benefit from teams!
ISBN: 1–55623–778–2

Available at fine bookstores and libraries everywhere.